THE EXTRA DIMENSION

The Extra Dimension

A Jewish View of Marriage

ROLAND B. GITTELSOHN

UNION OF AMERICAN HEBREW CONGREGATIONS

NEW YORK

Library of Congress Cataloging in Publication Data
Gittelsohn, Roland Bertram, 1910–
The extra dimension.
Bibliography: p.
1. Marriage—Religious aspects—Judaism.   2. Jewish
way of life.   I. Title.
BM713.G53 1983   296.3'878358   82–21776
ISBN 0–8074–0170–6

Produced in the United States of America
1   2   3   4   5   6   7   8   9   0

To Hulda

—whose love for me
and compassion for all
have opened new vistas in my life

EDITOR'S INTRODUCTION

Throughout his long and distinguished career as a servant of the Jewish people, Rabbi Roland Gittelsohn has transformed many lives in many ways. His books, articles, speeches, and broadcasts have touched people, moved them, and inspired them with the belief that our world can be a better place as a result of their personal efforts.

The Extra Dimension represents the latest product of Rabbi Gittelsohn's concern for the future of the Jewish family. His straight talk and courageous grappling with the tough issues in any relationship combine with the wisdom and experience gleaned from almost a half century of counseling to make this book must reading for any Jewish couple contemplating marriage. Indeed, even those readers who have been married for many years will find considerable Jewish teachings and insights within its pages.

We hope that you will find *The Extra Dimension* a valuable addition to your personal library and that it will fulfill its purpose of strengthening the Jewish family in the difficult times in which we live.

Rabbi Daniel B. Syme
Director of Education

PREFACE

Chronologically, a little over a decade has passed since publication of my first book for couples about to be married; but, in substance, at least half a century has gone by. Topics that were barely on the surface of our attention then are now at the very center. Among them: the women's movement, two-career marriages, second marriages, infertility, artificial insemination, child adoption, so-called "open marriages," the apparent weakening of the family.

New insights and knowledge have become available also on many problems which were covered in my earlier volume. There has, indeed, been so much change and growth that more than a simple revision is required. This book, therefore, while based on *My Beloved Is Mine* and repeating much that was and remains valid, is really a new work in more than title.

Not even the writing of many articles, sermons, and books qualifies one to thank adequately those whose generous cooperation is essential to such an undertaking as this. No one person can pretend to be an expert in all the disciplines touching upon the study of marriage. I have been extremely fortunate in receiving guidance and advice from others who read my manuscript or parts of it from the perspective of their professional competences: Dr. Sidney Slater Cohen as a gynecologist-obstetrician; Drs. James Wiener and the late Herbert Posin as psychiatrists; the late Professor F. Alexander Magoun, Dr. Samuel Glasner, and Edna Barrabee Grace as marriage counselors; Dr. Julius Kravetz as a scholar in rabbinic literature; Judith Fales as a sociologist; and Lillian Beauvais as a Jewish educator. Helpful practical suggestions came from several couples of married friends: Mr. and Mrs. Jackson Parker, Dr. and Mrs. Peter Braun, Mr. and Mrs. Stanley Godoff, Mr. and Mrs. David Stolper. All these are responsible for more than a few sharpened insights and improved expressions. I myself lay claim to whatever errors or omissions remain.

My debt to Rabbi Alexander Schindler is immeasurable. Without his never-failing energy and encouragement, this book would never have appeared. Rabbi Daniel B. Syme, director of the Commission on Jewish Education, was available to me at all times despite his very heavy burden of other responsibilities. The pleasing format of this volume is due to the skill and concern of Mr. Stuart Benick. My thanks go also to Mr. Douglas Tishler for his devoted help in research and technical detail.

Though *The Extra Dimension* is intended most immediately for Jewish couples, I would hope it might prove helpful to those of other faiths as well. The insights of Judaism on sex and marriage are universally relevant; the truths of psychology and science in these realms are, after all, the same for everyone. I am confident, moreover, that even couples who are already married can find in these pages suggestions which may bring them an extra dimension of life and hope.

If this work can improve the prospect of marital success or enhance the happiness of those who read it, every ounce of effort that went into it will be vindicated.

ROLAND B. GITTELSOHN

Boston, Massachusetts
November 1982

Contents

THE EXTRA DIMENSION

CHAPTER ONE

Hope...and Despair

How happy will your marriage be?

No human experience is so filled with sweet, confident hope as when bride and groom stand before their rabbi, awaiting those ancient words which will unite their lives as one. For every couple, the moment of marriage is a culmination of eager anticipation and inexpressible hope. Yet more than a few such couples are destined for great disappointment. For some, marriage will end in the divorce court; for others, it will degenerate into dull despair. During a recent period of seventy years in the United States, while population was increasing threefold and marriages fourfold, the number of divorces rose twentyfold! On the day they were married, nearly all the couples who failed would have staked their lives on success.

How happy will your marriage be?

A ten-year study under the auspices of a major American college discovered that only one couple in twenty is "quite unhappy." But no more than one in six reported to be "extremely happy." The poet Coleridge disclosed more about himself than about marriage when he said: "...the most happy marriage I can picture or image to myself would be the union of a deaf man to a blind woman." Professor F. Alexander Magoun was a great deal more realistic when he wrote: "Some marriages are sheer hell. Most marriages are pretty mediocre. A few marriages are positively delicious."[1]

1

How happy will your marriage be?

The question is not asked cynically, nor is the possibility of trouble introduced to chill your expectations at the start. It is precisely because marriage can be so wonderful, bringing you the most fulfilling happiness in the world, that it is worth the effort to distinguish those factors which assure success from those which presage failure. Your relationship to your wife or husband will be an entirely new kind of relationship, one which you have never known before, and which is difficult to describe in advance. No matter how close or loving you have ever felt toward any other person—a parent, a sibling, a teacher, a friend—this new relationship you are about to assume will require a dimension of intimacy you have never felt and cannot imagine. Even for those who have lived together before marrying, the wedding ceremony often alters the bond between them substantially. In order to increase the probability of your achieving the best in your marriage, it is necessary from the outset to be aware also of its potential worst.

How happy will your marriage be?

That depends on many things—the kind of persons you and your prospective mate are, the compatibility between you, your understanding of love, how hard you work together for happiness, your emotional maturity, your readiness for a mutually-fulfilling sex life, your knowledge of Jewish tradition concerning love and marriage, your attitudes toward religion.

The mere fact that you feel so strong an attachment and yearning for each other and that the words of the wedding ceremony will be properly uttered in your presence will not automatically assure you the happiness you seek. No more than an automobile, a tankful of fuel, and a desire to drive from Boston to Los Angeles add up to the promise of a successful journey. In order to reach your destination in good health and with joy experienced en route, you must know the nature of your car and of yourself, the rules for responsible operation of the highly powered machine at your disposal, the rights of others on the road, the route best calculated to carry you from coast to coast with a maximum of pleasure and a minimum of pain. Failure on any of these counts can bring disappointment ranging from minor inconvenience to major catastrophe. As you sit behind the wheel of your car, the ignition key you turn can activate unbounded happiness or tragic pain—for you and for innumerable others.

No less is true of marriage. Here too it is imperative that you know accurately all the factors involved, that you be realistically aware of human nature in general, of your nature and your beloved's in particular. Here too there is an accumulated wisdom of the ages which can be ignored only at great peril. Here too there are rules for responsible relationships; your happiness will be enhanced in direct proportion to your knowledge of these rules and your willingness to abide by them. Your wedding ceremony guarantees nothing; it promises much. It gives you a legal and ethical franchise to pursue—together with the person whom you love more than any other on earth—the highest happiness possible.

Despite recent increases in divorce rates, your chance for success is probably greater than that of any preceding generation. Like them, your resources include a great body of perceptive insight into the meaning of marriage, made available to you through Jewish tradition. But you can draw also upon much modern knowledge which was previously unknown. Many branches of science—biology, anthropology, sociology, psychology above all—combine to suggest the best routes to success. That success will require more than the reading of books. All that can even be attempted in these pages is to gather, in one convenient place, as much as possible of the wisdom provided by Judaism and science.

How happy will your marriage be?
That depends on how much you care. On how hard you try. On how scrupulously—at times perhaps even painfully—you seek the truth about yourselves.

How happy will your marriage be?
Only you can answer that question. You and your spouse. You and time.

CHAPTER TWO

"I Love You"

Probably the most misunderstood and abused word in the English language is *love.* People speak of *loving* their homes, their cars, their food, their dogs, their parents, their friends, their brothers and sisters, their husbands and wives. Obviously, a word that can be given so many meanings is in danger of having no meaning at all. Since marriage at its best is a permanent relationship between two people who are in love, it is imperative that we begin by trying to define love.

Many attempts have been made. Some have been intentionally humorous: love is "an itchy feeling around the heart that you can't scratch" or "a feeling you feel when you feel you are going to feel a feeling you never felt before."

More serious attempts to define love abound. Among them:

> From David Frost: "Love is when each person is more concerned for the other than he is for himself."

> From James Thurber and E.B. White: "Love is the strange bewilderment which overtakes one person on account of another person."

> From John Ciardi: "Love is the word used to label the sexual excitement of the young, the habituation of the middle-aged, and the mutual dependence of the old."

Alexander Magoun was one of the first university professors in this country to pioneer with courses on marriage. After devoting many years to an understanding of love, he suggested two definitions:

> Love is a feeling of tenderness and devotion toward someone, so profound that to share that individual's joys, anticipations, sorrows, and pain is the very essence of living.
>
> Love is the passionate and abiding desire on the part of two or more people to produce together the conditions under which each can be and spontaneously express his real self; to produce together an intellectual soil and an emotional climate in which each can flourish, far superior to what either could achieve alone.[1]

Several aspects of these statements merit further comment. First, let it be noted that love involves voluntary participation in the pains of another person no less than in his or her joys.

A chasidic tale expresses this truth eloquently. Two friends were drinking together one day in the corner of an inn. They had imbibed enough to reach the stage of sloppy sentimentality, throwing their arms around each other as they loudly professed their love. Suddenly one said to the other: "Ivan, what hurts me now?" Ivan's response: "How should I know what hurts you now, Peter?" To which Peter immediately demanded: "If you don't know what hurts me, how can you say you love me?" From the loosened lips of drunkards—no less than out of the mouths of babes—profound truth often flows.

No life can always be filled with sunshine; heartbreak and tragedy also are inescapable components of our human heritage. A willingness to share only the bright and happy experiences of another, while resenting an equal sharing of disappointments and doubts, betrays something less than either maturity or readiness for genuine love. Indeed, there is reason to believe that in a solid marriage the crises two individuals share do at least as much to unite them as their moments of rejoicing and success.

Jewish tradition has long been aware of this truth. One of the things we shall observe later about our marriage ceremony is that the wine shared by bride and groom symbolizes both the sweetness and bitterness of life, which they taste together.

In a good marriage, however, neither partner persistently takes advantage of the other. It is possible to tyrannize another person through weakness as well as strength. For husband or wife to play the role of chronic dependent, always demanding that the other bear most of their joint burdens, indicates a neurotic rather than wholesome relationship.

Dr. Erich Fromm, an eminent psychoanalyst, has written wisely about mistaking exaggerated dependency needs for love:

> . . . irrational love is love which enhances the person's dependency, hence anxiety and hostility. Rational love is love which relates a person intimately to another, at the same time preserving his independence and integrity.[2]

> Most people see the problem of love primarily as that of *being loved,* rather than that of *loving,* of one's capacity to love. Hence, the problem to them is how to be loved, how to be lovable.[3]

> Infantile love follows the principle: *"I love because I am loved."* Mature love follows the principle: *"I am loved because I love."* Immature love says: *"I love you because I need you."* Mature love says: *"I need you because I love you."*[4]

If husband and wife are compatible, each will contribute strength to the other. In some situations of stress, one will be for the moment stronger; in the next crisis, the opposite may be true. On one occasion, the husband will support the sagging spirit of the wife; another time it will be she who is able to save him from deep despair. The excitement and beauty of life are more than doubled when husband and wife share them in love. Tragedy and tribulation become easier to endure when love makes it possible for one to strengthen the other.

NO DICTATORS

It is equally important to observe, from the second definition suggested by Magoun, that love involves a mutuality which
precludes martyrdom on the part of either mate. Neither
should be expected to sacrifice or subsume self for the sake of
the other. This is true not only in marriage, but in all interpersonal relationships. Parents who constantly dominate a growing child, who persist in attempting to fashion that child in
their own image, who protest that they impose their will only
out of love are demonstrating many things in the way of self-
disclosure—but a capacity to love is not one of them. The
mother whose theme in life is her willingness to become a
martyr to her children is an eloquent exponent of masochism,
scarcely of love. The husband or wife who completely absorbs
the other, who *possesses* and controls the other, has not understood the meaning of love at all.

The essence of love is that two people unite their separate
lives inextricably, yet each retains his or her own individuality
while fostering that of the other. This is a very delicate, subtle
relationship, one which demands both maturity and sensitivity.
Each section of a symphony orchestra plays according to its
own timbre and tone, but in harmony with the others. If the
violins try to sound like horns, or the horns to emulate wood-
winds, the result, while novel, is not good music. By the same
token, however, if each plays from a different score—in utter
disregard of the others—the consequence is even worse. The
more truly each section exploits the maximum potential of its
own instrument, in a common undertaking with all other sec-
tions, the more richly does it enhance the music for all. So, in
a marriage which embodies mature love, each partner tries to
discover the highest potential of both, then to create an atmosphere and environment conducive to their maximum development.

You may have lifted a curious eyebrow when you noticed,
in Professor Magoun's second definition, reference to "desire
on the part of *two or more* people." A careful reading of the
entire definition will disclose that it could apply, not only to the
relationship between husband and wife, but also to that among

brothers and sisters or between parents and their children. Will one definition do for all these manifestations of love? I think not. True, there is valid similarity among them. It is doubtful whether a person who has never known a truly loving relationship with parents, siblings, and friends is capable of experiencing love with a mate.

Yet the uniqueness of the love which binds one woman to one man in marriage must not be lost in that which is admittedly common to the several varieties of love. The sexual aspect of love in marriage is in itself enough to make the difference one of kind, not merely of degree. Later we shall discuss the relationship between sexual attraction and love, as well as the extreme danger of confusing the two. For the time being, let it be said simply that sex is one of the most dominant needs of human beings and that a successful marriage between two normal young persons, without a mutually gratifying sex experience, is highly improbable.

At least in part as a consequence of their sexual bond, the partnership of husband and wife assumes that unique dimension of intimacy described in our opening chapter. The most loving association of two brothers living in the same household, of two sisters or friends—for all that it shares in many aspects of the partnership between husband and wife—falls so far short that any attempt to encompass both in one definition of love will confuse more than it will clarify. Our concern here is the kind of love which exists in a good marriage.

STILL NOT EASY

If it is possible to approach even as close to a valid definition of love as we already have, why do so many couples discover, some months or years after their wedding, that they have in fact been betrayed by self-deception? Their confusion inheres in the fact that there is a vast difference between achieving a reasonably accurate definition of love on paper and being able to identify or measure it within oneself. Often when youngsters ask their parents how they will recognize love, they receive some such answer as: "Don't worry; when you're really in love, you'll know it." As comforting as such certainty may be, it just doesn't happen to be true.

Not only is love, in and of itself, a complicated emotion, but it is also easily confused with infatuation and romance. Infatuation is a purely physical, sexual attraction between man and woman. The dictionary defines *infatuate* as *to inspire with ardent passion so as to deprive of ordinary judgment.* Romance is a warm feeling of comfortable attachment, induced and encouraged by soft music and lowered lights and the stuff of which daydreams are made. According to the dictionary, again, *to romance* means *to indulge in visionary fabrications, tell fanciful stories.* Where love is idealistic, romance is idealized. Love recognizes real virtues in the beloved and seeks to encourage their utmost fruition. Romance purports to see virtues which don't really exist.

A seventeen-year-old girl once wrote in her diary: "Love can blot out reality." She was hopelessly and disastrously wrong. It came as no surprise to me when, a few years and two children later, her marriage ended in divorce. People who convince themselves that love can defy reality are experiencing romance, not love. Sooner or later they are doomed to disillusionment. Genuine love is possible only when reality is recognized and accepted.

Both infatuation and romance are notoriously divorced from reality. However pleasant they are as momentary diversion, there is an inevitable moment of reckoning. Infatuation and romance are both necessary and valuable emotions for every person to experience; indeed, they may even be essential components of love. But it is disastrous to mistake a small part for the whole.

A cynical woman once said to me at the conclusion of a wedding ceremony: "It was nice . . . very nice . . . but, once the wedding is over, romance goes out the window." Her disillusioned comment reflected an all-too-frequent-and-unfortunate truth. The marriage devoid of strong physical attraction and moments of affectionate flight from reality is poor indeed. But a beneficial diversion can become fatal if confused with permanent policy.

There is no such thing as love at first sight. Often there is infatuation at first sight, followed at the earliest opportunity by romance. These can, in the course of time, develop into love, though, more often they don't. The newborn infant whose babbling sounds seem delightfully musical to its parents may become an opera star, but the objective observer will adopt a cautious policy of *wait and see.* The same procedure is wise in approaching the distinction between infatuation or romance and love. The first imperative, then—for you and your intended—is to ascertain, if you can, whether your attraction for each other is really love.

CRUCIAL DIFFERENCES

One way is by the test of time. Love has a lasting quality which is lacking in romance and infatuation. The latter are often like a match touched to a pile of combustible brush. The flame catches at once, bursts immediately into a fire which gives the deceptive appearance of lasting forever, then quickly subsides and dies. Love is more likely to be a fire built from small beginnings—first a few pieces of kindling, then larger logs to feed the flame, renewed nourishment whenever needed, glowing coals by which one is warmed.

The diagram below may help to clarify the distinction. Except for the rare instance where infatuation or romance leads to love, it begins more dramatically, develops far more rapidly, and expires while love may still be incubating.

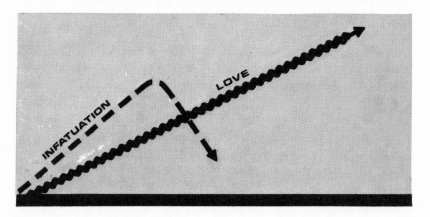

A second criterion for making this most essential distinction is whether the emphasis is on the self or the other person, on getting or on giving. The person who is infatuated is interested primarily in self; the other person is important only for what he or she can give. The frame of reference, whether vocalized or not, is: how-much-pleasure-it-gives-me-to-be-with-you. The person who is truly in love is at least as interested in the partner as in self. The frame of reference is: how-much-more-adequate-and-secure-each-of-us-feels-because-of-the-other.

A homely analogy may add to our understanding here. A parakeet, unable to tolerate loneliness, can be deceived into thinking it has a companion simply by installing a mirror in its cage. The foolish bird is convinced that it is no longer alone, when in fact it is looking only at itself. In a similar sense, psychologically, the individuals who are experiencing infatuation are really enjoying the image of themselves which they see reflected in the eyes of others.

Despite a superficial appearance to the contrary, these paragraphs do not contradict what has already been said about martyrdom. The individual who is involved in a true experience of love was not described as being *more interested* in mate than in self, but *at least as interested.* He or she must begin with a healthy, wholesome, balanced acceptance of and respect for self. No melodramatic self-sacrifice will do. Each must want the same opportunity for self-expression and self-realization that he or she would eagerly afford to the other. And each must strive for those circumstances and conditions which will enable both to achieve a degree of self-fulfillment which would be impossible for either of them acting alone.

This is where David Frost's proposed definition of love fails. Love does not require—or even allow—that "each person is *more* concerned for the other than he is for himself." Rather, the concern should be equal. True, there are bound to be crises in which the needs of one are so imperative that they must take precedence. But over a long span of time such crises will balance; in a good marriage the care and concern of each for the other will be equalized.

Erich Fromm has written eloquently of the capacity to concentrate on giving more than receiving:

What is giving? Simple as the answer to this question seems to be, it is actually full of ambiguities and complexities. The most widespread misunderstanding is that which assumes that giving is "giving up" something, being deprived of, sacrificing. The person whose character has not developed beyond the stage of the receptive, exploitative, or hoarding orientation experiences the act of giving in this way. The marketing character is willing to give, but only in exchange for receiving; giving without receiving for him is being cheated. . . .

For the productive character, giving has an entirely different meaning. Giving is the highest expression of potency. In the very act of giving, I experience my strength, my wealth, my power. This experience of heightened vitality and potency fills me with joy. I experience myself as overflowing, spending, alive, hence as joyous. Giving is more joyous than receiving, not because it is a deprivation, but because in the act of giving lies the expression of my aliveness.

. . . The most elementary example lies in the sphere of sex. The culmination of the male sexual function lies in the act of giving; the man gives himself, his sexual organ, to the woman. At the moment of orgasm he gives his semen to her. He cannot help giving it if he is potent. If he cannot give, he is impotent. For the woman the process is not different, although somewhat more complex. She gives herself too; she opens the gates to her feminine center; in the act of receiving, she gives. If she is incapable of this act of giving, if she can only receive, she is frigid. With her the act of giving occurs again, not in her function as a lover, but in that as a mother. She gives of herself to the growing child within her, she gives her milk to the infant, she gives her bodily warmth. Not to give would be painful. . . .

What does one person give to another? He gives of himself, of the most precious he has, he gives of his life. This does not necessarily mean that he sacrifices his life for the other—but that he gives him of that which is alive in him; he gives him of his joy, of his interest, of his understanding, of his knowledge, of his humor, of his sadness—of all expressions and manifestations of that which is alive in him. In thus giving of his life, he enriches the other person, he enhances the other's sense of aliveness by enhancing his own sense of aliveness. He does not give in order to receive; giving is in itself exquisite joy. But in giving he cannot help bringing something to life in the other person, and this which is brought to life reflects back to him; in truly giving, he cannot help receiving that which is given back to him. Giving implies to make the other person a giver also and they both share in the joy of what they have brought to life.[5]

This capacity to *receive-by-giving* is so important an ingredient of love that it deserves further comment. Because of it, the partners in a love relationship are able to discover and develop in each other rich resources of ability and character which they may never have suspected. Each becomes a finer, nobler, more decent human being because of the other. According to Jewish tradition, before Akiba fell in love with his future wife he was only a humble, illiterate shepherd. She agreed to marry him on condition that he study Torah; obviously, she recognized in him a capacity for intellectual and spiritual achievement of which he had not become aware himself. Akiba agreed. After they were secretly married, he left her for two periods of twelve years each, during which he studied assiduously and became the most illustrious rabbinic scholar of his time, the famous Rabbi Akiba.[6] Not every person possesses the potential for great scholarship. Not everyone is a possible genius. But all of us—without exception—have ability and character far beyond that which we have discovered in ourselves. Love—like the warm, beneficent rays of the summer sun—draws this innate energy and goodness to the surface, promoting the growth both of lover and beloved. The famed philosopher, A. N. Whitehead, must have had this is mind when he said: "By myself I am only one more professor, but with Evelyn I am first-rate."[7]

Rabbi Eugene Borowitz expresses his understanding of love as follows:

> Our beloved is so concerned with our welfare . . . he cares not only for what we are but for what we yet will be. He recognizes our potential and helps us try to reach it. Love thus validates our existence as nothing else can and, with an unparalleled immediacy, helps turn us into the people we always were meant to be.[8]

Infatuation may be compared to the sound waves projected by a bat as it flies. It emits a squeal, too highly pitched for the human ear, which bounces back from surrounding objects, thus enabling the bat to avoid colliding with them. This is nature's prototype for sonar, the transmission of sound waves through water by a ship, in order to locate submerged submarines. Both bat and ship are interested only in themselves and their own needs; everything in the environment is "sounded" only in order to guide themselves. In like manner, the emotional beams projected by people who are infatuated are intended to yield benefit only to themselves. Their objective is the pleasure received from the reflection of themselves. With love, the primary concern is to find and benefit someone else though, in the very act of finding, we feel gratified and fulfilled.

Another analogy, suggested by Alexander Magoun, may help. People who are infatuated are like tourists who visit a foreign country for their own edification and enjoyment. The sights seen, the information obtained, the new possessions acquired: these constitute the sum total of their experience. People who are in love may more accurately be likened to members of the Peace Corps who spend time abroad to benefit the local population. Their primary purpose is to give rather than to receive, yet—paradoxically—they probably end up seeing more, learning more, and acquiring more than the casual tourist. So it is with love, compared to infatuation.

TO BURN OR BLESS?

A third criterion for distinguishing love from infatuation or romance is actually an extension of the second. Not only is each partner in a true love relationship concerned with the other, the two of them together are very much involved with people beyond themselves. Infatuation and romance are likely to be ingrown kinds of relationship; to the degree that the two people concerned truly share with each other, their vision goes no farther than that. They prefer to spend most of their time alone. Even when they are with others, their interest is primarily centered on themselves. While it is true that those who are in love also enjoy spending some time alone with each other, they seek a wider circle of interest, too. In the words of a French philosopher, "Life has taught us that love does not consist of gazing at each other but in looking outward together in the same direction."

Only a loving person is capable of becoming a lovable person. And the boundary lines of love are broader by far than those of romance and infatuation. There is no such thing as loving only one person in the world, to the exclusion of all others. Indeed, some of the most beautiful love relationships in history have been between two individuals whose love prompted them to bring great benefit to others. Elizabeth and Robert Browning wrote exquisite poetry—each with a different style—yet each stimulated and encouraged by the other. Marie and Pierre Curie together discovered radium, bringing blessing and healing to multitudes. Louise and Stephen Wise established a great synagogue and labored creatively for those less fortunate than themselves. Apparently our ancient rabbis understood this special quality of love. They incorporated the following story in midrashic literature:

> There once lived a pious man who was childless. He prayed for a son, vowing to invite to his wedding-feast every poor person in the city. A son was eventually born to him, and he gave him the name of Mattaniah, namely, a gift from God. The boy grew up and his wedding day approached. The father invited all the students of the Torah and all the poor, who together filled six rooms.

God wished to test the bridegroom, so He sent the Angel of Death, in the guise of a man attired in soiled raiment, to beg for a place at the wedding. The bridegroom refused on the plea that all who could be accommodated had been invited. Moreover, the man's garments were objectionable.

In the night, the Angel of Death revealed himself, declaring that he was about to take away the bridegroom's soul since he had failed in the test. The bride gave voice to this prayer:

"O Lord of the universe, you have said in Your Torah that, when a man takes unto himself a wife, he shall bring her cheer for a full year and not leave her. May it be Your will that my husband live before You, and I shall teach him to practice loving-kindness to everyone without discrimination." Her prayer was heard on high, and the Angel of Death was commanded to leave.

What was the nature of this young woman? Her mother was accustomed to draw cool water from a spring for school children. When she became old, her daughter said: "You need not abandon your good deed. I shall lend you the strength of my arm and carry most of the weight so that you may continue to perform the *mitzvah*."

It was this consideration for her mother that made her deserving in the eyes of the Lord.[9]

ONE MORE DIFFERENCE

We have seen, then, that love can be distinguished from romance and infatuation by virtue of the facts that (a) it is more enduring, (b) it is characterized by the joy of giving rather than the self-gratification of only receiving, and (c) it stimulates two people to benefit others through their affection. There is one more criterion of immense importance.

Infatuation is purely physical; love is both physical and spiritual. Perhaps I should pause to clarify the meaning of *spiritual.* I use it here for those aspects of a human being which go beyond the purely physical, for the extraphysical or trans-physical characteristics of human experience. My brain is physical; a surgeon can easily identify it and, if necessary, explore parts of it. My mind is spiritual; though it is dependent on my brain, it is not of itself an anatomical entity to which a physician can point. True, when I think, certain electrochemical currents are released in my brain. But these are not my thoughts, they are just the physical manifestations of thought, the way my brain functions while thought is being produced.

The spiritual phases of life are referred to as a person's soul. They include our capacity to create and/or appreciate truth, beauty, and moral goodness. Just as thought and truth are not physical, so beauty and ethical values are not physical. We often recognize them in physical form, but they are themselves spiritual.

To return, then, to our fourth and final criterion of distinction, infatuation is a purely physical experience; love is physical plus spiritual. The only bond between individuals who are infatuated is their bodies, especially the physical comforts and pleasures they can obtain from each other. The bonds between lovers include all this, plus an irresistible impulse to create or to appreciate with each other increasing quantities of truth, beauty, and goodness. To say that love is a spiritual as well as a physical experience is to imply that there is something sacred in the love of man and woman for each other. This is exactly what Judaism has always taught.

TWO COUPLES

Does my attempt to distinguish infatuation from love sound ponderous? It has its light side too. And we can often learn while chuckling. I particularly like a newspaper column by Anatole Broyard. In it he describes the time when he and his wife hosted a couple younger than themselves, a friend and his "girl":

He is lit up, he leaves a flaming trail. During the introduction, he is almost dancing. As I carry their bags
downstairs to the guest room, I feel that they are packed
with delight and it gives me a pang. How long has it
been since my heart leaped up like a dolphin or a flight
of birds? . . .

We lunch on cold cuts in the living room, where the fire
is going. While I am ordinarily the better talker, my
friend is scintillating today. He scatters wit all over us,
he crackles with associations. . . .

The fire hisses and pops. My friend and his girl look at
it with a proprietary air, as if they owned all the warmth
in the world. They too are combustible. I'm glad for
him. It does me good to see him happy. But, while I am
not competing with his happiness, it is difficult all the
same, inhuman, in fact, not to covet it just a bit. . . .

Feeling myself carried away by the sheer spectacle of
the girl, I search for balancing consideration. She and
my friend, I tell myself, are still only picnickers, people
on a holiday. They are tourists of the emotions, while
my wife and I are natives. So far, this infatuation of
theirs is an indefinitely extended date, a contradiction
in terms. They are falling stars and we are the Big
Dipper.

When I was in the Army, I learned that there are two
kinds of explosives. One has a progressive effect, and
this is the kind that launches the rocket or sends the
projectile out of the cannon. This is the wife, adding
her energy to her husband's. The other explodes in-
stantaneously and detonates everything around it. This
is the girl. She has blasted my friend sky-high and he
hasn't come down to earth yet.

Yes, but there is no denying the force of that detona-
tion, the blinding flash, the tremendous swell and lift of
it, the stunning destruction of all structures, all de-
fenses.

Yet I knew that once and no longer wanted it. I remember girls coming down from colleges, spending the weekend. Friday night was delirium, Saturday we were amazed by ourselves. But Sunday, Sunday afternoon, I would wish I had children to play with. When the sun was shining, I could see right through myself and those girls.

I remember the emptiness between fullnesses, the valleys between peaks. I remember the finiteness of affairs.

Still, isn't it nice not to have to take your past, present, and future in your arms? To act out a little pantomime of freedom, or of irresponsibility? My friend and his girl are gamblers and my wife and I are investors who have given hostages to fortune. They are a studio and we are a house.

And so I seesaw through the afternoon, counting my riches and estimating my losses. The light is dying in the room and, when it is long gone, I will lie in my licit bed and they in theirs. If I had it to do over again, I would do it over again, but there is sadness here, too. When children grow up, they never feel that they have played enough.

Through the window of the living room, we watch the sun go down. It is an unusually striking sunset, and we all get up to look. Suddenly the girl is eclipsed. I realize that the world is bigger and more beautiful than she is. Thank God.[10]

BACK TO YOU

If I have tried at some length to define love, this is because your hope for happiness in marriage depends on the quality of love between you and your future mate. Nothing is more important at the immediate outset than for the two of you to utilize all the wisdom and skill you possess to evaluate your relationship. It will not be easy to do so. The physical attraction which is common to infatuation and romance as well as love is so overpowering that under its impact objectivity becomes extremely difficult. Yet your future happiness hinges on how well you can see—in the light of the four criteria enumerated in this chapter—whether your feelings toward each approximate genuine love.

Love is not a static thing; it is a dynamic process. Love either increases or diminishes; it seldom remains the same. Love is largely a matter of right emotional relationship. Perhaps an analogy will help. The parts of a watch must be located and operated in the right relationship in order for one to have a timepiece. If the spring is too large or too small, too strong or too weak in proportion to the other parts, there can be no watch. If all the parts, though they be of proper size, are thrown into an envelope instead of being connected in the right relationship to one another, everything physically necessary for a watch will be present, yet there will be no watch. To have a watch, the sum total of the parts in right relationship to each other must be more than the sum total of the same ingredients disorganized. The same is true of love.

Love is a consuming desire to share one's whole life—both physically and spiritually—with a person of the opposite sex; to share sorrows and pains no less than pleasures and joys. In love, one is at least as anxious to give as to receive. Love is a relationship in which each partner is able to develop his or her own abilities, to fulfill his or her own hopes, in far greater measure than either could have achieved alone. Only those who are truly, deeply in love can expect to enjoy a happy marriage.

CHAPTER THREE

More Than a Matter of Age

Our preceding chapter failed if it did not convince you that love is a far more complicated emotion than most people suppose. Since marriage demands so much understanding of oneself and one's mate, it is for adults, not for children or half-mature adolescents. We live at a time when better and longer educational preparation is required for every profession or skill. How odd it is that precisely at such a time we act as if marriage did not call for at least as much preparation and effort as any vocation.

There have been periods in the past when youthful marriages were more common than today. The Talmud, for example, tells us that "he who reaches the age of twenty and does not marry spends all his days in the thought of sin." We must bear in mind, however, that the Talmud was compiled in a part of the world where young people matured much faster than in the temperate zones and that life was much less complicated then. For that matter, even our earlier rabbis realized that under certain circumstances marriage must be postponed. Two of their qualifying observations are pertinent:

> A man should build himself a home, plant himself a vineyard, and then bring into the home a bride. Fools are they who marry while they have no secure livelihood.

> In olden times the pious sages were willing to go about hungry, and to devote all their attention to Torah and *mitzvot* [the performance of religious obligations]. God came to their succor and aided them on their way. In our times, however, there are no such sincere scholars, and they must not rely upon the aid of God if they do nothing for themselves. Nowadays, no one should marry until his livelihood is secure.[1]

In our western civilization today, there are both advantages and disadvantages to early marriage. One of our most serious moral problems grows out of the fact that young people today are biologically ready to wed long before their social and financial circumstances make marriage possible. The earlier marriage occurs, then, the less insistent will be the pressure toward premarital sexual intercourse.

Unfortunately, this is but half the story. The record of success in youthful marriage is anything but encouraging. Two experts on marriage estimate the divorce rate where both spouses were under twenty-one at the time of their wedding to be six times the rate where both were over thirty-one![2]

The same authorities have summarized their conclusions on this point as follows:

> It is our conviction that many persons marry when they are too young, not necessarily in years but in maturity, in experience, and in the ability to meet the many responsibilities of family living. Such marriages are "bad" marriages, not perhaps because the couple is unsuited to each other, not because of any deficiencies in the persons concerned other than those which time can erase, but because they have assumed life's major responsibility before they were ready to do so. It injures a young horse to do heavy work too soon, the best automobile should not be overtaxed when it is new, a plank breaks when it is overloaded. . . . Marriage means much more than the legality of sharing a common bed.[3]

AGAINST THE ODDS

How can we explain the fact that many couples defy the risks of marrying at younger ages? Well, for one thing, boys and girls today begin to date at a much earlier age than they did a generation ago. When I compare the social sophistication of today's high school sophomores to the naiveté and inexperience characteristic of my friends and myself at that age, the difference is astounding. Youngsters in America today learn to dance earlier, start to smoke and drink earlier than ever before. Many of them, by the time they reach their upper teens, begin to feel bored with casual social contacts and consider themselves ready for marriage.

Until recently very few young men gave serious thought to the possibility of marriage until they were able to provide a living on their own. This is no longer true. Increasing numbers of parents are now willing to subsidize their children, making marriage feasible while they are still students. There has also been an upsurge in the number of marriages where both partners continue to work. These two phenomena—subsidization by parents and two incomes—carry favorable and unfavorable implications for marital success. At a later point we shall consider the pros and cons; for the present, we are interested only in noting that this too is a factor encouraging youthful marriages.

One of the most interesting social changes in recent American life has been the tendency of high school boys and girls to "go steady." Obviously, a boy and girl who have already grown to depend upon each other for regular social contact in their mid-teens are more likely to enter into marriage at an early age than if their social lives had been more diversified.

Closely related to the foregoing is the undeniable fact that sexual standards among adolescents have changed. While the increase may sometimes be exaggerated, the fact remains that greater numbers of both boys and girls indulge in sexual intercourse during their high school and early college years today than in the past. This lowers the average age of marriage in two ways: (a) more single girls are moved to marry because they have become pregnant, and (b) some couples who would probably have broken up in the course of time have gone so far in their sex relations that they would feel guilty were they not to marry. On the former of these counts, certain studies suggest that a third to a half of all high school girls who marry are pregnant at the time of their weddings, while a half to three-fourths of high school grooms feel forced to marry for this reason.

A final factor, though less immediate or obvious, is also responsible for more than a few youthful marriages. We live at a time of increasing anxiety and tension which often overload young people today with emotional pressure. Sometimes marriage is sought as an antidote to uncertainty and stress. It appears to offer a safe harbor from the ominous storms of life.

Of what practical consequence to you and to the success of your marriage is this excursion into the reasons for so many marriages which involve youthful brides and grooms? For one thing, if you are yourselves still in this younger age group, it is important that you examine your own motivations. Among the explanations just given, it is not too difficult to distinguish those which are wholesome and realistic from those which are deceptive and quixotic. But even for couples whose chronological age is more advanced, this discussion should provide food for thought. Readiness for marriage is not just a matter of the number of years one has lived. We have grown accustomed to measuring intelligence by the I.Q. of an individual, his or her *intelligence quotient,* the ratio of intellectual age to chronological age. It would be a great boon for happy marriages if there were an exact way of determining one's E.Q., his or her *emotional quotient,* the ratio of emotional growth to age in years.

Unfortunately, no such device has been invented, nor does one appear likely in the near future. We find ourselves caught in a quandary. Nothing is more essential to success in marriage than emotional maturity, yet few things are more difficult to evaluate. The difficulty must not deter us, however, from trying. No matter what your age or that of your loved one, wisdom dictates that you catalogue the criteria of emotional maturity, then apply them to yourselves.

MEASURING YOUR E. Q.

Even without precise means of measurement, there are valid standards by which to estimate emotional maturity. Emotionally mature individuals display the following traits:

1. They learn from experience, from both successes and failures. Recognizing that they are imperfect human beings—indeed, feeling no need to be perfect—they realize that they will continue to make mistakes all their lives but successfully avoid repeating the same mistakes endlessly.

2. They willingly assume responsibility for their own acts. When the outcome is good, they are ready, without becoming egotistical or boastful, to give themselves due credit; when the outcome is bad, they accept as much of the blame as was really theirs, without feeling threatened by it and without needing a scapegoat.

3. There is purpose to their lives. The routine of daily detail does not stand by itself, isolated from any larger context. Having projected important long-range goals, they plan their activities as progressive steps toward the attainment of those goals. Thus they are able to measure their accomplishment day by day and to feel fulfilled through growth.

4. They learn to live with unhappy situations which they can neither change nor honorably avoid. Understanding that life cannot always be exactly as they would want it, they distinguish between those circumstances within their power to improve and those to which they must become reconciled. They exemplify and follow the well-known prayer which has been attributed to a number of famous individuals: "Lord, give me the courage to change what can be changed, the patience to endure what cannot be changed, and the wisdom to distinguish the one from the other."

5. They accept themselves—their virtues as well as their faults. Since they do not expect to achieve perfection they need not castigate themselves for falling short. They are able to evaluate realistically both their abilities and deficiencies. They can accept criticism and disappointment as those are balanced by achievement and success. So long as they have done reasonably close to their best, failure does not represent disgrace.

6. They are able to do what needs doing now, in the present, neither reliving the past with regret nor preliving the future with undue dread. Emotionally immature or unbalanced persons often live each experience three times: once in fearful anticipation, once in fact, once in morbid remembrance. Thus they drain off two-thirds of their effective energy from the task at hand. This does not mean that mature persons live without careful planning or serious inventory; we have already referred to the need for a meaningful context or plan. The emphasis to be remembered here is that, having planned as carefully and wisely as possible, having carried out that plan as efficiently as circumstances and their own abilities permitted, having briefly absorbed whatever was to be learned from the experiences just concluded, they then proceed to plan the next step, without wallowing in remorse or becoming obsessed with what they did wrong.

7. Mature persons do not need to dominate or control others. They find sufficient satisfaction in improving themselves, in exercising their own freedom, in exploiting their own capacities, so that they gladly extend the same privileges to others. When they find themselves in positions of authority, they are able to discharge the responsibilities of leadership without becoming arrogant or destroying the integrity of those who work under their direction. When they are subordinates, they are able to follow reasonable instructions without feeling diminished.

8. They are able to defer a pleasure currently available for the sake of a greater fulfillment which cannot come until later and which depends on renouncing the enjoyment immediately at hand. Mature persons deny themselves the rich dessert they crave if they are already overweight and their health demands lower caloric intake; their immature friends glut themselves, regardless of what their physician has advised. Mature persons can forego satisfaction of many immediate wants for the sake of benefits which will not accrue until several years later. Immature persons want what they want when they want it—which is usually at once.

9. Another category of qualities which distinguishes mature persons is rather difficult to label. Perhaps it can best be

identified by such terms as spontaneity, openness, and humor. Mature persons enjoy a good joke, whether directed joshingly at them or others. They are neither sadistic in the employment of humor toward others, nor masochistic in interpreting it as a threat when aimed in their direction. Their conduct is frequently characterized by a free and even joyous spontaneity. They give evidence of enjoying life, not of fearing it.

10. A final attribute of mature persons is their capacity to grow. Their personality is not static nor stagnant. Marriage itself can be a most effective instrument for improved maturity. But it can succeed only if bride and groom bring to it the raw materials of at least reasonable maturity at the time of their wedding. This involves an ability to be flexible, to change opinions in the face of new facts, to seek new kinds of experience.

FROM THEORY TO FACT

These criteria of maturity will be only of academic value unless they are accurately applied. There are no substitutes for maturity, no easy detours, no clever little self-deceptions which will succeed permanently. It is imperative that you and your future spouse evaluate yourselves honestly, that each of you rate yourself separately, then compare your estimates. Using the chart suggested below and without prior consultation, let each rate self and spouse/fiancé, giving *four points* for *superior maturity, three points* for *above average, two points* for *average* and *one point* for *below average.* If there are wide discrepancies between your self-evaluations and the ratings given by the other, this merits discussion of how realistic you have been.

There is another point to be made in connection with these evaluations. In a seven-year study of married couples, Dr. Eleanor Braun Luckey of the University of Connecticut discovered the immense importance of mates agreeing in their estimates, each of self and of the other. She said: "Couples who agree with each other about the kind of person the other one is, whether I might agree or not, tend to be the most satisfied partners."[4] In addition, therefore, to measuring your respective degrees of maturity on the following scale, it will be instructive to learn whether you agree on the ratings each gives the other.

Where two individuals are attracted to each other by romance rather than love, it is entirely possible for them to agree in their ratings, yet for both to be inaccurate and unrealistic. An effective check against this can be provided by asking one or more intimate but objective friends to rate the couple too, then to compare all the ratings for each person.

In making these evaluations, several additional factors should be kept in mind. First, remember that very few people, if any, are fully mature by all these standards and in every situation. Each of us is a combination of maturity and immaturity. An individual can be mature in one situation or at one time, inconsistently immature in another situation on the following day. One who is admirably mature in the office or socially may be childishly immature at home or in rearing children. Yet for most of us there is a discernibly consistent trend; it should be possible to characterize us as tending in general to be at a certain point on the spectrum of maturity. Incidentally, if there is too wide a variance in the maturity an individual displays from moment to moment or day to day, that in itself may be evidence of emotional imbalance.

It is also desirable to base your ratings of your partner on as wide a variety of circumstances and settings as possible. An individual's conduct should be appraised not only in terms of behavior with a prospective mate but also with respect to family, friends, and larger social groups. It is possible for one to "put on a good act" toward a person one wants very much to impress; the probability of successfully maintaining such a pose over a long period of time and toward a large group of associates is considerably lower.

HOW MATURE ARE WE?
1. Below average
2. Average
3. Above average
4. Superior

COMPARING OUR MATURITY	MY RATINGS		YOUR RATINGS	
	Of Myself	Of You	Of Yourself	Of Me
1. Learns from experience				
2. Assumes responsibility				
3. Has purpose in life				
4. Accepts the inevitable				
5. Accepts, respects self				
6. Concentrates on the task of the present				
7. No need to dominate				
8. Able to postpone pleasure				
9. Demonstrates spontaneity and humor				
10. Possesses capacity to grow				

Granted that the most desirable match is between two individuals both of whom are at least reasonably mature, suppose you discover that this is not the case with you and your intended? Which combination augurs better for success: two persons, both of whom are immature? Or one who is perceptibly more mature than the other? No one can pretend to possess a sure or certain answer to this question. It is my own suspicion that, while neither alternative promises an ideal marriage, the first is probably more favorable than the second. As we shall see in our next chapter, compatibility is a factor of enormous importance in marriage. The more two persons are alike—in personal characteristics and temperament as well as in values and goals—the greater the probability of achieving happiness together. It seems to me, therefore, that a wide divergence in maturity between husband and wife would be productive of even more tension and frustration than a sharing of immature traits.

Even this, however, is subject to careful qualification. Immature needs are of different kinds. In either of the imperfect situations proposed above, it is possible for the needs of two individuals either to aggravate or to complement each other. For example: if one partner to a marriage has a need to dominate, while the other has an equal need to be dependent— provided that their respective needs are not too extreme and that the individuals are reasonably compatible in most other respects—the prospect for success in their marriage may not be hopeless. In any event, few responsibilities of an engaged couple are more important, more productive of future happiness, than a careful, honest evaluation by each of the emotional maturity disclosed by both.

PAST . . . PRESENT . . . FUTURE

Maturity is not a set, static goal which can be attained once and for all time, then forgotten. It is a product of the past, a level of achievement in the present, a hope for the future. The wise man or woman strives for increasing maturity throughout life.

As a person matures, values and goals change. At a given point in life it is perfectly proper for a marble or toy to be one's most prized possession. Later, in successive stages, top priority goes to a bicycle, a popular record, a souped-up convertible, a college education, a job, a subscription to the symphony, participation in the struggle for civil rights or world peace. If —at the moment of marriage or through subsequent growth on the part of either mate—an individual who is still at the convertible stage is wedded to one who has reached the symphony level, trouble may be in the offing.

The gravest danger in undertaking marriage when either partner is manifestly immature is that the future is unknown.

If husband and wife mature along parallel lines, the prognosis can be favorable. If, however, their paths of maturation proceed in divergent directions, they may well be even more poorly matched on their fifth anniversary than on their wedding day. Hence the extreme importance of both personalities being rather clearly shaped and the permanent values of both being identifiably charted before their lives are joined. When two sculptors have barely begun to shape their respective masses of clay, it is too early to tell whether their final works of art will go well together. Only after both have proceeded well along the way is it possible to judge their compatibility.

The importance of maturing along similar lines persists throughout marriage. If, after their wedding, the interests of husband and wife diverge too drastically, they will come to enjoy less and less in common. It is pathetically sad to see couples in their fifties who have drifted so far apart through the years that they share only bed and board. Conversely, there is abundant fulfillment for the couples who increasingly enjoy together their recreations, their hobbies, their most serious social and spiritual concerns. To be retained in later years, however, such mutuality must be cultivated from the beginning.

There are stages through which one grows to the maturity essential for marriage. From birth on, we grow into and through periods when the principal object of our affection is, respectively: ourselves; our parents, first mother, then both; our clique, consisting of our own sex; members of the opposite sex in general; one particular member of the opposite sex, on whom we have a "crush," the targets of such "crushes" normally and healthily changing from time to time; then, finally, the one person of opposite sex whom we desire and need as a permanent partner.

Persons who have skipped any of these stages are not likely to have achieved full maturity. By the same token, those who exhibit as adults too many lingering traces of traits which were appropriate only to an earlier level of life are also poor candidates for marriage.

It is in this context that the practice of "going steady" at an early age is likely to be dangerous. The person who has enjoyed a wide range of social experience, who has dated many members of the other sex, who has had the opportunity to relate socially to a variety of personalities is thereby better able to judge the type of individual best suited as a partner for life.

The relationship of a mate to a parent of the opposite sex is of special importance. Modern depth psychology has helped us understand scientifically a truth which was intuitively suspected even by the ancients. At one period of childhood every normal boy experiences a strong sexual attraction toward his mother and every girl toward her father. In most instances, moreover, this feeling is reciprocated: fathers feel an unconscious sexual attraction to their daughters and mothers to their sons. In psychiatric jargon this is known as the Oedipus Complex. There is nothing abnormal or immoral about it, provided it be a stage from which both parent and child emerge.

Sometimes, however, a young woman may still be too strongly attached, on an unconscious level, to her father or a son to his mother. This is frequently the case when a bride is many years younger than her groom or a husband too much younger than his wife. Each may then be searching—again unconsciously—for a father-substitute or mother-substitute rather than a mate. It is important, therefore, not only that the age differential between you and your beloved be confronted (more about this in the next chapter), but also that you be aware of the relationship of each partner to the parent of the opposite sex. Neither extreme is good. Just as a woman errs in seeking a husband who duplicates her father, so, if she has harbored deep resentment of her father, she makes a possibly fatal mistake in selecting a man as different from her father as she can.

The Oedipal relationship can be no less troublesome when it is the parent who hasn't outgrown too strong an attraction to a son or daughter. A mother who insists that no girl is good enough for her son or who finds fault with every girl in whom he is seriously interested—a father who exhibits the same pattern of behavior toward his daughter—these are in all probability parents who haven't emancipated themselves yet from an intensity of relationship which is quite normal at one stage in life but fraught with explosive possibilities if it persists.

RUNNING AWAY?

There are two additional complications to be considered on the immensely important topic of emotional maturity. It sometimes happens that—consciously or unconsciously—marriage represents an escape-hatch from a situation or condition which appears to be intolerable. It can be an unhappy home or parental pressure or a frustrating job or indecision in choosing a vocation or almost any other kind of tension. Marriage can serve either as a convenient escape or an effective psychological weapon with which to strike out against an offending parent, sibling, or boss.

This danger is compounded by the fact that the mechanism for escape or rebellion is an unconscious one. About all you can do is to be aware of the possibility, to give it special credence if either you or your intended has been generally an unhappy, frustrated individual. One marriage expert has summarized this situation with exceptional eloquence:

> How often is this "love" which some feel the desire to get away from a quarrelsome, bickering family, a dominating mother, or a tight little office in which one feels stifled? It is understandable that people should strive to get away from that which annoys them, although the basic reasons for the annoyance may be in themselves. When you marry, you *assume* responsibilities; you do not *escape* them. A good marriage will mean that life will be much richer and more worthwhile, but it will not be easier. Marriage creates as many problems as it solves. The success of your marriage will depend upon what you are getting into, not what you get away from.[5]

An important implication of this statement is that the person who is suffering a serious emotional disability should not undertake marriage as a cure. Those who are experiencing difficulty handling themselves and their problems while single will nearly always confront even graver trouble when married. Marriage is not therapy. True, it can contribute to the maturity of a person who is reasonably adjusted at the start, and husband and wife can be of enormous help to each other at times of emotional turbulence, but serious personal problems are best resolved before marriage. If, therefore, either you or your future mate is in the midst of psychotherapy, the wisest course is to delay your wedding until your therapy is either completed or very nearly so.

We spoke of two complications. The second is the danger of falling into a bad marriage on the rebound. Quite often a person who has just been jilted or has recently broken off a romantic relationship will almost immediately take up with a new partner and rush with undue haste into a permanent attachment. Though psychologically simple to understand, this is fraught with immeasurable harm. To terminate a relationship on which one has depended for emotional security and status can be painful in the extreme. To seek reinforcement for damaged self-esteem and pride is natural. An emotional vacuum is as difficult to tolerate as a physical vacuum. For that very reason, however, one's objective judgment is, under these circumstances, likely to be less than its best. If either you or your beloved, then, has recently rebounded from disappointment in what had seemed to be love, there is every reason to proceed now with extra caution and delay. Make sure you are being positively attracted to something wholesome and good, not negatively repelled by a frustration or defeat which is difficult to endure.

THE QUESTION REMAINS

We have not finally and firmly answered the question with which this chapter commenced. Are you and your beloved ready for marriage? Only the two of you can answer this question. By the same token, the two of you stand to benefit most if your replies are valid, to suffer most if they are not. There is no set age in years and months, no exact point of time, at which everyone is ready to marry. Some persons in their late teens may be better prepared than others whose age is twice as great. Competence for marriage is more a matter of emotional maturity than of chronological age. There are couples who should marry at an early age, others who should avoid marriage until one or both have achieved more maturity. The exasperating, often agonizing dilemma of marriage counselors and rabbis is that the couples who need most desperately to wait are frequently the very ones most impulsively determined to proceed in haste.

Are you really ready?

CHAPTER FOUR

Water and Oil

Can we assume that a man and woman who know the meaning of love, who are capable of giving and receiving love, and who are both reasonably mature are automatically assured of happiness in their marriage? Unfortunately, no. While the prognosis for success is obviously better with affirmative than with negative responses to the questions raised in the preceding chapters, we have only begun our inquiry. Even two fine, adult individuals —both ready for a mature love relationship—can fail if they are not properly matched. A marriage can be bad, not because of glaring defects in either person, but because they were just not right for each other.

Water and oil cannot be permanently blended. No matter how successfully they be momentarily homogenized, before long each will resume its chemical identity, separate from the other. So it is with man and woman in marriage—if by disposition and nature they just don't naturally mix.

In some civilizations the responsibility of selecting a mate rested, not on the bride and groom, but on their parents. For many centuries an important functionary in the Jewish community was the שדכן (shadchan) or matchmaker, whose professional task it was to negotiate with parents for the matching of their children in marriage. There are other culture groups in which this practice is carried to such an extreme that bride and groom do not even meet until the day of their wedding.

Before dismissing this procedure out of hand, we should

36

recognize that it had some advantages. Parents can sometimes be more objectively sensitive than their children to such factors as similarity of background, parallels of personality, or financial competence and prospects. There can be no question, however, despite vestigial remains of such parental initiative among some immigrant groups, that in our social setting the pendulum has swung to the opposite extreme. From having had everything to say in the choice of a mate for their child, parents are now often excluded from the decision entirely.

Balancing the rights and demands of parents against the rights and needs of their grown children is a subtle, at times an excruciating, experience. A medieval rabbi, Judah ben Samuel of Regensburg, knew this. He wrote:

> Parents may not hinder a son's marriage that he may continue to work for them; let him take a wife and remain with them still. If he can find no wife at the place where his parents live, and these be aged and need his care, let him not leave that city; and, if, taking a wife, he can no longer care for such helpless father and mother, let him remain unwedded. If he can pay for the support and care of his parents, then he has a right to seek a wife and settle elsewhere, only let him see to it that they [presumably, the support and care] are not such as are repugnant to the parents' feelings. If his choice has fallen on a worthy girl of honorable parentage, but his father or mother wish to force him to take one not worthy, because her relatives offer money, he need by no means yield to his parents' wishes, for their proceeding is blameworthy.[1]

Where the general relationship within a family has been healthy and loving, parents will be invited into the process of selecting a mate; their advice will be welcomed, though not necessarily always followed. The primary responsibility, of course, must rest upon the couple.

Jewish tradition has not been unaware of how heavy this responsibility is. The Talmud advises: "Be quick in buying land; be deliberate in taking a wife."[2] Rabbinic literature also contains a not-so-subtle suggestion to parents that theirs is at most a minor role in the selection of mates for their grown children. This is the inescapable inference from the story of how perturbed King Solomon is reputed to have been when it was revealed to him in a dream that his beautiful daughter was destined to marry one of the poorest young men in his kingdom. He disapproved the match and was determined to prevent it. So he built a palace on an inaccessible island and surrounded it with an impregnable stone wall, locking his daughter and her servants in to isolate her from her prospective groom.

Some time thereafter the young man Solomon had seen in his dream was wandering one cold night in the forest. Lacking enough clothing to keep from freezing, he came upon the carcass of a bull and climbed into it for warmth. As he slept, a huge bird snatched up the carcass, flew with it many miles, and dropped it on the roof of the island palace. When the princess went to the roof the following morning, she beheld the handsome young man; at once they fell in love. After a time they were married in the presence of her servants.[3] Our rabbis apparently were aware that not even the utmost effort of a strong-minded king could prevent his daughter from marrying whom she would.

NOT SO EASY

The scholars of Judaism recognized that it is no simple matter to match men and women for marriage.

> A matron once asked Rabbi Jose ben Halafta: "What has your God been doing since He finished making the world?" "He has been matching couples in marriage," was the reply. . . . The matron declared that she could do as much herself; nothing was easier than to couple any number of slaves with as many slave-girls.
>
> "You may think it easy," said Rabbi Jose, "but it is as difficult for God as dividing the Red Sea."
>
> The matron accordingly tried the experiment with a thousand males and as many female slaves, setting

them in rows and bidding this man take this woman, etc. The next morning they came to her, one with a broken head, another with gouged-out eyes, a third with a broken leg; one man saying: "I don't want her," and a girl saying: "I don't want him." Thus was the matron constrained to say that the mating of man and woman was a task not unworthy the intelligence of God.[4]

Does this talmudic tale imply that marriages are made in heaven? It would seem so, from the comment made elsewhere: "Forty days before the formation of a child, a Voice proclaims in heaven: 'So-and-so's daughter is to marry so-and-so's son!' "[5] Post-talmudic rabbis, however, emphasized that human cooperation is also needed for divine choice to be effective. This we find especially in the final sentences of the following quotation from the זהר (*Zohar*), great sourcebook of medieval Jewish mysticism:

> Each soul and spirit, prior to its entering into this world, consists of a male and female united into one being. When it descends on this earth the two parts separate and animate two different bodies. At the time of marriage, the Holy One, blessed be He, who knows all souls and spirits, unites them again as they were before, and they again constitute one body and one soul, forming as it were the right and left of one individual. . . . *This union, however, is influenced by the deeds of the man and by the way in which he walks. If the man is pure and his conduct is pleasing in the sight of God, he is united with that female part of his soul which was his component part prior to his birth.* [6]

In a later chapter we shall turn our attention to a modern interpretation of the connection between God and love. For the time being, let it simply be noted that our ancestors expressed their conviction that marriage is a noble, sacred enterprise by associating it with God. While recognizing that in a very real sense God enters into every successful love experience between man and woman, we cannot pass the buck to God in the selection of a mate. We must attempt to discover for ourselves what it takes for two people to be successfully matched for life. And any two individuals who are contemplating marriage owe it to each other and themselves to ask in depth: are we really well matched?

A DIFFICULT DEFINITION

What we have been leading up to in preceding paragraphs, obviously, is the subject of compatibility. Usually this word is assumed to mean sexual compatibility. While a good sexual adjustment is of undeniable importance, to restrict the meaning of compatibility to this one area is to distort monstrously the nature of love. There are numerous kinds of compatibility; the wise couples will attempt to judge their congeniality with respect to all of them.

There is, for example, *intellectual compatibility.* Marriage is a meeting of minds as well as bodies. Husband and wife presumably intend to live together for many years; if they have nothing in common intellectually, no serious concerns to discuss and share, they face a future of tasteless boredom. For a bright, egotistical man to marry a dull, doting girl may temporarily meet the needs of both, but before long their relationship will grow tedious. Our rabbis knew this long centuries ago. Addressing themselves to a man of intelligence, they said:

> A man should sell all he possesses with the object of marrying the daughter of a scholar or giving his daughter in marriage to a scholar. This is like uniting grapes of the vine to grapes of the vine, which is good and acceptable. But let him not marry the daughter of an ignoramus, because that is like uniting grapes of the vine to berries of the bush, which is something ugly and unacceptable.[7]

It should go without saying that the same danger exists where intellectual incompatibility favors a wife rather than her husband. It has been my experience through years of premarital and marital counseling that most couples do rather well in meeting this criterion of compatibility, perhaps better than on some of the others to be discussed in a moment. Where two particular persons contemplating marriage differ from each other too widely in intellectual capacity, there is reason to suspect that they are attracted by infatuation, not love.

A fourteen-year-old patient once told her psychiatrist she could always tell which were the married couples in a restaurant. When questioned concerning her method, she replied: "It's easy! They're the ones who have nothing to say to each other during dinner." Two people who share so little intellectually that, as a general rule, they have nothing to say to each other beyond their immediate problems and needs can expect little enduring happiness in their marriage.

The enormous stress which Jewish tradition places on intelligence in the choosing of a mate is reflected in this passage from the עָרוּךְ שֻׁלְחָן (*Shulchan Aruch*), sixteenth-century code of law by which Orthodox Jewish life is still governed:

> A man ought always to strive to win in marriage the daughter of a Torah scholar, and to give his daughter in marriage to a Torah scholar. If he cannot find the daughter of a Torah scholar, let him seek to marry the daughter of a renowned communal leader; if he cannot find one of these, let his choice be the daughter of a congregational leader; if not one of these, then the trustee of a charitable fund; if not one of these, let him select the daughter of an elementary Hebrew teacher, but let him not marry off his daughter to an ignorant man.[8]

In reading a reference such as this, it must be remembered that the advice is obviously directed to one who possesses considerable intelligence himself. It recommends, then, not only the value of intelligence as such, but also the need for this level of compatibility.

By the way, the obvious sexism in some of my quotations from Jewish sources may bother you. Most medieval and premodern authorities seem to have concentrated only on males. To alter their wording in the light of our broader understanding would mean, I believe, to distort their views. Needless to say, however, in considering marriage today we must be equally concerned with the nature and needs of both sexes.

Cultural compatibility is implied in our emphasis on the importance of being well-matched intellectually. It is important enough to be asserted explicitly. Do you and your prospective mate both like theater? Art? Music? Books? Opera? Are your tastes in these areas similar or quite different? During your engagement have you found yourselves battling over cultural preferences, or ignoring each other's desires, or learning from each other? Cultural differences can become either a weapon with which two people beat each other, or a priceless opportunity for each to expand the horizons and enrich the life of the other. The probable success of your marriage can be in part predicted by the pattern of cultural accommodation you have already established.

This is an important consideration in the creation of culture as well as in appreciating it. It is surely not essential for both husband and wife to be creative in the same field, though this can be an asset if neither feels competitively threatened by the other. What is essential—if either is creative—is that the partner appreciate what is being created and encourage its continuance. A scientist who has no use for art, who is allergic to museums and exhibits, would probably make a poor husband for a painter whose skill with the canvas is exquisite but to whom a laboratory is first-cousin to a horror chamber.

Insofar as love is concerned, the old adage, "opposites attract," is nonsense. Opposites—in personality, in temperament, in values, in cultural proclivities—may for a time be infatuated with one another. They will never know the meaning of love.

Religion is a part of culture, viewed in its broadest context. The ultimate values and ideals of a man and woman—which means to say, their religious orientation—also call for a high order of consistency if their marriage is to succeed. Our very brief listing of *religious compatibility* at this point is due only to the fact that an entire chapter will be devoted to it later.

Social compatibility is also important. The minute this is mentioned, I expose myself to criticism as a snob. The risk is worth assuming if I can succeed in emphasizing the fact—and it *is* a fact—that, all other things being equal, two individuals who emanate from similar social backgrounds have a higher probability of marital success than two who do not. Cinderella-type matches of rags and riches lead to happiness more often in print or on film than in life. All serious studies of marriage show this to be true. Similarity of social background reduces the likelihood of wide discrepancies in the customs, values, expectations, and ambitions with which husband and wife confront each other and their friends. The point to be made here is not that one social setting or class is superior to another, only that—whatever the class—it is wise for bride and groom to come from the same one.

MONEY TALKS—AND TELLS

Next is *economic compatibility.* What we have in mind here is not the financial resources of bride and groom respectively—that would really be included in social background—but rather their attitudes and ambitions on financial matters. The marriage of an extravagant spender to a compulsive saver does not augur well. Neither does that of a country club devotee to one who would prefer to buy paintings and books. In short, it is important, not only that both mates agree generally on saving versus spending, but also that they see alike on the direction their spending is to take. In Chapter 6 we shall consider at greater length the role of financial management in marriage. For the present our concern is with consistency between the financial attitudes and needs of husband and wife. This is essential for its own sake, in order to avoid excessive controversy over money.

It is even more significant, however, because one's approach to money and its uses tells a great deal about one's personality as a whole. Money is a symbol—next to sex, perhaps the most important symbol in many lives. This is especially true in our type of economically oriented culture. The feelings of an individual toward money disclose significant aspects of that individual's total character. The compulsive spender is an altogether different kind of person from the obsessive saver; in marriage, they are likely to clash in many areas quite beyond the domain of the dollar.

Here are good questions to explore with utmost honesty: If we unexpectedly found ourselves with a surplus of ten thousand dollars, would we agree on how much of it to spend and how much to save? And having decided that, would we both want to utilize in the same way the part we planned to spend?

The answer to this last question opens up the entire area of values and goals. Unless the prospective partners to a marriage pursue similar purposes in life, their prognosis for happiness is not good. Here it becomes necessary to be as specific as possible and to consider motives as well as objectives. A friend of mine whose first marriage failed tells me, by way of illustration, that both he and his wife wanted a garden. On the face of it, this concurrence of desires might seem to indicate great compatibility. Actually, it disclosed nothing of the sort! He wanted a garden because he loved flowers; she wanted one to impress the neighbors. What may at first glance have given the appearance of compatibility was in fact quite the opposite!

A husband who desires to purchase paintings as an investment is on that score not well matched to a woman who chooses paintings for the beauty of the art itself. In short, it is necessary to compare *reasons* and *motives,* not just superficial symptoms, if one would truly measure compatibility.

Before leaving the subject of financial compatibility, a word should be added on marrying for money. According to an old quip, it is just as easy to fall in love with a rich person as with a poor one. Yet the matter is not so simple. If the wealth of either bride or groom was an inconsequential or minor consideration in the attraction between them, it need not unduly concern us. But if such wealth was a primary and proximate cause of the attraction, there may be trouble ahead. For one thing, unless both were wealthy, our previous comments about social compatibility would be pertinent here. Aside from that, a whole complex of problems could develop out of a relationship in which one mate feels inferior to or excessively dependent upon the other.

The Talmud contains two epigrammatic admonitions on marrying for money:

> He who weds for money will have delinquent off-spring.[9]

> He who looks for the earnings of his wife sees never a sign of blessing.[10]

Compatibility is also essential in *a wide variety of personality traits,* any one of which may seem by itself to be only of minor consequence, but all of which together build up to major proportions. If one mate, for example, is rigid while the other is permissive and lax—if one is punctual, the other careless of time—if one is neat, the other sloppy—if one is a shy introvert, the other an exuberant extrovert—their future together may well be rocky. Not only will they constantly quarrel over the direct issues they confront—over the disciplining of their children, the budgeting of their time, the management of their household, the intensity of their social life—these apparently superficial divergences also bespeak deeper differences in personality which will plague them. In the daily commerce of sharing bed and board, little annoyances are symptomatic of bigger problems and soon assume major significance themselves. In his extravagantly amusing play, *The Odd Couple,* Neil Simon portrayed how true this is even for two men sharing an apartment. It is far truer for husband and wife.

Since a primary enterprise of marriage is the rearing of a family, *similar attitudes toward children* constitute yet another valid dimension of compatibility. To improve your prospect for a happy marriage, you should agree on whether or not to have children, on the number desired and how they should be spaced, on at least the major principles of educating and disciplining them. While it is too much to expect a complete program of child development before you are even married, there are significant and revealing questions that should be asked right now. Do you both like or dislike being with children? Are you attracted to the same kinds of children? Do you agree or disagree on the way your parents reared you, on the way your friends are rearing their offspring? Alert attention to this kind of comparison now can avert considerable tension and heartache later.

STILL MORE

As long as this list has already become, we have by no means finished yet with the kinds of compatibility which are essential in marriage.

Similarities in leisure time interests are too frequently overlooked by couples contemplating marriage. Yet they are extremely important. Our economic system is such that—with the relatively rare exception of the husband and wife who work together in a profession or business—most couples will be destined to spend by far the greater portion of their waking hours apart. The amount of time they manage to spend together, then, becomes crucial in shaping the success of their marriage. Two of the earliest scientific students of marriage in this country concluded, after extensive investigation, that couples who share and enjoy all their leisure activities together have fifteen times as much chance for marital happiness as do couples who lack such sharing.

There is grave danger that a marriage may degenerate into nothing but a convenient fiscal arrangement for managing a household and providing sexual satisfaction. Couples who permit this to happen in their relationship are cheating themselves. Only if there are parallel leisure time preferences at the start, and a strong desire by both to spend as much, not as little, time together as possible, can their marriage be realized in full. A good question, then, to face right now is whether, in addition to enjoying each other's company, you also enjoy doing the same things together.

The importance of this factor has been underscored by Dr. Henry A. Bowman, a University of Texas sociologist who specializes in the study of modern marriage. He has emphasized that "leisure pursuits serve as common interests or as points of departure for conflicts." They therefore can either exacerbate or dissipate tension. Trouble is in store for couples who strongly disagree either on the use of their leisure or on how much time they want to spend together.[11]

The immediately preceding paragraphs should not be misconstrued to mean that husband and wife must spend every minute of their leisure time together. Separate hobbies or avocations can certainly be tolerated in marriage—provided they do not dominate most of a couple's spare time and if the proportion of time spent together is agreeable to both.

Much has been written recently about each partner's retaining his or her independence in marriage. This becomes a more vexing problem as more wives pursue careers of their own. There is no magic formula, no perfect balance between independence and dependence, which can serve as a guideline for all couples. No two individuals are identical; the relationship between each husband and wife is unique. You and your spouse will have to discover for yourselves the proportion most likely to enhance your own marriage, while giving both of you full range to develop your individual capacities. If you are wise, this will be an area for discussion and experimentation during your courtship. The more nearly alike the two of you are on a spectrum between the two extremes of dependence versus independence, the greater will be your probability of finding happiness together.

Marriage involves many paradoxes; not the least of them is the fact that, while two people in a very real sense merge their lives, neither surrenders the right to privacy. Both husband and wife are entitled to quiet moments alone. This will be especially necessary and true where two careers are involved. I know of two mates—both professionals—whose back-to-back desks are in a single large study. They often enjoy working at the same time, neither interrupting nor disturbing the other. I have heard of two other mates who—as a result of friction about privacy in the early years of their marriage—have adopted a unique set of signals. When he puts on his golf hat or she her scarf, the other immediately knows that there is a need at that moment for privacy.

Compatibility in age has already been mentioned in Chapter 3.

While no one can project an iron-clad formula, there is no doubt that too great a disparity in age is not good, regardless of whether the husband is much older than the wife or she than he. In addition to what has already been said regarding the dangerous unconscious factors which can be involved in such cases, there are two extremely serious practical problems when the bride is substantially younger than the groom. The first emerges from the fact that the life expectancy of women in the United States is appreciably greater than that of men. The average wife must therefore anticipate that her husband will probably predecease her, leaving her later in life as a widow. The greater the age-spread between them, the longer her possible period of loneliness. Admittedly, this isn't the pleasantest kind of consideration, especially at the approach of one's marriage. Yet the wise person will not, for that reason, avoid it. Marriage is meant to be a partnership for life. No sensible person would enter into a long-range business contract without considering the remote as well as the immediate circumstances. No less should be true of marriage.

The second serious practical problem, when a husband is many years older than his wife, has to do with their sexual relationship. A woman of twenty and a man of thirty-five can enjoy a mutually gratifying sex life together. But when she is fifty-five and he seventy, their sexual adjustment may be complicated. Even though both are still sexually active, the frequency of their desires and capacities can differ greatly.

During the very week this chapter was first being drafted, the impending marriages of two Hollywood stars were announced. One, at the age of sixty-one, was marrying a woman of twenty-seven; the other, fifty-nine years old, was matched with a girl of nineteen. It was the third or fourth time around for both grooms. Couples such as these may be able for a time to tantalize and titillate each other; the probability of their achieving an enduring marriage is remote.

The insight and wisdom of Judaism are manifest here too. According to the Talmud, "he who weds his daughter to an old man, and he who gives a wife unto his minor son, commits a wrong."[12] The Torah directs that, when a man dies without having given his wife a child, his brother is obliged to marry the widow so that a child can be conceived to carry on the dead man's name. This obviously preceded the time when monogamy was introduced into Jewish practice. The Book of Deuteronomy tells us that, if the brother of the deceased is reluctant to fulfill this obligation, "the elders of his city shall call him and speak to him." In commenting on this passage, the Talmud says:

> This teaches that they gave him advice suitable for him. If he was young and she old, or vice versa, they would say to him, "What sense is there in your marrying one much younger than yourself?" or "What sense is there in your marrying one much older than yourself? Go, marry one who is about your own age and do not introduce strife into your house."[13]

Evidently the rabbis considered too great a discrepancy in age so significant an obstacle to successful marriage that they were willing, on this account, to defer another biblical custom which they deemed to be important.

Interest in other people is yet another area in which compatibility is important. The kind of people whom one likes usually resemble oneself, or at least one's conscious impression of self. Thus our friends are often reflections of our own personalities and values. A man and woman who like each other's friends, who react similarly to a third person whom they both have met for the first time, are in this respect compatible. It is worth observing also that, according to reliable studies of marriage, individuals who have many friends of their own sex seem to make better marriages than those with few friends.

A PERENNIAL PROBLEM

There have probably been more indisposed jokes about in-laws than about any other kind of human relationship. Yet there is nothing funny about a couple whose marriage must scale the rapids of tension with parents. In many years of counseling engaged and married couples, the in-law problem is one mentioned to me frequently as an obstacle to happiness. True, in-laws are sometimes just convenient scapegoats, plausible disguises by which husband and wife distract their attention from more fundamental sources of aggravation. But they are also the primary source of difficulty often enough to merit our serious consideration. Hence the urgency of *compatibility with your mate's family.*

There is an almost irresistible temptation to object at this point: "But I'm not marrying a family; I'm marrying an individual!" True, yet at the same time not entirely true. The family of your future mate has already become so vital a part of that mate that no one can completely divorce them. If you propose to live in the same community with either or both of your families, it will be especially necessary to work out a harmonious relationship. Even if you intend to live at a remote distance from them, emotional ties are much more persistent and pervasive than geographical bonds. A wife whose husband is at odds with her parents can be torn to pieces by conflicting loyalties and loves. A husband whose wife is at war with his parents is in no less lamentable a position. Many a marriage has been wrecked on the rocks of in-law trouble.

On an even more elementary level than this, you are indeed marrying a family. Some of the characteristics you resent in your future in-laws may well be integral aspects of your beloved's personality, though the blinders of romantic infatuation may prevent you from seeing them. If in fact they are present, the more realistic light of daily intimate encounter will expose them. Both the physical and emotional health of your mate have been affected by and are largely dependent upon his or her family and the relationship between them. Your children will inherit half their heredity from your mate's family; what an ironic twist of fate it is when one perceives in one's own child a trait abhorred in the in-laws!

Our sages can be forgiven their genetic error in supposing that children resemble their maternal uncles; the larger point they were attempting to express is nonetheless valid: "Before taking a wife, investigate her brothers, for most children resemble their mother's brothers."[14]

IN GENERAL

Any professional who spends considerable time trying to help unhappy couples salvage something of their marriages is amazed over and over again at how infrequently these people gave serious attention in advance to the levels of compatibility outlined in this chapter. You may feel that I have gone to the opposite extreme, that my discussion makes love and marriage seem like cold, rational, almost mechanical relationships rather than primarily matters of emotion. True, in reacting against one extreme I may have swung suspiciously toward its opposite.

Yet there need be no fear that marriage will cease to be for the most part emotionally motivated. There is greater danger by far that it will be *only* emotional. The role of reason with respect to emotion is rather like that of skillful tacking in sailing a boat. Wind of necessity remains one's motive power. But if wind is permitted to have its way, to carry a small vessel wherever it will, the sailor will never reach his desired destination. So, without deploring or denying the value of the wind, the prudent sailor sets his sails carefully and holds his rudder firmly—the better to utilize the power supplied by wind to go where his mind and will have planned. Normal, average human beings need have no apprehension that emotion will be lacking in their love experience. Their realistic concern should be instead whether they have injected enough reason in their relationship to channel their emotions constructively. One does not walk about with a pencil and chart, rating a candidate scientifically before proposing. Nor can computers replace human instincts and emotions. The wise person, however, when becoming more than casually or platonically interested in another, will pause to reflect on their compatibility before seriously approaching the possibility of marriage.

The Bible offers an instructive passage on this point. When offered any gift he might want of God, King Solomon asked for "an understanding heart." Now, one usually associates understanding with the head rather than the heart. Is it far-fetched to suppose that Solomon had in mind the very issue we have raised here? What he was really requesting was a combination most desirable in life generally, in marriage especially: rich emotion tempered by firm intelligence.

It would be a serious error to suppose that husband and wife can or should be carbon copies of each other. Even if such duplication were possible, it would produce an insufferably dull and boring marriage. Our goal should be, not to seek exact facsimiles of ourselves, but to make sure that we and our contemplated mates are reasonably similar in most important respects, that we do not differ too irreconcilably in any, and that our divergences complement rather than aggravate each other.

The individual who marries in the expectation of being able to remodel the mate, so to speak, is making a foolish mistake. Our personal characteristics and temperament have been pretty well established for life by the time we are old enough to consider marriage. Short of either a traumatic experience or psychotherapy in depth, we will remain basically for life the same kind of person. Unless you like that kind of person —could gladly live with that kind of person, with both the virtues and faults you perceive—beware of a permanent entanglement! Two people who live together in a loving marriage can indeed affect each other, can learn from each other; it has been said that sometimes husband and wife in the course of time come not only to think alike, to anticipate each other's conversation, but even to resemble one another physically. But this is true only if they began with essential compatibility. You won't be able to practice plastic surgery on your beloved's personality or emotions.

Professor Magoun has put the matter very well:

> The only person one ever has the right to try to change is one's self. Immaturity often manifests itself in an attempt to reform the betrothed. A mature person sees faults, balances them against virtues, and accepts another individual for what he is.[15]

True compatibility means that you must like as well as love your mate. Actually, this statement begs the question; if you don't like your mate as a person, you are experiencing infatuation, not love. Quite aside from the romantic, sexual magnetism you both feel, is your beloved the kind of person you respect and admire, with whom you would be anxious to spend much time, from whose friendship and companionship you could learn and grow even if there were no sexual involvement?

Some years ago I visited an elderly man whose wife had just died. The tears he shed were a tribute to genuine loss, not a symptom of self-pity. Nodding his head sadly from side to side, he repeated over and over again: "Did I lose a friend! I lost the most wonderful friend a man could have!" In his humble, unliterary manner, he came eloquently close to summarizing the truth that, if, in addition to everything else which binds them together, a husband and wife can feel that they are solid friends to each other, their marriage is likely to succeed.

The reverse side of the coin is illustrated by a woman who said to me, after twenty years of marriage: "Rabbi, I married a man with whom I don't have a single thing in common!" What a miserable pity it is to enter upon so intimate and sacred a relationship with so little knowledge of one's partner! Enormous amounts of suffering could be averted if prospective brides and grooms would more accurately assess their probable compatibility before accepting the responsibilities and opportunities of marriage!

Others with whom we become emotionally involved can have a variety of effects on us. They can make us feel

inferior, or

superior, flattered, possessing an inflated ego, or

satisfied with ourselves as we are, or

acceptable to ourselves as we are but *eager to improve.*

Neither the first nor the second of these alternatives augurs well for marriage. Both are in the nature of illusions. Time has a cruel way of shattering such façades; when it does, little will be left of the marital bond. I can live a long and reasonably happy life with one who makes me feel satisfied with myself as I am. The only truly creative relationship, however —as we observed in trying to define love—is one which enables me to see, not only what I am today, but also what I have the potential to become, and which encourages my growth toward that goal.

NO CRYSTAL BALL

Did compatibility seem like such a simple thing before you read this chapter? And does it give the appearance now of being almost hopelessly complicated? The momentary confusion will be constructive if it enables you to evaluate more realistically how well you are matched.

There are professional tests to help, if you feel the need. Any serious doubt should prompt you to ask your rabbi or a marriage counselor to administer and interpret such a test. It will not be an oracle, giving you sure and certain answers. It can be in the nature of a thermometer which indicates whether your compatibility-temperature is normal or requires further investigation. For most couples a simple questionnaire of twenty items like the following will suffice. I have adapted it by permission from a volume called *Better Ways of Growing Up*. [16] To be qualified as compatible, a couple should rate *much alike* (4) on at least half the listed items, *somewhat alike* (3) on most of the others, and *very different* (1) on no more than three or four at most.

The chart suggested in Chapter 3 was filled out by each of you separately, then compared. In this case the ratings should be given by the two of you together. Try to be as objective and honest as possible; self-deception is as dangerous for the future as it is tempting in the present. To be impartial and unbiased about a sexually-colored emotional relationship demands almost superhuman effort. But there is enough involved —either of misery or of joy—to make that effort imperative.

HOW COMPATIBLE ARE WE?
1. Very different
2. Mildly different
3. Somewhat alike
4. Much alike

	Traits	Ratings
1.	Home and social background	
2.	Personal standards of right and wrong	
3.	Ideals regarding home and family	
4.	Desire for and feelings toward children	
5.	Differential in age	
6.	Educational background and interests	
7.	Intelligence	
8.	Religious interests and preferences	
9.	Vocational ambitions and attitudes	
10.	Desire for money and social standing	
11.	Spending and saving habits	
12.	Relative emphasis on home and outside activities	
13.	Cultural tastes: art, music, drama, books, etc.	
14.	Personal habits: eating, sleeping, smoking, etc.	
15.	Circle of friends	
16.	Recreational and leisure interests	
17.	Temperament and mood	
18.	Punctuality and neatness	
19.	Attitudes toward parents of both	
20.	Tendency to be critical or to praise	

CHAPTER FIVE

Promise Is a Seed

A theme established almost at the outset recurs. There is no guarantee of success in marriage. Marital happiness—like every other kind—must be earned. The promise implicit in the words of a rabbi at your wedding ceremony is a seed; it can be either frustrated or fulfilled; the choice is mostly yours.

Love is so dynamic a relationship that very seldom, if ever, does it remain on one level through the years. Like an airplane, which either maintains a minimum forward motion or falls to the ground, the love of husband and wife either increases rewardingly or diminishes disastrously. When love is reduced below the slowest speed at which it can remain airborne, so to speak, it crashes into hate. Though it may seem logically paradoxical, it is psychologically true that love and hate are first-cousins. Hate is not the opposite of love; indifference is. Hate is a distortion of love.

Many competent observers of human behavior are convinced that no one is born with an innate need to hate. At birth every infant possesses an almost insatiable hunger for love. Even while still in the hospital nursery, tiny babies can intuitively sense its absence; careful research has demonstrated that, when an unloving nurse is on duty, the amount of crying among the infants increases sharply. When a newborn child's need for love is met, he or she in turn is able to love. When that need is left unfulfilled, the capacity to love is cruelly transposed into hate. As drastically different as these two emotions are, they spring from the same psychological root.

This has a doubly significant bearing on your marriage. First, the quantity and quality of love received in childhood by each partner in a marital relationship influence to a great degree the amount of love that person is able to receive and give as husband or wife. People who become emotionally conditioned early in life to the dread suspicion that no one loves them because they are unlovable find it difficult at best to thaw even under the beneficent warmth of a spouse's affection. People who spend the most important and impressionable years of their childhood and youth exclusively in the arctic wastes do not have an easy time adjusting to tropical heat.

The second impact on your marriage of the organic connection between love and hate is that patterns of childhood rejection are often repeated in adult experience. A person who has become overly sensitive because of early emotional starvation may interpret—or misinterpret—the slightest aggravation or affront as more of the same. Without even being aware of the process, the wife who criticizes or complains—however mildly or justifiably—is seen as the mother who failed him in his need. The husband who disappoints his wife's expectations in even the most incidental detail duplicates the father who—in either fantasy or fact—had rejected her. When these complicated emotional transferences grow beyond the ability of an individual or a couple to handle, professional psychiatric help may be needed. For most of us, fortunately, an awareness of the possibilities and an alertness to them will suffice.

As you approach marriage, it is enormously important that both you and your beloved understand your relationships to your respective parents, especially to the one who is your sexual opposite. Does your intended in any way resemble—physically or emotionally—either of your parents? Is the resemblance in a trait you admire or one you dislike? Is either of you still emotionally too dependent upon parents? Too fiercely or rebelliously independent? These questions—whether you face them now or not—will inevitably affect your marriage for good or bad. All else being equal, the person who has a warm, loving, mature relationship with parents who themselves have a good marriage is the best candidate to enjoy such a marriage in turn.

Disappointed marital love seldom leads to its real opposite, indifference, but more often to a distortion of itself, hate. Even where an unhappy husband and wife remain together, living what Thoreau called "lives of quiet desperation," their feelings toward each other are more likely to degenerate into smoldering hate than casual neglect. The bride and groom who are eager for their love to blossom into the most compelling and creative ecstasy in life, rather than be corroded into sordid hostility, must strive to learn and follow those laws of human nature which alone can yield the desired result. It would be wonderful—almost too wonderful and simple—if there were a precise blueprint which could guarantee marital success. Marriage is far too personal and intimate a relationship, individual human beings are too unique in their natures, to make such a blueprint possible. Yet there are directives culled from the experience of other couples, refined by scientific observation and religious insight, which can be priceless to you. In some measure they have already been considered. Our concern now is to ask—in addition to a realistic comprehension of love and emotional maturity and many-levelled compatibility—what factors will determine the quality of your marriage?

LONG ARM OF THE PAST

One is the love relationship each of you has already had occasion to observe in your respective parents. In some ways you can probably remember—in more important ways that have been repressed beneath the surface of consciousness— you have been influenced and affected by that relationship since the moment of your birth, perhaps even since you were conceived. How your parents have felt toward each other has helped shape their feelings toward you. The way they have treated one another has had a more consequential effect than their words in the formulation of your attitudes and expectations of marriage. Needless to say, the same is true of your future spouse.

This is more than just theory. Dr. Paul Popenoe, an outstanding authority in the field of marriage counseling, has studied the effect of their earlier home life on the happiness of 4,000 married couples. Of those who had grown up in happy homes, 67 percent had achieved happiness in their own marriages. Of those who had emerged from unhappy homes, only 43 percent were themselves happy.

Does this mean that, if your parents or your future parents-in-law were unhappily married, you are doomed to duplicate their failure? Fortunately, not at all. It does mean that you and your future mate should give careful attention to the reasons for their failure. What is there about the unsuccessful parental couple—about each of them as individuals, about their maturity or lack of it, about their understanding of love, about the extent of their compatibility—which can aid you to understand their disappointment and do better yourselves? Is either of you —in your attraction to the other—unduly motivated by a haunting sense of having been rejected or abandoned by your opposite-sex parent? In short, a disastrous marital experience for either set of parents can be a liability or an asset to the next generation. By learning from it wisely, you can acquire an advantage over the couple who has never been close to such trauma. If, on the other hand, your parents have been fortunate in their marriage, you have enjoyed a living example which is worth more than many volumes of advice.

WISE USE OF THE PRESENT

A second determinant of your future happiness is the kind of courtship you have experienced. I refer here not necessarily to a formally announced engagement, but to the period of time the two of you have planned together for marriage, and how you have used that time.

An engagement as we experience it today is unknown in Jewish tradition. Rabbinic law describes three stages in the marriage process. First came שדוכין *(shiduchin)*, consent by both parties or their parents to proceed with formal arrangements. The second step was ארוסין *(erusin)*, or betrothal. But this was not just an agreement that could easily be broken. It was actually the first step in marriage. The parties were bound

to each other both religiously and legally, though not yet permitted to live together; in fact they were not even allowed to
see each other alone. A quasi-divorce was required by rabbinic
law in order for this relationship to be dissolved.

If the prospective bride were a virgin, a year had to pass
between ארוסין and the completion of the marriage, known as
נשואין (nissuin). Only then could the match be sexually consummated. When the bride was a widow, a month was deemed
sufficient interval between the two ceremonies. Both ארוסין
and נשואין were marked by religious ceremonies which included the recitation of appropriate blessings and the drinking
of wine.

In the course of time the intervention of an extended
period between betrothal and final marriage was deemed to be
clumsy. The two ceremonies were therefore combined. The
Jewish wedding ritual as it is performed today will be described
in a later chapter.

While the foregoing is of great historic interest, it is the
engagement period as we know it now which will play a significant role in determining your happiness.

The length of an engagement is important; reliable studies
indicate that couples who have been engaged for approximately a year have, on the average, a better prognosis for
marital success than those whose engagements are either
shorter or too much longer. You will recall our earlier reference to the test of time as an important instrument for distinguishing love from infatuation. One of the most significant
functions of the engagement is to provide precisely such a test
of time.

I must confess to fearful apprehension whenever two people tell me, in a premarital conference, that they have known
each other only a few months. I feel very little relieved when
they add that they have spent so many hours together in that
period that they really know each other well. Valid and complete knowledge of another person is not that easily or quickly
obtained. True, one never fully knows another until they have
lived together under the same roof. But reasonably accurate
knowledge is possible, provided enough time and effort go into
the search for it. A hundred hours spent together over a period

of several months can provide a far more accurate index than the same number compressed into a few weeks.

It disturbs me also to hear a prospective bride and groom confess that they have never faced a serious disagreement, that as a consequence neither really knows how the other would react to controversy or handle dissension. Or to listen, as I did on one memorable occasion, to the voice of an intended groom saying: "I know that Jane is able to give in when I become stubborn; she has done so many times. But I have no idea whether or not I would be capable of compromise on an issue too important for concession on her part. We just never have faced such a situation!" Let no one be so foolish as to suppose that abrasive situations will not occur in marriage—in *every* marriage. The time to test the capacity of two individuals to confront and resolve them is not after, but before the wedding!

To serve its proper function, then, an engagement must afford couples an opportunity to evaluate their probable compatibility on as many levels as possible. This they can hope to achieve only by seeing each other in a maximum variety of circumstances—when they are angry and sullen as well as when contented and joyous, when frustrated as well as fulfilled, in dirty jeans as well as when dressed formally. I sometimes ask a prospective groom in the presence of his beloved: "Have you seen her with her hair in curlers? Do you know how she behaves when her emotions are in curlers?" Similar questions are equally pertinent in reverse.

In the course of counseling couples involved in troubled marriages, I have on occasion asked the husband or wife who was complaining about annoying characteristics or habits in the other whether those traits weren't evident during their courtship. Not infrequently, after a moment of reflection, the answer will be something like, "Well, yes, I guess they were, but then I just thought they were cute quirks." A good use of an engagement is to distinguish between habits, phrases, mannerisms which will continue to be cute and those which the passage of time and constant exposure will transform into annoyances.

What all this adds up to is the importance of evaluating each other realistically, of knowing the defects as well as the virtues of your future mate. For be sure of one thing: both defects and virtues are there! If you are unable to identify the former with some degree of exactitude, they will become evident soon enough after the wedding. It is far better to know in advance the kind of caprice or quirk to which you will have to adjust than to be shocked by it later. In a good marriage neither partner expects perfection from the other, because neither is so presumptuous as to pretend to be perfect.

Your engagement is the most priceless opportunity each of you will have, short of marriage itself, to learn the truth about the other. But a special effort in this direction may be needed. Too many of us have been reared since earliest childhood to disguise our emotions, to construct a social façade for ourselves, to project an image rather than reveal what we really are. This becomes especially pernicious during our dating years when, understandably enough, each of us strives to create the best possible impression. The fine art of camouflage, which no doubt serves a legitimate purpose in casual dating, can be calamitous if carried through an engagement and into marriage.

A marriage undertaken with less than true knowledge is precarious in the extreme. Alexander Magoun has written wisely on this point too:

> The only thing in the world as strong as love is truth, and there are reasons to believe that as far as marriage is concerned they are different aspects of the same thing. A deep and abiding love is the emotional response to an intellectual recognition of the truth about another person.[1]

It will help you toward the attainment of such truth if you observe carefully how your intended behaves, not only toward you, but also toward family and friends. And, for reasons which should not now require lengthy elaboration, it is important also to note the relationship between his or her parents and to discuss them openly if they give rise to apprehension.

Engagement should also be a time to plan for the future. While details pertaining to the wedding ceremony and honeymoon will, of course, be included, they are the least of the matters to be carefully explored together. There should be conversations in depth also on such topics as your first year's budget, the amount of income to be expected, how much is to be spent and how much saved, what proportion is to be set aside for investment and insurance, where you are to live—in rented quarters or your own home—how many children you hope to have and approximately when, whether both of you are to work, the nature and intensity of your religious identification, and many other matters no less significant. Two people who cannot amicably, intelligently, lovingly make such plans during their engagement had better hesitate cautiously before marrying.

Wise candidates for marriage will be alert during courtship to the manner in which their intended mates react to a variety of disappointments: to a flat tire when both are dressed formally; to the unavoidable cancellation of a long-anticipated party due to the sudden intrusion of a business responsibility; to interference of illness on an important social evening. They will also initiate such joint ventures as shopping together and preparing a dinner for friends in order to estimate how well the two of them can work together. They will explore together their feelings about women's liberation, especially about the respective responsibilities of husbands and wives in maintaining their home, preparing and serving meals, and the eventual care of their children. Each will explore the opinions of the other on important world events, on politics and religion, thus to ascertain how much they really have in common.

Some years ago, near the end of a premarital conference, I was startled when the prospective bride burst into tears. They were turbulent tears, not gentle ones. When they had subsided enough to make coherent speech possible, she said: "Rabbi, I want to be married, but I'm also desperately afraid. I don't know whether I'll be able to meet my responsibilities, sexually or otherwise." Such fears are, in reasonable measure, not too uncommon. Many a bride finds her eager and hopeful anticipation at least partially shaded by fear. More than a few grooms worry over surrendering a portion of their freedom and assuming a kind of responsibility they haven't previously faced. The period of engagement, if used wisely, should help to alleviate such fear. If it fails to, if either bride or groom approaches *the day* with a heavy burden of dread or doubt, the ceremony should be postponed until they have had a chance—by themselves or with professional help—to resolve their foreboding. Undue apprehension is a fragile auspice under which to enter marriage. If more than normal doubt persists, better a cancelled engagement than gambling future happiness against inordinate odds.

Yes, your engagement is crucial. It can and should be a testing-ground of your maturity and compatibility, either warmly reassuring the two of you about your probable future or flashing ominous warning lights which it would be hazardous to ignore. Dr. Gerald Albert, a psychologist who has specialized in marriage counseling, identifies some of these possible warnings:

> . . . the revelation during courtship that either of the partners cannot confide in the other, or feels persistently disturbed by the other's activities, beliefs, or attitudes, a tendency toward dramatic changes of mood, quickness of temper, unwarranted jealousy, a strong need to dominate, and frequent feelings of self-blame and remorse.

A TEST OR A GAME?

Should the testing of engagement include living together? Isn't that, after all, the best way to determine how well-fitted two people are for marriage? Increasing numbers of American couples seem to be answering these questions affirmatively. But many students of marriage remain unconvinced.

I recall counseling two mates a few weeks prior to their wedding. They had been living together for two years. As I questioned them, however, it became apparent that they really knew very little about each and had no idea of the problems they would probably face. After two years of living together! I was finally forced to say: "You two haven't been living together. You've just been playing house!"

It would be grossly unfair to assume that this is true of every such couple. Yet recent studies cast grave doubt on the value of premarital cohabitation. The divorce rate among couples who have lived together is no lower than among others. It is by no means uncommon to hear of two people who lived together, then married, then were divorced.

Dr. Nancy Coatworthy, associate professor of sociology at Ohio State University, after studying one hundred married couples between the ages of 18 and 35, concluded: "The findings do not support the hypothesis that a period of living together before marriage better helps to select a compatible mate or aids in adjustment to marriage." To the contrary! She found that couples who had *not* lived together were "just a little bit happier and more successful. There were fewer divorces."[2]

We can only speculate on why this is so. Some couples may have been so blinded by romance and/or sex as not to test their compatibility in other crucial areas. Some may have been incapable of or frightened by any long-term commitment. Others may have found "forbidden fruit" more enticing than a socially sanctioned relationship. Perhaps they resemble those unfortunate men who are able to enjoy sex only with prostitutes or mistresses, not with their wives.

However strong the emotional ties between two individuals who are just living together, there is still likely to be an element of pretense in their relationship; after marriage, one or both of them can change a great deal. Not all such changes are so superficial or amusing as the case of the man who had slept in the nude during his entire period of cohabitation with the woman he eventually married. From the night of their wedding on, he wore flannel pajamas. Why? When asked to explain, he confessed that he was constantly cold when they slept without clothing but went along with what he thought was his friend's preference. Now that they were married, he felt, it was no longer necessary to endure such discomfort.

Whatever the reason, cohabitation is less than a reliable augury of happy marriage. Without the element of commitment and responsibility which goes with mature marriage, the alleged test isn't really a test at all. When two individuals live together on a trial basis, their premise is that if the wind blows too vigorously, or the water gets too rough, all they need do is ask out. This is an altogether different relationship from one in which the two partners are pledged to work out their problems, however vexing, and to use their failures as well as their victories to cement a closer, more significant partnership. A woman in our congregation, after listening to a sermon dealing with this topic, reminded her husband of troubled times early in their marriage and said: "My God, what happiness and growth and joy we would have missed if we had just walked out then instead of remaining together to work at it!" This kind of reaction makes me wonder whether some of the couples living together don't risk cheating themselves in the long-run.

William Safire is even more suspicious than I about the value of living together as a test of compatibility. He wrote:

> The unmarried state of people living together is less a mark of independence than a mark of uncertainty; less an expression of the strength of mutual respect than a confession of the weakness of people to commit themselves to each other; and less a challenge to society than a refusal to rise to the greatest individual challenge of all—symbolically to make permanent a union with another independent person.[3]

A final word before we leave the subject of your engagement: I strongly recommend that a month or two before your wedding premarital conferences be held with both a physician and your rabbi. Not every doctor is competent to conduct such a conference. Nor is every rabbi. In addition to basic knowledge, these professionals must feel comfortable about their own sexuality and about marriage. If they have known you or your intended over a long period of time, so much the better. Any questions remaining after you have read this book, as well as all discomforts or doubts you may still have about marriage, should be discussed openly and honestly during your premarital sessions.

Most states require blood tests before a marriage license can be issued. Though not required by law, you should also be tested for Tay-Sachs disease, a genetic disorder which seems for some strange reason to afflict especially Ashkenazic Jews. No responsible Jewish couple of Ashkenazic origin should marry or conceive a child without such screening. Either your rabbi or physician can tell you where Tay-Sachs tests are available in your area. (For an excellent article on this subject, see *Death in the Family* by W. Stockton in *The New York Times Magazine*, 12 August 1979.)

LIGHT AND SHADOW

A third contingency on which marital happiness hinges is the kindness and consideration each partner shows the other. How pitiable and pathetic it is to see the contrast between the sweetness with which some couples wooed one another and the sullen indifference or hostility which marks their later relationship. Some of us never speak with such nastiness to strangers as we do to those whom we presumably love. Near the beginning of this volume we compared love to a slow, steady flame, infatuation to a spectacular but speedily spent brushfire. Let it not be overlooked that a flame must be continually fed. Kindness and tenderness are the fuels needed to keep the flame of love burning. A great painting, abandoned in a dump to be covered with grit and grime, is indistinguishable after a while from the refuse surrounding it. A Stradivarius violin, carelessly discarded to accumulate dirt and dust, soon loses its purity of tone. The more precious a possession, the greater the continuing care which it deserves and needs. No possession on earth is more priceless than the love of a husband and wife. It therefore requires the most diligent care.

I recall an emotionally undemonstrative man in his seventies yielding to profuse tears a few hours after his wife had died. He said: "I don't think I ever realized how much she meant to me or how deeply I loved her until I learned she had cancer!" What happened to all the potentially rich years of affection—experienced and expressed—prior to the onset of this woman's fatal illness?

Gilbert Chesterton once said that the way truly to appreciate anything is to remember that one day it may be lost. Carried to its most morbid extreme, this thought can blight love. Understood in proper perspective, it can prevent us from neglecting or ignoring that which will certainly be lost if we take it for granted.

Jewish tradition clearly understood the importance of constant kindness between mates. Thus the *Zohar* tells us:

> A wife who receives love gives love in return; if she receives anger, she returns anger in equal measure.

An earlier *midrash* is more explicit on the same point:

> A wise woman said to her daughter who was about to become a bride: "My daughter, if you will respect your husband like a king, he will treat you like a queen. If you will serve him like a slave-girl, he will serve you like a slave. But if you will be too proud to serve him, he will assert his mastership by force and will treat you like a maid-servant. If your husband is about to visit his friends, persuade him to bathe and wear fine raiment. If his friends come to his house, welcome them heartily and set before them more than they can eat, so that they will respect your husband. Watch well your home and all of your husband's possessions. He will be delighted with you, and you will be the crown of his head."[4]

We must not interpret too literally this mother's suggestion that her daughter serve her husband as if she were his slave, and the admonition to supervise his bathing and dress could easily lead to nagging. We must also transpose the theme into a male key, emphasizing the equal obligation of husbands to be tenderly considerate of their wives.

Each must be especially sensitive to times of crisis in the other's life. A wife whose best friend is mortally ill . . . a husband whose livelihood is threatened or who feels driven to a change of career . . . a woman or man worried over inadequate sexual responses: these are individuals who require and deserve utmost consideration and kindness from their mates.

No one can be expected, over the long run, to give evidence of kindness that is not honestly felt. But it can be safely assumed—can it not?—that at least in the beginning marriage partners do feel genuine kindness and compassion toward each other. Why do their tender emotions sometimes deteriorate into something less laudable? In attempting to answer this question, we come upon a paradoxical psychological truth. We know that our actions normally emerge from our feelings. We behave in a given manner toward other persons because we feel about them in certain ways. What is less commonly known, unfortunately, is that the opposite is also true of the relationship between emotion and action. Which means to say: the way we feel about a particular situation or individual is also influenced by our behavior.

During the Second World War, I served as Jewish chaplain with the Fifth Marine Division on Iwo Jima. Because I was more desperately and almost uncontrollably afraid than ever before or since in my life, I wanted more than anything else to run away. My emotion of fear dictated a clear-cut course of action. But I could not run away. Quite aside from the fact that my conscience would have troubled me if I had, there simply was no place to run. More than 75,000 marines and unnumbered Japanese combatants were crowded into an area of eight square miles, surrounded by the menacing sea. My conduct, then, was forcibly shaped more by outer circumstance than by my strong internal feelings. Thus did I learn from my own visceral experience what I had previously known only from books—that my conduct could have perhaps as much effect on my emotions as my emotions undeniably exercised over my conduct. Forced to act as if I were unafraid, I in fact found myself growing less afraid!

This diversion from marriage to combat is not meant to be cynical. The dynamic of behavior so evident in the one situation is no less applicable to the other. We begin marriage with the kindest, most compassionate feelings for each other. If we express those feelings by appropriate action, they become strengthened and reinforced. If we take them for granted, if we assume it is unnecessary continually to communicate them, if our daily conduct is incongruous with our emotions—soon we begin to cease feeling as warm and loving as we once did.

Haven't you noticed how often during courtship individuals in love will bring gifts to each other even without a special occasion—just as a warm expression of affection? The only thing that can make such gifts even more significant and touching is when they continue into the years of marriage. There is, in short, a mutual, two-way connection between what we do and how we feel. They constantly interact on each other for either evil or good.

Erich Fromm excels in expressing the subtle yet corroding difference between the way some couples feel and act toward each other before and after they have wedded:

> During courtship neither person is yet sure of the other, but each tries to win the other. Both are alive, attractive, interesting, even beautiful—inasmuch as aliveness makes a face beautiful. Neither yet *has* the other; hence each one's energy is directed to *being*, i.e., to giving to and stimulating the other. With the active marriage this situation frequently changes fundamentally. The marriage contract gives each partner the exclusive possession of the other's body, feelings, and care. Nobody has to be won over any more, because love has become something one *has*, a property. The two cease to make the effort to be lovable and to produce love, hence they become boring, and hence their beauty disappears. They are disappointed and puzzled. Are they not the same persons any more? Did they make a mistake in the first place? Each usually seeks the cause of the change in the other and feels defrauded. What they do not see is that they no longer are the same people they were when they were in love with each other; that the error that one can *have* love has led them to cease loving. Now, instead of loving each other they settle for owning together what they have: money, social standing, a home, children. Thus, in some cases, the marriage initiated on the basis of love becomes transformed into a friendly ownership, a corporation in which the two egotisms are pooled into one: that of the "family."[5]

NO ANGELS

The preceding excerpt must not be misinterpreted to mean that any one of us can be never-failing in kindness. There is room for anger in human relations too, room and need. One who cannot honestly handle hostility and express it openly will also be incapable of expressing love. The success of your marriage will depend also on your ability—while endeavoring to maintain a pervasive atmosphere of kindness—to articulate on occasion your resentment of each other and to criticize each other constructively.

Even the kindest person, enjoying the most wonderful of marriages, will not always—at every moment of every day—feel well-disposed toward a spouse. There are circumstances and times when we must learn to suspend or delay the expression of our negative feelings. But to suppress them as a matter of general policy would be catastrophic. Any strong emotion which is regularly muted or denied becomes a burning acid which destroys both its opposite feeling and the person who hosts both of them. Professor Magoun's advice is worth remembering:

> The wise man does not try to avoid anger; he determines what, for him, is worth being angry about, then is angry at the right person, in the right way, at the right time. *He expresses the anger in a constructive way,* and he gets over being angry as soon as this is accomplished.[6]

Criticism and anger can be expressed either constructively or destructively. The difference is crucial, though sometimes subtle. A wife, disturbed over the way her husband flared up at her mother, can react in either of the following ways:

The minute they are alone, she can explode with: "You had your nerve talking to my mother that way! After all the things she has done for us, you were positively insulting. You just wait until the next time your parents are here; I'll show them as much love as you did to my mother!"

Or, waiting for a more propitious moment after the emotional temperature of both has subsided, she can say: "Sweetheart, you're usually thoughtful of mother and I'm sure you didn't realize quite how you sounded this afternoon in arguing with her. I can't really blame you for getting excited; I do it myself. But I don't think she meant to offend you any more than you really wanted to hurt her. Next time, if you can tell me your criticism and let me talk about it when I'm alone with her, perhaps that would make things easier for all of us."

In both cases the wife has made her point, in the second more effectively and with less emotional abrasion to either her husband or herself.

There will be outbursts and flares of temper between almost any two people living in the intimacy of marriage. What we must do is strive to keep them to a minimum, to get over them as speedily as we can, to avoid as far as possible saying things we don't really mean, and to apologize when we have been wrong. A good check point for every married person, preferably two seconds before the lightning strikes, is to ask: "Which is more important in the end—this thing about which we're quarreling or our love?" Properly handled, even the arguments in marriage can cement a closer relationship between mates.

You will recall my earlier suggestion that this is another of the crucial areas to be explored during your engagement. How have you handled your disagreements, especially on matters which at the time seemed vital to either or both of you? How long does it take for the quarrel to be resolved? Is it usually the same one who gives in, or is there a pretty even balance in this respect? How deep have the scars been and how enduring the pain? Your honest answers to questions like these can be most revealing as you anticipate the handling of stresses and strains in your marriage.

A rabbinic directive is relevant here: "Love without admonition is not love."[7] This certainly is not meant to recommend regular indulgence in carping criticism. Love should bypass minor imperfections and eschew nagging. But, if it fails to yield constructive admonition, it cannot realize one of its most essential values, helping the loved one to fulfill more of his or her richest potential.

AN INVALUABLE KEY

It will help inestimably to maintain the difficult combination of overall kindness and honest expression of hostility if husband and wife can accept each other as unique human personalities, with a temperament and set of problems peculiarly their own. Basic to such acceptance is a recognition of the fact that men and women differ in their essential natures and needs. It made for enjoyable entertainment in *My Fair Lady* when Henry Higgins plaintively wailed his impatience with Eliza Doolittle through the song, *Why Can't a Woman Be More like a Man?* But the fact of the matter is that women are, in some important respects, not at all like men, nor are men like women. If, moreover, the two sexes were to become emotionally and intellectually identical, far more would be lost than gained.

The altogether proper call for equal rights on behalf of women becomes hopelessly distorted if it presupposes no essential differences between them and men. Such differences, as a matter of fact, show themselves at a very early stage in the development of children. Dr. Evelyn Goodenough of the Gesell Institute for Child Development has conducted some fascinating experiments which disclose this. Children between the ages of two and four were ushered into a room where they found a box of brightly colored plastic blocks which they had not seen before. An observer and a tape recorder were also in the room. The reactions of the boys were nearly always focused on practical interests dealing with the arrangement and structure of the blocks. They asked such questions as: "How many blocks are there? How strong are they? How do you think I can stack them?" There was little deviation from this line during the ten-minute period of observation.

Little girls, exposed to the same stimulus, reacted quite differently. Their interest in the blocks themselves was sustained for no more than about three minutes. By the end of that time, if not sooner, they would look up from the blocks and ask the observer some such question as: "Did you know I'm going to a party tomorrow and my mother bought me a new dress?"

Or, "Do you know that my grandpa has a new car?" They were also inclined to flit from topic to topic, having little or no connection to the blocks at hand.

When the mothers and fathers of these children were interviewed, most of them felt that by and large male thinking was apt to be direct, analytical, and resourceful; female thinking impressed them as illogical, indirect, and excessively sentimental.[8] Two caveats are necessary before we assign excessive importance to these opinions. Even at so young an age, cultural influences have affected these children. The behavior they have already witnessed in their homes as well as the expectations of their parents, teachers, and friends have in some measure determined their reactions. In addition, the observations given subsequently by their mothers and fathers, however objective they have honestly tried to be, were to a certain degree colored by their own stereotypes and assumptions.

Dr. Goodenough's observations are reinforced by those of Erik Erikson, who sees a correlation between the anatomies of boys and girls respectively and differences of personality and temperament which distinguish them. He refers to studies of ten- to twelve-year-old children at play. Each sex was asked to construct "exciting movie scenes." Boys tended to build ruins or tall structures that were susceptible to collapse, to show exterior action scenes with a great deal of motion. Girls were more likely to build peaceful interiors, with females busy in them at enjoyable or productive pursuits like playing the piano.[9] Is it too far-fetched to recognize a similarity between the bodies of each sex and the interests that sex is apt to pursue?

It is dangerous to generalize too extravagantly, and of course there are exceptions to all sweeping descriptions. Obviously, the younger the age at which boys and girls are studied, the more important and impressive are any divergences noted between them; cultural conditioning is still at a minimum. On this basis, Dr. Richard Restak, a neurologist, concludes that there are substantial differences in brain function between the sexes. He calls our attention to the fact that from birth on female babies are more sensitive to sound, while males show early visual superiority. Girls also seem to show more sensitive skin, especially in their fingertips. There are social differences as well:

> By four months of age, a female infant is socially aware enough to distinguish photographs of familiar people, a task rarely performed well by boys of that age. Also at four months, girls will babble to a mother's face, seemingly recognizing her as a person, while boys fail to distinguish between a face and a dangling toy, babbling equally to both. . . . A boy will react to an inanimate object as quickly as he will to a person. A male baby will often ignore the mother and babble to a blinking light. . . .

Dr. Restak also cites certain tests measuring how the two brain hemispheres function and indicating quite a difference between male and female infants.[10] While not all psychologists have accepted his findings, many are impressed with the evidence of substantial inherent differences between the sexes. The fact that environmental factors undeniably reinforce such differences does not mean they don't exist biologically.

Indeed, more recent research appears to go even beyond that of Dr. Restak. Studies of hamsters and rats disclose that the "brains of male and female animals differ physically and chemically in ways that may help explain some basic behavior patterns of the sexes."[11] Further inquiry will be needed before we can conclude that similar structural and chemical sex distinctions exist also in humans, but the evidence is at least suggestive that not all behavioral sex differentiation by any means can be attributed to cultural factors.

Later we shall turn our attention at greater length to the women's movement and its effect on marriage. For the moment, let's simply note and remember that there *are* substantial differences between men and women: anatomical, physiological, and—allowing for many degrees of variation and exception —most probably also psychological and emotional. Our aim— in both marriage and society at large—should be, not to act as if these differences don't exist, but to accept and respect them.

What does this have to do with your marriage? Just as neither you nor your mate has any right to mold the other into an image of self, so neither of you is wise to expect men and women to react precisely the same. There are situations in which male propensities can be most helpful, others in which typically feminine traits will avail better, and many more in which the approach best calculated to succeed is a combination of both. A good marriage becomes more probable in the proportion that husband and wife accept each other's individual and sexual uniquenesses, trying to benefit from them, not to beat each other down. It almost goes without saying that the more understanding of this sort an individual gives, the more he or she will receive.

TOO BUSY

Another factor of immense consequence is the amount of time husband and wife spend together. We have already mentioned in connection with compatibility, the importance of sharing many leisure time activities. In an earlier and simpler economy most people had no choice. There were enough responsibilities revolving around the household to keep not only father and mother but also their growing children occupied in a variety of joint ventures. Today—with smaller quarters, frozen foods, electronic gadgets for cleaning, more voracious vocational demands keeping both men and women away from home, the increasingly strident distractions of the entertainment industries abroad and television at home—corrosive inroads threaten both the structure and integrity of our families. Even when husbands and wives are together for their leisure hours, too often they share only a passive spectatorship as they watch experts display their prowesses. Far from truly and deeply sharing in meaningful activity, too many mates today seem scarcely to know each other. A study made in California even before the wholesale advent of television showed that 76.4 percent of total leisure time activity was being spent watching others perform, rather than actively participating oneself. With television as ubiquitous and popular as it is now, the figure would unquestionably be even higher.

I recall an occasion when I sat with a stunned and shocked husband whose wife had died a few hours before. They had been married over thirty years; while their marriage had not been one of preeminent success, it wasn't too different from many others. In an attempt to encourage the ventilation of his inmost thoughts and feelings, I asked the man what his wife's interests had been outside her family and who her closest friends were. After a moment or two of troubled silence, he responded: "Rabbi, I'm afraid I can't answer that question. . . . I just don't know." Each of them had possessed his own circle of interests and friends; the two circles had almost never converged.

We must be realistic. Unless husband and wife are engaged in a joint profession or business, their opportunities to spend meaningful time together during most of the week will of brutal necessity be limited. All the more reason, then, not to shun each other completely on the weekend. It is understandable that a man should want to fish or play cards or compete in golf with other men, that a woman might wish to spend part of her leisure time with female friends playing tennis. But if they make these activities their primary weekend pursuits, leaving only a grudging remnant of time and concern for each other, they cannot expect much in the way of marriage. Husbands and wives who use their home as a motel, a convenient place to sleep, change clothes, and eat—occasionally but not necessarily doing some of these things together—cannot hope to experience love at its best. What they will more probably come to know is, in the perceptive words of Marya Mannes, "the intolerable hell of two alone together."

Dr. James A. Peterson has expressed this very well:

> Hard physical effort such as scaling a mountain or hiking a great distance or lugging a canoe over a portage or playing a hard-fought set of tennis—all of these enable us to release some of the aggressions built up within us. We invest ourselves in these activities and when they are finished there has taken place a kind of catharsis that has value.

There is a type of psychological help for children called play therapy which is based on the definite recognition that creative play enables the child to release feelings hitherto inhibited. In the same way the play of husband and wife releases pent-up feelings and clears the way for more positive feelings.

Recreational events are the sunshine among shadows, the highlights of sometimes gray marital experiences. But every experience in the family influences all other experiences. When a couple solves their difficulties in a game they are provided with a new pattern for resolving difficulties in other areas. After several such recreational experiences the budget-planning session will be conducted in a little different atmosphere with more gaiety and good humor.[12]

LOUD AND CLEAR

Another component of happy marriages is too important to be assumed, yet too obvious to allow for elaboration at length. Husbands and wives must at all times strive to keep their lines of communication open. Nothing is more conductive to contamination in the marital relationship than a person who retreats into sullen silence at the first sign of disagreement. Better by far an explosive moment—if no better choice seems possible—than refusal to communicate at all!

One couple who came to me for aid in repairing a badly damaged marriage had reached the point where their only means of verbal exchange—living in the same house!—was to write each other letters which were duly deposited in locations where they would surely be noticed. Needless to say, it was by then too late for my help to avail. Whatever bothers either mate about the other, or about their relationship, should be articulated. Not in a key of carping criticism and complaint, but in an honest desire to come through to each other "loud and clear." Moody withdrawal and obstructed channels of communication are twin blights which will shrivel even the most promising marriage.

FOR BETTER . . . FOR WORSE

I have intentionally saved for last one of the most essential ingredients of good marriages: a strong sense of commitment and responsibility. As the most important difference between marriage and cohabitation, this deserves more than the passing reference it has already received. Judaism has always perceived the relationship between husband and wife as a sacred covenant, second only to the covenant between the Jewish people and God. Each partner in a good marriage offers his or her mate, not just what the giver may wish to give, but what the other most urgently needs. I know men and women who see marriage primarily as an arrangement for the satisfaction of their own wants . . . period. So long as their needs are reasonably fulfilled, the partnership endures; if these needs appear to be unmet, the marriage is quickly dissolved. The element of mutuality is ignored, the fact that *two* people are involved, that *commitment* and *responsibility* are essential components of marriage.

Marriage means assuming the fulfillment of my spouse's needs as well as my own. You recall, I hope, the perceptive words of Erich Fromm cited earlier, describing how a mature person is a *giving* person, one who in a very real sense gains at least as much from what he or she is able to do for a loved one as from what is received.

Commitment carries with it vulnerability and risk. There are significant numbers of men and women—perhaps more now than in the past—who have avoided marriage because they fear such involvement. Is this part of the *me first* philosophy of our time, the narcissistic concentration of individuals only on their own desires and needs? Perhaps so. Perhaps also in part it reflects the fact that life generally is in some ways more hazardous and threatening now than in the past. The ultimate of this view is the conviction of the Zen Buddhist that the only way to escape certain kinds of pain is to avoid emotional involvement with others.

True. But this also means denying oneself the ecstasy yielded by love. A rabbinic legend portrays the angels debating whether God should or should not have created human beings.

God, in effect, responds: "The matter is really moot. I have already created them; they must now do the best they can." We have been born with a capacity—more, even a need—to love. To deny that need is to deprive ourselves of what makes us unique among the creatures of earth. Life is a constant battle between risk and opportunity. Each time we fly, or ride in a car, or even walk down the street, there is a risk of accident or injury. To eschew all such risk means to become a house-imprisoned hermit—where, by the way, we still face the risk of bacterial infection, accident, or injury.

To marry without perceiving the vulnerabilities involved is foolish. Permitting these potential hazards to dominate, however, denies us the companionship, the security, the support, the love which can enhance and ennoble our lives.

Here is another of the decisions each of us must make. We must weigh advantage against disadvantage, cost against benefit, being emotional hermits against the richest kind of relationship we humans can know.

There are times when love entails sacrifice. This is especially true when one mate suffers a prolonged illness and the other is called upon to exhibit great sensitivity and patience. To sustain a relationship with another person only so long as the books balance in my favor, so to speak, is a tenuous premise even for friendship. In marriage it should be unthinkable. To marry means to a great degree replacing *I* with *we, me* with *us*. It means assuming as strong a sense of responsibility for and commitment to another human being as I feel for myself.

No one is likely to disagree with this in theory. The facts of life, however, are often far more complicated than so simple a statement. There can be a delicate, even excruciating calculus between responsibility and masochism. Shakespeare gave us exquisite poetry when he wrote, ". . . love is not love which alters when it alteration finds." But is this always true?

Suppose only one of the mates in a marriage feels so full a sense of responsibility? Suppose the other is either incapable of or unwilling to assume a similar measure of commitment? Suppose either husband or wife is an emotional infant, intentionally or unwittingly forcing the other to serve as surrogate mother or father? Suppose one is cruelly afflicted with a totally incapacitating illness—perhaps paralyzed or comatose or senile? What then? Must the other be trapped, doomed forever to forego any possibility of happiness?

We must be careful about answering such questions for others. What may be miserable martyrdom for me could be fulfilling love for you. What strikes you as insufferable masochism, I may feel as gratifying responsibility. Each of us—if called upon to confront so painful a dilemma—must respond in terms of his or her nature and need. And we must respect each other's integrity, whether we agree or not.

What no one of us can gainsay is that marriage certainly involves a very strong sense of commitment, not to be lightly minimized, never to be entirely abdicated. Even when circumstances justify a legal separation or divorce, no responsibly decent man or woman will be indifferent toward the needs of a former mate. Commitment can carry with it vulnerability and risk. No man or woman who fails to understand this, who is unwilling or unable to accept it, should enter marriage.

NOT FORGOTTEN

Two additional factors of enormous significance in determining the prospects for your marriage have been eliminated from this part of our discussion, not because of neglect, but because entire chapters will be devoted to them later. They are the influence on marriage, respectively, of sex and religion. Suffice it to say for the present that both are indispensable ingredients in any recipe for marital happiness and success. Before turning to them, however, a few pages on certain financial problems which play a significant role in determining the outcome of every marriage.

CHAPTER SIX

Money Is the Root...

*The importance of financial compatibility as a barometer of person-*ality adjustment has already been mentioned. Money enters into marriage in a more direct manner too. While it is true that financial difficulties often reflect more fundamental causes of dissension, the management of money is itself an immediate problem of marriage which the wise bride and groom will include in their planning. Either too little or too much money can frustrate your hope for happiness. That insufficient means for comfortable living can impose a severe strain on a marriage needs no argument. That the opposite is also true may not be quite so apparent.

I once counseled an attractive young couple at whose wedding I had officiated a year or two earlier. They were troubled with considerable tension. Near the end of our time together I said: "Part of your trouble is financial." "Oh no," was the immediate and joint response, "you're wrong; we don't have any financial problems at all. We both have quite a bit of money as well as stocks left to us by our grandparents." And they proceeded, without any prodding, to tell me the extent of their liquid assets. But neither one of them had comprehended what I had said. Their trouble *was* in part financial; they suffered from too much opulent luxury, handed to them on their wedding day with no effort on their part at all. True, they may have experienced trouble even without such easy affluence, but, whether as symptom or

cause, financial abundance was an integral part of their problem. In terms of socio-economic background they were compatible; but their values were distorted and they had no economic goals for which to strive together.

It is naive to suppose that those with a great deal of money
are automatically assured a happier marriage than those with
very little. One marriage counselor has reported an interesting
study he made in the area of Los Angeles. In an exclusive
suburb he came upon a family whose income was $100,000 a
year, but whose home was filled with ugly conflict. In a trailer
court he met a crippled man who lived with his arthritic wife
and adolescent daughter. They were remarkably happy on the
very small income he managed to earn as a part-time watch-
man. These two couples scored lowest and highest respectively
on a marriage adjustment test given to a large number of
families in Los Angeles county.[1]

This does not mean that poverty is conducive to happiness; rather that wealth is by no means a guarantee of success.
Much depends, as we have already had occasion to see, on the
expectations and values of a given couple. Economic security
in reasonable measure is important. There are some people,
however, who feel less secure on $2,000 a week than others on
$200.

Whatever their income, married couples must learn to
manage their resources together. For either one to be the
business manager for both is wrong. The family budget should
be planned together; in fact, as soon as children are old
enough, they should be involved in the process too. Decisions
as to how much to lay aside for insurance, for investment, for
a nest egg, for deferred spending on large items—all these
should be made together. If you and your future spouse are
already accustomed, each of you, to project and administer a
budget for one person, you have a head start toward carrying
on the same kind of enterprise now for two. If either of you is
entering upon marriage with a backlog of debt or of extraordinary financial commitment, this should be made known to the
other and should be included in your budget.

The rabbis whose sermonic excerpts are recorded in the
Midrash were aware of the fact that financial cooperation be-

tween the partners is an essential component of successful marriage. They used the following parable:

> Once a man engaged in robbery by night, keeping his family in luxury as a consequence. The wife of a neighbor complained to her husband: "What ill-luck is mine that I am married to you. The man across the way keeps his family in every comfort." The husband replied: "But rumor has it that he is a thief. Do you wish me to become like him?"
>
> The wife answered: "I care not what your occupation is, provided you give me the luxuries I crave."
>
> Being enamored of his wife, the husband begged his neighbor to allow him to participate in his next enterprise. The police were informed and laid a trap for him. The experienced robber succeeded in escaping the snare but the novice was captured and hanged.[2]

In our day no less than theirs it is essential that husband and wife want the same material things, plan together on how to obtain them, and keep each other fully informed on their joint financial status. If the economic ambitions of either mate or of the two together outstrip their income, their marriage can be jeopardized.

Is it wise, in this connection, for two people to marry when they know that at least temporarily they will be dependent upon financial help from their parents? No categorical answer can be given. Much depends on the kind of people they and their parents are. Ideally, parents should be happy to provide such assistance and young couples should be able to accept it without reactions of either resentment or guilt. Yet there are psychological booby traps in such arrangements; no couple should make this decision without at the very least being aware of them. There is an almost irresistible temptation for parents who are supplying all or part of a young couple's income to interfere in how it is spent. More subtle but no less contaminating is the tendency of the recipients to feel guilty over their dependency on parents and, as a consequence, to resent the very hand that feeds them.

It is my own strong conviction that, especially at a time when the gap between sexual and psychological readiness for marriage and its practical possibility is growing wider, parents who can afford to should make it possible for well-matched, mature couples to marry before they are financially independent. But such help should not be proffered unless the giver is prepared to exercise no control over how it is spent and the recipients are able to accept it without any loss of self-esteem. In some circumstances it may be the wisest course for parental help to be extended, at least ostensibly, in the form of a loan; this may aid in the preservation of integrity. To wipe such a loan off the books at a later date may be less threatening than an immediate and outright gift.

Those who are inclined to suspect that this is only a post-modern problem will be interested in the comment of a chasidic rabbi:

> A passenger on a ship patiently awaited the day when it would reach port. When the ship was nearing the harbor, a storm drove it back to sea, much to the chagrin of the traveler. Likewise a man is afflicted with anxiety for his sons and daughters until he succeeds in rearing them to maturity. Then he hopes to be freed from worry regarding their lot. But his oldest son comes with his troubles, seeking paternal counsel and the father's retirement is delayed. The daughter also comes with her problems, and once more his hope of a quiet life is postponed. Few of us are ever entirely free from worry and the necessity of continuous labor in this world.[3]

BUTCHER, BAKER, CANDLESTICK MAKER

The ways in which men and women earn a living impinge upon their marriages to a greater degree than you may think. In the paragraphs to follow, bear in mind that wives with active careers are still a relatively recent phenomenon on the American scene; prior to the last decade or two such women were rare. Later we shall spend considerable time thinking through the relationship of the women's movement to marriage. I mention it here only to explain why much of what immediately follows is couched in terms of the effect a husband's career is likely to have on his wife and their marriage. As more wives pursue careers of their own, as more knowledge is gained from their experience, our frame of reference too will change: the effect of occupation or profession on marriage will become more of a two-way road than it has been in the past.

Most brides know in advance the probable occupation of their grooms. Yet all too few take this into serious consideration in contemplating the probable success of their marriages. No factor so significant to a man as his profession or business can fail to have an important impact on his marriage. We know, for example, that certain vocations seem to carry with them a higher probability of marital happiness than others. These include the work of professors, chemical engineers, and the clergy. Those tending to show a lower score are laborers, mechanics, and traveling sales representatives. This correlation must neither be pushed too far nor altogether ignored. It can easily be understood in terms of the personality traits which might direct a person toward one or another occupation, also as the result of environmental circumstances peculiar to particular pursuits.

Jewish tradition was acutely aware of this. The rabbis therefore stipulated that the wife of a tanner could, if she wished, ask a rabbinic court to pressure her husband for a divorce. Apparently in ancient times animal dung was used in curing hides. Especially before the institution of the daily bath, a man who spent most of his day at this inelegant business could scarcely have smelled very attractive at dinner or in bed. If his wife found the odor too offensive, she could ask that their marriage be dissolved.

The tanner today poses no exceptional problems for his wife; other occupations do. The wife of a traveling salesman, for example, must certainly be prepared for periods of lonely separation from her mate. So must the husband of a woman whose work necessitates extensive travel. The wife of one whose work must be done at night will have to accommodate to a topsy-turvy kind of personal and social schedule. So will the husband of a woman whose business or professional hours don't dovetail with his. A wife whose husband's vocation brings him into daily, perhaps even intimate, contact with other women must learn to curb whatever inclination she possesses toward jealousy. No less is true of the husband whose wife spends her working hours mostly with men.

Two professions in particular—for the most part limited in the past to men—are vulnerable to extraordinary marital pressures: medicine and the clergy. The fact that I am a rabbi and the son of a physician enables me to perceive that in some respects the problems are similar. In both instances, for example, the practitioner's spouse must settle for the enforced absence of a mate, sometimes at the very moment that mate is wanted or needed most. Young interns or residents face regular night duty in the hospital. After they have commenced their private practice they are constantly subject to emergency calls. Their families must grow accustomed to the possibility that, just as they are ready for a dinner appointment, a picnic or party, a theater engagement, the shrill intrusion of the telephone bell rudely interrupts their plans.

The intrusions on the life of rabbis can be equally annoying. The serious illness or death of a congregant commandeers them too. Endless meetings, conferences, and pastoral visitations expropriate the evenings they would prefer to spend with their families. The tensions and frustrations frequently forced upon them by insensitive members of the congregation and board are sometimes unjustly ventilated against their spouses and children. The family often bitterly resents the time and attention seemingly given so generously to everyone else.

A role performed by both male doctors and rabbis is that of father-substitute. Especially the women among their patients and congregants respectively are apt to develop strong emotional attachments to them. On occasion such attachments and emotional dependencies seem to reflect the search more for a surrogate-husband than for a father. All this both the male doctor or rabbi and his wife must understand and accept. There can be no doubt that it increases the tension with which their love must cope. If they are mature individuals and their love is strong enough, they will carry these extra stresses not only adequately but even with shared touches of humor.

As more women become physicians and rabbis, more men will have to cope in their marriages with problems which in the past have caused trouble only for wives. Will it be harder for the husband of a rabbi or physician to manage a good marriage than for the wife of a physician or rabbi? Only the future will tell. What we can be sure of at once is that problems there will undoubtedly be.

While the mate of a busy professional—or business executive—must be prepared for adjustments, the busy one needs a word of caution as well. It is so easy for the ambitious young physician to exaggerate the amount of time he or she really needs to spend away from home; so tempting for the neophyte rabbi to assume that no building can be dedicated, no banquet digested, without his/her personal benediction. It is almost irresistible for the aspiring business executive to act as if the entire future of the firm depends on an extra hour or two at the office. There are various reasons why men and women become *workaholics.* Obsessive work may be either the cause or the result of a bad marriage; seldom are they unrelated.

Certain studies indicate that, the more successful a person is at work, the less happy in marriage.[4] This poses a fascinating question of cause and effect. Does such a person's marriage suffer because business or professional responsibilities drain so much time from it? Or is that person driven to work compulsively because of personal frustrations at home? Perhaps either, perhaps both. In any event, the correlation is both important and intriguing. The conscientious person, determined to give his/her profession everything it demands, with no more than meager leftovers for the mate, will soon have no marriage left worth cherishing. A balance must be established from the start, with major priority assigned to both objectives, with a recognition by husband and wife that sometimes their marriage will temporarily be subordinated to pressing business or professional demands, but at other times the priority must be reversed. Every busy person owes as much deliberate budgeting of time to marriage as to career.

True, each man marries a woman and each woman marries

a man. But a career is both an extension of its participant's personality and an influence in the further development of that personality. For that reason above all, it must be included in the calculus of marriage.

So far as possible, you and your future spouse should explore during your courtship the ramifications and involvements of your probable careers. It has been said of the Baal Shem Tov, founder of modern Chasidism, that he was betrothed to a very young girl named Hannah by her father, who died shortly thereafter. After years of wandering, the Besht returned—unknown and in beggar's garb—to claim his bride. Her brother, taking the suitor to be in fact a beggar, refused. After she saw her father's written agreement, Hannah was ready to go with him. But the Besht delayed until he had taken her aside, secretly revealed his true identity, and described the difficulties his chosen career would impose upon their marriage. Happy ending: Hannah accepted and they were married. Obvious lesson: engaged couples should give serious consideration to the impact of their careers on their life together.

SUMMING UP

In several ways, then, financial factors enter into marriage. Earlier we saw that love is realistic while romance is illusory. To contemplate marriage as if there were no financial complications is to be patently guilty of a purely romantic approach.

No one—in a chapter, a book, a whole set of books—could successfully encompass all the behavioral conditions on which a good marriage depends. I have tried here and in the preceding chapter to suggest only the most important: the love relationship of your parents; the quality of your courtship; the continuing kindness and consideration you extend to each other; the honesty and maturity with which you are able to handle hostility; your ability to accept each other as unique individuals and to welcome the differences in temperament and nature between women and men; the amount of time you spend together and what you do with that time; your success in the joint management of family finances; the wisdom with which you anticipate the special circumstances imposed on your marriage by vocational or professional demands; your attitudes toward religion and sex.

It is to the last of these that we now turn our attention.

CHAPTER SEVEN

Sex and Love

We have completed six chapters without mentioning, except for an occasional casual comment, the subject of sex. A generation ago that would have been impossible. The very best books on marriage available then dealt chiefly, if not entirely, with sex. It was believed even by experts that, if newlyweds were furnished with accurate, reliable information that would help them achieve a good sexual adjustment, everything else they desired would follow. The basic premise underlying this view was that sexual satisfaction was either synonymous with love or was its precondition and cause.

Today we know better. Not that we place a lesser value on the role of sex in marriage, but we recognize the relationship as being reversed. Sexual fulfillment is a consequence rather than a cause of love. Intercourse gives two persons who already love each other an ecstatic way to express and at the same time enrich their love. To pretend that sexual adjustment produces love makes as much sense as to claim that one's body temperature produces disease; it confuses symptoms with causes.

No one has understood this more perceptively or expressed it more eloquently than Dr. Erich Fromm. He has epitomized the older view as follows:

> The underlying idea was that love is the child of sexual pleasure and that, if two people learn to satisfy each other sexually, they will love each other.

He proceeds to summarize a newer and more accurate approach in these words:

> Love is not the result of adequate sexual satisfaction, but sexual happiness—even the knowledge of the so-called sexual technique—is the result of love. . . . Fear of or hatred for the other sex are at the bottom of those difficulties which prevent a person from giving himself completely, from acting spontaneously, from trusting the sexual partner in the immediacy and directness of physical closeness. If a sexually inhibited person can emerge from fear or hate, and hence become capable of loving, his or her sexual problems are solved. If not, no amount of knowledge about sexual techniques will help.[1]

A good marriage between two young, normal, healthy partners, without a mutually gratifying sexual relationship, is virtually impossible. But the place to begin is with love, not sex. Hence our deferment of sex to this point.

Fortunately, knowledge of sex is more commonplace and accurate today than it once was. So much so that I am not including here the basic information you need concerning the anatomy and physiology of sex or recommended methods of birth control. If you or your future mate have any doubts on these scores, let me suggest that you turn to chapters eight and nine of my book for high school students, *Love, Sex and Marriage —A Jewish View* (Union of American Hebrew Congregations, 1980). For present purposes, I shall assume you already possess the information given there.

Nothing is more important for the couple about to be married than an awareness of uniquely *human* sexuality. This can best be appreciated against a background of what sex means among subhuman animals. With some—especially certain fish—after the female has laid eggs, the male—without even seeing her—fertilizes them by depositing on them a substance from his body. In others—chickens, for example—the male sprays a fertilizing fluid onto the female while the egg is still forming within her and before the shell has appeared. The egg thus contains its fertilizing agent within itself. In a number of species the male is almost incidental. There are some male fish who attach themselves permanently like leeches to the body of the female, living out their lives that way for the one and only purpose of being available when fertilization of eggs is needed. Among some insects, once the male has fertilized the female's eggs, he becomes superfluous; either he quietly goes off to die by himself or is immediately devoured by his mate. The female praying mantis bites off the head of her mate during intercourse; his death throes increase his copulatory thrusts. Then she eats his body, storing food from it for her offspring. So far as we know, in none of these procedures is there any sensation of pleasure for the participants; their conduct is purely instinctual, serving only the purpose of propagation.

Among mammals—with the exception of whales—sexual intercourse is physically similar to what we experience in human life, yet there are profound differences. Before describing these differences, it is worth noting that certain animals have evolved closer to the human pattern than others. The bald eagle and wild goose, for example, mate for life with only one member of the opposite sex. The wolf mates with only one female during her life span and will take a second partner only upon the death of the first. While these instances are fascinating forerunners of human sexual behavior and emotion, we must not make too much of them. They are still a far cry from the full role of sex in our lives.

Among the differences between animal and human intercourse are the following:

1. Only among humans do the male and female generally face and see each other during coitus.

2. Only among humans does intercourse serve purposes other than propagation of the race. In the animal kingdom it occurs only when the female is ovulating and can be impregnated. At all other times she will resist—if need be, with violence—any attempt by the male to mount her. Intercourse between human mates takes place whenever husband and wife wish to express and at the same time enrich their love. It is not limited either to the time of ovulation or the purpose of procreation.

3. Only among humans is coitus a spiritual as well as a physical experience. When an impassioned male dog meets a female in heat—which means to say, ovulating and therefore ready for copulation—he goes about his business, experiences an orgasm, injects her with semen, and casually departs. There is no love, no permanent relationship, no anticipation of a family—nothing but gratification or pleasure for him and probably just instinctual fulfillment for her. The next time either of them experiences intercourse it will almost certainly be with a different partner and with no more permanent consequence than before.

Nowhere is the meaning of intercourse as a purely physical experience among animals more vividly illustrated than in the observation of Julian Huxley, eminent British biologist:

> . . . many birds will attempt to mate with a stuffed dead female as readily as with a real live one—provided that it is set up in a certain pose; and the sperm for artificial insemination in cattle and horses can be obtained because the mating urge of bulls and stallions is aroused by suitable dummies as well as by live cows or mares.[2]

There are, to be sure, men and women for whom intercourse means little more than that, but it is questionable whether their sex life can in that event be called truly human. With us, if we wish, intercourse can be an expression not only of physical desire but of emotional tenderness, yearning, compassion, and love. It can leave husband and wife not merely satisfied and spent physically but more closely bound to one another in their pursuit of the true, the beautiful, and the good.

All three of the foregoing distinctions mark human sex life as superior to that of animals. There is one respect, however, in which it can be more degrading and depraved. We seem to be the only species in which it is possible for the male to overpower the female, forcing himself upon her sexually against her will. In short, only among human beings do we find the contemptible practice of rape. Our sex life can be either incomparably more glorified or unconscionably more debased than that of any other creature on earth. The choice is our own to make.

BY NO MEANS THE SAME

Before proceeding to additional detail regarding that choice, another word about the common mistake of assuming that sex and love are synonymous. Harlan Ellison titled his short story collection *Love Ain't Nothing But Sex Misspelled.*[3] As a device for capturing attention, this may be successful. As a statement of fact, it is both misleading and harmful. Though inseparably related in marriage, love and sex are by no means the same.

Coitus is not the only expression of love between husband and wife; nor is every instance of coitus an evidence of love. One of the serious mistakes of the Kinsey reports is their reduction of all sex experience to sheer quantity. Sexual fulfillment is measured entirely by the number of so-called *outlets* experienced, as if each orgasm is qualitatively similar to every other. The word *love* does not appear even once in forty-eight pages of index to the basic Kinsey volumes!

A person who is masturbating alone experiences an orgasm but not love. A fiend who rapes a child also achieves an orgasm; it manifests anything but love. A man who reaches an orgasm with his wife may be as self-centered as the masturbator, as sadistic as the raper, or superbly loving. No one has understood the qualitative dimension of coitus better than the distinguished psychiatrist, Dr. Karl Menninger:

> The orgasm of a terrified soldier in battle, that of a loving husband in the arms of his wife, that of a desperate homosexual trying to improve his masculinity, and that of a violent and sadistic brute raping a child are not the same phenomena. The muscles and nerves and secretions may be the same but the orgasms are not the same, and the sexuality is not the same.[4]

Sexual satisfaction, in short—outside or within marriage—can be good or bad, desirable or degrading, wholesome or diseased.

The tendency to equate sex with love is deplorable. It is a gross distortion to call intercourse "making love." A popular magazine hit painfully close to much of our current confusion when it published a cartoon in which an ardent young man says to the rumpled and disarrayed girl he is passionately embracing: "Why speak of love at a time like this?"

Our society too often promotes sex on its lowest and cheapest level. Lurid ads, revealing dress, erotic entertainment —all conspire to impress upon us the purely sensual aspects of sex, rupturing it brutally from everything that makes it human. No less corrosive is the influence of those who would convince us that sex is only a physiological urge, comparable to hunger or an itch and as easily satisfied. They overlook the fact that civilized people accept certain restraints even in the way they eat or scratch themselves. This evaluation of sex, moreover, settles for a stage of evolutionary development reached a million or more years ago.

We are sometimes told that the exercise of control in the satisfaction of our sexual urges can be harmful to mental health. No psychologically literate person would deny our enormous need for sexual release or the value of wholesome sex fulfillment in striving for mental as well as physical well-being. But we have other needs too, on which the sometimes delicate balance between illness and good health hinges. Among them is our need to be truly human, to match with our attitudes and behavior the level of evolution we have already attained. A rock is fulfilled just by being; nothing more is required in order for it to satisfy its *rockness*. A dog, rooted to one spot of earth, restricted to the immobility of the rock, would not have fulfilled its *dogness*. Grass justifies itself simply by sprouting a green blade; no more is expected of it. A rose bush restricted to the level appropriate for grass, limited only to the production of green stems, would have failed to achieve its *roseness*. All of which means that each product of evolution must be itself, must actualize its potential, must realize its margin of superiority over the stages of development which preceded it. We cannot achieve emotional health if we settle for being less than we are. In addition to following all the environmental prescriptions recommended by biology and psychology, to be healthy persons we must find out who we really are and strive to be more than animals.

The most perceptive of our psychoanalysts themselves are aware of this. Thus Erich Fromm has written:

> The complete satisfaction of all instinctual needs is not only not a basis for happiness; it does not even guarantee sanity.[5]

Dr. Povl W. Toussieng, a Danish psychiatrist at the Menninger Clinic, has expressed a similar conviction:

> The history of mankind is man's struggle against his impulses. He has never completely won that struggle and there are many defeats, but we cease to be human if we merely give in to our impulses.[6]

All of which adds up conclusively to the fact that not every orgasm is conducive to mental or emotional health. Only those which are expressive of our best, which emerge out of truly human love, can contribute to our long-range welfare.

MORE THAN ONE MEANING

Rabbi Eugene Borowitz provides us with immense help by calling our attention to the fact that even in human experience sexual intercourse can take place on several levels.[7] With only minor modifications of my own, the arrangement which follows is his; the levels are numbered in reverse.

Level five is that of conquest or force. We have already noted that rape is found only among human beings. If a male dog were to force himself sexually upon a female against her will, at a time when she is not ovulating and is therefore not receptive to his advances, not only would she resist him ferociously, if necessary she would even attack his sex organs. Human females are sometimes less successful in defending themselves against rape. Women have organized in recent years—and properly so—to advise each other on how to avoid or resist being raped, offering compassionate guidance and help to those who have been thus victimized. To the rapist, sex is plainly and only an instrument of power, a way of imposing himself and his will on someone weaker, a vain attempt to simulate a self-confidence which doesn't exist.

Level four is that of the "healthy orgasm." It emerges from a perception of our sexuality as a strong physiological need (admittedly true) which it is healthy to express, unwholesome to repress. The underlying assumption or code is simple: when hungry, we eat; when thirsty, we drink; when afflicted with an itch, we scratch; when desirous of sex, we seek intercourse. One writer, in commenting on this level of sexual activity, has said that "sex, presumably, will become purely fun, like surfing —or hygiene, like Swedish calisthenics."[8]

The most popular expression of the "healthy orgasm" philosophy of sex is in *Playboy* and similar periodicals, in books with such titles as *The Love Machine,* and in such promotional slogans as "Two Views of the Sex Game." Sex is interpreted as little more than mechanical adjustment or sport. The ultimate aim is to become a sexual athlete or gymnast, to discover exotic positions and procedures for intercourse that one has never thought of before.

The trouble with sex as recreation is that it is seldom anything more than that. Many psychiatrists and psychologists have observed that, the more permissive the sexual behavior of society or individuals becomes, the less it means to the participants. In the perceptive words of Norman Cousins, "People who insist on seeing everything and doing anything run the risk of feeling nothing."

This brings us to *level three which Rabbi Borowitz labels "mutual consent."* Where level five definitely and level four probably exemplify the desire of an individual to fulfill his or her own sexual needs, the partner being only a means to that end, here on level three we come to consideration for both participants. Two people feel a desire for sex at the same time. Finding each other to be physically attractive, they agree to satisfy their mutual need. The situation is really not much different from that of a man and woman who agree to scratch each other's itchy backs. Neither is imposing personal will upon the other or taking advantage of the other. Instead of one individual's seeking a healthy orgasm for self, two agree to do so mutually and simultaneously. It is clear—isn't it?—that thus far each level has been a bit more restrictive than the preceding one; which means to say, each category of intercourse imposes additional criteria which must be met before two individuals proceed to the experience of intercourse.

The same thing is true as we proceed to *level two, that of love*. Here, for the first time, intercourse becomes part of a relationship between two whole personalities, not just two genital systems. As one competent observer has commented: "Penises and vaginas can't love each other; only people can do that."

Those who advocate that intercourse be restricted to love say that various types of human behavior are appropriate to different degrees of relationship. One politely nods toward a casual acquaintance, shakes hands with a person to whom he has just been introduced, affectionately hugs an old friend, passionately kisses a mate. To shower a casual or new acquaintance with hugs and kisses would be highly questionable if not comic behavior. The question, then, is: At what degree in the relationship between two persons is sexual intercourse appropriate? The answer, for those who take their stand here: On the level of love, not before.

Rabbi Borowitz expresses this view eloquently:

> I think highly of friendship, but sexual intercourse seems to me a rather extravagant way in which to express it. One should think so much of self, and what his most intimate giving of self means, that he should not do so without the most worthwhile reason. Or, to put it more positively, I value intercourse too highly as an interhuman experience for me to find it an appropriate act with a person who is only a friend.[9]

Finally, there are those who would *reserve intercourse for marriage*. They would point to the fact that it is easy, under the persistent urging of sexual desire, to confuse love with infatuation. A psychiatrist has described a young girl, one of his patients, as saying: "I believe one should have intercourse only when in love, so I am constantly in love." Without being quite so obvious, many individuals act on a similar premise. Adherents of level one remind us of the time test we used earlier to distinguish love from infatuation. To this, they would add that there is a difference between "love for now" and "love forever." When two persons not only feel the strongest kind of interpersonal relationship but are ready on that basis to commit themselves to each other, to assume what they hope will be permanent responsibility for each other, then intercourse between them becomes appropriate and proper. Rabbi Borowitz summarizes this level in the following words:

> Lovers do not make love simply to achieve or produce rich sensation but because they love each other. They do not love for the sake of achieving orgasm, but achieving orgasm is fully appropriate between them because they love. Indeed because they know and trust each other fully, they may hope to find in their lovemaking a personal fulfillment and joy that no other setting for sexual intercourse could provide.[10]

FACING FORWARD

As you approach marriage, you have in all probability already chosen among these five levels of sexual intercourse. The past can never be undone; only the possibility of learning from our mistakes and correcting them justifies concentration on it. Your concern at this point, therefore, should be the level on which you and your future husband or wife will live sexually. True, the probability of your reaching the highest sexual level will be enhanced if you have already achieved that option. But in any event the two of you should consciously plan together the kind of sex life you desire.

Loving brides and grooms, husbands and wives, will remember: their sexual relationship must at all times express and enrich their total love. Coitus is something they do *with* each other, not *to* each other. They cannot hope to achieve a good sex relationship if either approaches it from the perspective of: what's in it for *me?* . . . how can I meet *my* needs? . . . how can *my* desires be satisfied? The sex life of husband and wife must be a paradigm of their entire love relationship. We have long since established that love is distinguished from infatuation by its emphasis on receiving through giving. It follows that people truly in love must be as desirous of giving an orgasm to their mates as of experiencing one themselves—not just because it affords them a sensation of manipulative power, but because they cannot be happy in their own orgasms unless they are also extending the same kind of joy to those whom they love.

Intercourse between mates must be consistent with every other aspect of their relationship. They cannot expect to neglect or ignore each other generally, to indulge in selfishness or abuse at all other times, yet to enjoy a good sex life. That kind of coitus may be normative for animals, surely not for men and women. This is one of several areas where women are generally more sensitive and subtler than men. Sometimes a husband will desire intercourse directly after a marital quarrel —either to appease his guilt or to ritualize the reconciliation. At this point his wife is likely to want no part of his proposal. For her even more than him, each act of intercourse is inextricably related to the totality of their relationship, especially to the incidents and mood of the immediately preceding moments.

The intercourse-quotient of a couple will be no higher than the general quality of their interpersonal relationship. Sex cannot be the only level on which they possess intimate contact. Their mutual ecstasy through coitus will be precious precisely in the proportion that it supplements their many other avenues of intimacy. Thus do they enhance their sex life in the present, while at the same time establishing firm foundations for an abiding love which will bless them long beyond their years of intercourse.

Sex will be important to you in your marriage, extremely important. A mutually enjoyable, satisfying sex life is indispensable to normal, healthy, young or middle-aged couples who want good marriages. But no marriage can succeed if the relationship between husband and wife is limited only to sex or if their sexual experience is not part of their total partnership.

There has been so much concern in our time with methods, positions, and techniques that some couples make almost a caricature of sex, as if they were dutifully following a set of technical instructions to assemble a complicated piece of plumbing equipment rather than expressing their love. I do not mean in any way to decry the importance of accurate knowledge or of discovering how best each of us can arouse himself/herself as well as his or her partner. Knowledge of technique, however, can never substitute for kindness, tenderness, and patience. It will help married couples to remember that they are not involved in sexual competition, in aiming at a world's record for quantity or quality of orgasms. They are in bed because they love their mates, love each other both physically and spiritually. And they are expressing that love in a way God has reserved for human beings alone.

No mistake is more surely fatal to a good marriage than assuming that sex can be developed as a special skill, separate from all other aspects of a couple's relationship. This has been clearly recognized and eloquently expressed by the two experts who, probably more effectively than any others, have studied the physiological phenomena which occur during sexual intercourse. Dr. William H. Masters and Virginia E. Johnson have learned how often couples fail to achieve mutually fulfilling sex lives:

> They pull sex out of context; that is, they consider the physical act of intercourse as something in and of itself, a skill to be practiced and improved. The usual analogies are with dancing or tennis but such comparisons are misleading. Sexual intercourse is not just a skill to be mastered, an activity to exercise the body, or a game to be played. . . . To reduce sex to a physical exchange is to strip it of its richness and subtlety and, even more important, ultimately means robbing it of all emotional value.
>
> Unless there are emotional bonds which link a man and woman and which exist entirely apart from the pure physical relationship, unless they share interests and values which exist outside the bedroom, sexual functioning is not sufficient in itself to establish enduring friendships. . . .

Anyone who suggests that intercourse is in itself a good foundation for friendship proves, with that single statement, an ignorance of two different relationships; such a person knows nothing of the meaning of sex in the context of an emotional involvement—and such a person knows nothing of the meaning of friendship, neither of its origins nor how it is developed nor the part that it can play in the lives of any two individuals.[11]

Judaism perceived intuitively long centuries ago what Masters and Johnson have only recently discovered empirically. It is more than a linguistic coincidence that the Hebrew Bible uses the word יָדַע (*yada*)—meaning "knew"—for intercourse. Thus we read in Genesis: "Now the man knew his wife Eve and she conceived and bore Cain. . . ." Our ancestors knew that coitus on the human level was meant by God and nature to be something more than just physical contact and release. It involves two individuals *knowing* each other—respecting and caring for each other deeply in both physical and spiritual dimensions— loving each other maturely enough to desire a permanent sharing of their lives and partnership in the creation of new life.

The eminent Jewish philosopher, Martin Buber, eloquently articulated the distinction in human relations between "I-It" and "I-Thou." "I-It" means treating another person as if he or she were only a thing. If I move a chair aside because it stands in my way, there is an "I-It" relationship between the chair and myself. It makes no difference to the chair where it is placed or how often it is moved. But, if I rudely bump you because you happen to be in my way, it does make a difference to you. You are a "Thou," not an "It"; you are a human being, with feelings, fears, hopes, and needs very much like my own. I have no right to manipulate or use you for my own purposes if they do not coincide with yours. I must relate myself to you on an "I-Thou" basis. To fail this is to act as if only I were created in God's image, not you. And, in the last analysis, to treat you as if you were only an impersonal means for the satisfaction of my needs degrades myself too.

In no sphere of interpersonal relationships is this truer or more important than in sex. Within or outside marriage, when one person exploits another only for the gratification of personal sensual desires or the inflation of a personal ego, he/she has violated one of the most precious principles of Judaism and of sound human relations.

FOR WOMEN TOO

One of the positive results of the women's movement has been widespread recognition of the fact that sexual desire and need are as strong in women as in men. We shall shortly see that ancient Judaism was surprisingly aware of this. Until recently, however, it was assumed by too many people that woman's sexual role was a passive one, that her sole responsibility was to fulfill her husband's needs. Not so! It may be, indeed, that the capacity of women to enjoy sex is even greater than that of men. Many women, for example, are capable of achieving more than one orgasm during intercourse; most men are not.

The most excitable part of a woman's anatomy is her clitoris, a small organ located between the lips of her vagina. When this is gently manipulated—by contact either with a man's penis or his hand—she can be aroused to the point of climax. Freud mistakenly thought there are two kinds of orgasm which occur in women—clitoral and vaginal—and that the latter is superior. More recent research has shown that an orgasm is an orgasm, regardless of the technique by which it is achieved. It is probably true that the motion of a man's penis in a woman's vagina increases the excitement of her clitoris, and there may be increased emotional gratification from this, but there is only one kind of orgasm. Some women find that indirect stimulation of the clitoris by contact with its surrounding vaginal tissues is more stimulating than too much immediate contact. Some are, as a matter of fact, able to enjoy more repeated and passionate orgasms through manual fondling of their clitoris than through penile contact. Like so much in sexual experience, individuals and couples vary greatly in their preferences.

Whatever the method or technique employed, it is important that a wife too enjoy orgasms. There is no excuse for a man's achieving his climax, then allowing a sexually aroused woman to be frustrated short of fulfillment. There may be occasions when a woman doesn't want or isn't able to reach a climax during or following intercourse, but these should be exceptions, not the rule.

Among the popular assumptions which have been pretty well dispelled by now is the notion that husband and wife should aspire toward simultaneous orgasms. Where this is wanted and achievable, fine, but at best it requires timing which is exceedingly difficult to achieve. A professor of psychology with extensive experience in counseling and teaching college courses on marriage puts it this way:

> The effort to give one's partner the fullest measure of concern and satisfaction is essential to rewarding sexual activity. If either person is primarily concerned with gratifying self or is caught up in an impending orgasm, he or she cannot give full attention to his/her partner. Similarly, if one is concentrating only on the partner's sexual gratification, appropriate concentration on one's own responses and pleasure is impossible.
>
> Furthermore, men and women react quite differently in bodily movements at the time of orgasm. The man's tendency is to plunge into the vagina as deeply as possible at the moment of orgasm and to hold this position, followed perhaps by one or two deep, deliberate thrusts. The woman's tendency, on the other hand, is to want the same stroking, plunging movements of the excitement and plateau phases continued during the orgasmic reaction, with perhaps an acceleration of the thrusts and an increase of pressure in the vulval area. These two highly pleasurable patterns of movement are obviously incompatible. Since both cannot be executed at the same time, whichever pattern is carried out during simultaneous orgasm must detract from the full pleasure of one of the partners.
>
> The arguments would appear to be stronger against than for simultaneous orgasm. . . .[12]

Far more important than whether their orgasms occur simultaneously is striving for both to achieve climaxes as an expression of their deep and abiding love.

Another aspect of female sexuality should be mentioned before we move on. Women vary greatly in their feelings and actions during menstruation. A considerate husband will soon discover whether or not his wife requires special tenderness during her menstrual flow and immediately preceding it. If she prefers not to be approached sexually at that time, if she is easily angered or hurt then, he will act accordingly. Despite the fact that the Bible forbids intercourse during menstruation, if neither mate objects, from a modern point of view there is no valid reason to avoid it; this is a matter of personal preference. Intercourse during menstruation should not be attempted, however, if it is distasteful or uncomfortable to either partner. A wife who is unusually sensitive at this time of month is entitled to extra tenderness from her husband; she should not, however, misuse her menstrual difficulty as an excuse to deny him too long.

CHAPTER EIGHT

"As You Sow..."

The mates who discover from the very beginning that intercourse is mutually pleasurable are probably an exception, not the rule. Like every other aspect of marital happiness, a good sex adjustment comes as the result of correct procedure plus patient trial and error, not as a gift. It may take weeks, months, perhaps even a year to discover the positions, the techniques, the timing which are best calculated to stimulate and satisfy both. There is no one formula of sexual success which will suit everyone. This most intimate of relationships must be worked out for both mates on their own.

Essential to success is an understanding of the differences in sexual nature and need between men and women. Men are both more easily aroused and more simply satisfied. While women achieve every bit as high a degree of both desire and pleasure, they are aroused to a readiness for orgasm more slowly. This places the primary responsibility for patience and tenderness at the beginning of their relationship on the husband. If he is concerned only with himself, his own passion and its fulfillment, there can be no sexual mutuality in their marriage. Hence the extreme importance of a husband's restraining himself patiently and indulging in enough loving foreplay to prepare his wife for penetration and orgasm. One of the major misfortunes of our sex mores is that so much petting occurs before marriage, so little afterward. Petting is nature's way of insuring a readiness for intercourse on the part of both male and female; its most appropriate place is the marriage bed. The whispering of sweet endearments, the gentle fondling and kissing of her breasts, caressing her clitoris—these are a husband's way of bringing his wife to that pitch of desire and need which will make an orgasm probable for her too. They also afford time for her vagina to expand sufficiently at its slower rate so that it may receive his penis without discomfort or pain. When the size of her vagina has expanded and its outer lips are bathed in liquid secretions from within, she is ready for penetration. No kind of sexual foreplay which is enjoyed by both participants and is repulsive to neither is wrong. The two of them are the only persons in the world with the right to judge what is acceptable sexual procedure for themselves.[1]

Most women like to have their breasts fondled as a prelude to intercourse, finding the sensation sexually stimulating; there are, however, occasional exceptions. A loving husband will always quickly discover his wife's preferences and conform to them. In this connection, a gross superstition should be dispelled. There is no correlation between the size of a woman's breasts and her sexual excitability, any more than there is between the size of a man's penis and the intensity of his sexual urges.

Afterplay is no less significant than foreplay. Coitus itself is not an isolated act, but rather the climax of an entire syndrome. What precedes and follows determines the quality of the climax. The husband who—directly after orgasm has been attained—turns over at once to fall asleep or jumps out of bed to raid the refrigerator is, in effect, telling his wife that physical release of tension was really his only aim. Though many men may be unaware of it, their need for a continued expression and demonstration of love after coitus itself has been completed is almost as imperative as that of their wives.

YOUR HONEYMOON

The first days or weeks of marriage can be crucial. For most couples they offer the first opportunity to establish foundations for their future relationship on every level as husband and wife. The ideal place for a honeymoon is where there are interesting things to do together, but not so many as to cause excessive distraction or fatigue. I have known married couples who seemed almost afraid to be alone, who sought constant distraction as protection against getting to know one another. The honeymoon is a time when newly-weds should spend just enough time with others to highlight their primary purpose of becoming better acquainted than ever before with each other.

If bride and groom have deferred intercourse until after they are married—and especially if the bride is a virgin—their first coitus can be crucially important. If she is fearful or experiences pain at her husband's first attempt to penetrate, he should try to proceed at a pace which will minimize her discomfort.

Any failure to achieve mutual gratification and pleasure in the early intercourse of the honeymoon should be accepted by bride and groom as part of the normal trial and error of marriage. If they appear to be making no progress in this respect over many months, professional aid should be sought.

For understandable reasons, sex is likely to play a larger role during the honeymoon than it will after a few years of married life. But even the honeymoon should be more than just sex. This is a couple's first precious opportunity to nurture a total love relationship—a joyous meeting of bodies and minds, of hearts and souls—to which their sexual union will testify. Sex, in short, should occupy its proper and proportionate place from the start.

Remember that to some extent a honeymoon is unreal, that is, it occurs under circumstances devoid of many pressures you are bound to confront later. There are no household chores on most honeymoons, no conflicts between career and home, no tensions caused by children or relatives or friends. To take full advantage of such ideal conditions is wise; to expect that life will always be so close to perfection would be naive.

My earlier emphasis on the importance of open and honest lines of communication between husband and wife is especially pertinent in their sexual relationship, commencing with the honeymoon itself. There is unfortunately reason to believe this is not always the case. Several studies of marriage indicate that the average husband believes his wife reaches orgasm more often than she actually does. They disclose also that most wives estimate the frequency of intercourse as higher than do their husbands. Whatever this shows about the relative enjoyment of coitus by the respective partners in marriage, it certainly bespeaks a clouding of communication between them.

The same sad conclusion is supported by a more recent study of one hundred married couples. Eighty-three percent of them reported that they enjoyed happy marriages; ninety percent said that, given a choice again, they would marry the same mate. While one-third of the wives in this group admitted they experienced difficulty maintaining excitement during sexual intercourse, only one-seventh of their husbands were aware that their partners were experiencing this kind of difficulty.[2]

Husbands and wives should not play games of pretense with each other. If she is not achieving orgasm, if either or both are failing to feel fulfillment in their sex relations, it is essential that they convey the truth to each other. Only thus can they lovingly experiment together toward better results.

This honesty is especially essential where a man and woman differ in the intensity of their sexual desires and expression. Such differences are not uncommon. I couldn't hope to say what needs saying here as well as Masters and Johnson have:

> The question is whether a husband and wife can learn to respect and accommodate themselves to differences in the strength of their sexual desires. . . .
>
> If these two are to achieve a compatible sexual relationship, they must reach a mutual understanding of their individual natures. They must accept the fact that variations in sexual drive do exist, that neither partner should apologize to the other for having more or less sexual energy, that one is not "better" or "worse" than the other. The husband must make his wife feel that he

accepts her nature for what it is and that any regret he may have about her inability to experience a more intense degree of sexual pleasure is genuine regret, not dissatisfaction. The wife in turn must make her husband feel that her muted response is not a reflection on his skill as a lover or in any way a personal rejection but her natural expression of sexual fulfillment. Thus, instead of acting as two separate individuals with contrasting—or even conflicting—standards of sexual behavior, they become a couple who honor the sexuality of their marriage.

Limited sexual responsiveness is, of course, often enough true of the male. The same principle applies—an acceptance of variations in sexual natures. This means rejecting the idea that the husband is any less a man because his sexual needs are less urgent than his wife expected, and it also means rejecting the idea that the wife is at fault because she fails to stimulate her husband to greater activity.[3]

There is no such thing as a *normal* or *average* pattern of sexual procedure, of frequencies and routines which will be best for everyone. The sexual relationship between husband and wife is the most uniquely personal, most intensely intimate bond in human experience. How and how often you and your husband or wife express your love together can be determined only by the two of you. Whatever you both enjoy, whatever binds you closer together physically and spiritually, is right for you.

Too many couples are tyrannized by the notion that there is some kind of universal sexual standard they must strive to attain. It is no more necessary—or possible—for all to experience their sexuality in the same way, than for everyone to enjoy the same foods, eat the same portions, shed the same number of tears in grief or joy. What is incontrovertibly true is that everyone must eat a reasonably balanced diet and be able to express his or her emotions. Similarly, married couples should share and enjoy sex together. How frequently or in exactly what manner—this they must discover by and for themselves.

ONE AND ONLY ONE?

A proper understanding of the relationship between sex and love leads us to certain ineluctable consequences, among them the extreme danger of extramarital sexual encounters. The seventh commandment is not the only prohibition of adultery in Jewish tradition. Among the objects of covetousness against which the tenth commandment warns us is our neighbor's wife. The writer of Proverbs, referring to "the evil woman" and "a harlot," warns his readers not to lust after them:

> Can a man take fire in his bosom,
> And his clothes not be burned?
> Or can one walk upon hot coals,
> And his feet not be scorched?
> So he that goes in to his neighbor's wife;
> Whoever touches her shall not go unpunished.

Similarly, the prophet Hosea makes it clear that the law against adultery applies to men no less than women. He cautions his listeners that they cannot expect their women to be punished for such offenses while they themselves are equally guilty:

> I will not punish your daughters when they commit harlotry,
> Nor your daughters-in-law when they commit adultery;
> For you yourselves consort with lewd women,
> And you sacrifice with harlots.

The Talmud too underscores the importance of sexual faithfulness between husband and wife: "In marriage a person reserves his partner for himself as a sacred object."[4]

In the earliest stages of Jewish legal development adultery was a crime for which only women were indicted; men were apparently free to indulge in extramarital adventures. The fifth chapter of Numbers prescribes a grim, humiliating public test to be imposed on any married woman suspected of having cohabited with a man other than her husband. The Talmud, obviously perceiving the unfairness, mitigated the severity of the biblical procedure. It decreed that a wife could not be convicted of adultery unless it were proven that she had been warned in the presence of two witnesses not to have any communication with the man in question, yet had afterward met him secretly under circumstances conducive to the crime.[5]

Rabbinic law also made it clear that men were not immune from the charge of adultery. Thus, one who was suspected of having experienced coitus with another man's wife was not permitted to marry her if she were subsequently widowed or divorced![6] It was decreed, moreover, with reference to the biblical test of bitter waters intended to expose a woman's infidelity:

> Only when the man is himself free from guilt, will the waters be an effective test of his wife's guilt or innocence, but, if he has been guilty of illicit intercourse, the waters will have no effect.[7]

This excursion into ancient Jewish tradition would be incomplete without acknowledging that legally a husband could be convicted of adultery only if his sexual exploit had been with a married woman. Extramarital intercourse with a partner neither married nor betrothed was frowned upon, but not considered a crime. This was one of many kinds of evidence attesting to a double standard of sexual ethics.

Our modern knowledge and insight can tolerate no such dichotomy. A man must be no less sensitive to the damage he inflicts on his wife and himself, or on the future marriage of a single girl, than to the harm he does to another man. The most persuasive argument against adultery emerges from the significance of sex and love on the highest human level. Surely if intercourse climaxes a total physical-plus-intellectual-plus-emotional-plus-spiritual partnership, rather than merely a transitory physical liaison, it must be limited to one's husband or wife. Any exception to that rule will be destructive both to the individuals involved and to their love.

Among contemporary writers Dr. George N. Shuster has put this aspect of the problem very well:

> . . . we are coming slowly to recognize that the psychological impact of infidelity—on the man and the woman

involved, on the injured partners, and particularly on the children of the married couple—is far greater than we had previously thought. Anyone who thinks that adultery, gone into however lightly and however gracefully, cannot completely shatter the life of the injured partner is terribly mistaken.[8]

To assume that monogamy is just one of many convenient but arbitrary arrangements—not much better or worse than others —imposed upon the individual by an authoritarian society is miserably to misunderstand the meaning of love and marriage. A faithful one-to-one relationship between husband and wife has been found by millennia of experimentation to be the very best plan possible for the preservation of love and the achievement of happiness. It is arbitrary only in the sense that it conforms to human nature at its best and cannot be violated, therefore, with impunity.

Dr. Frank Caprio, a practicing psychiatrist, has made an extensive study of marital infidelity. He concludes that it is nearly always a manifestation of illness:

> *Infidelity, like alcoholism or drug addiction, is an expression of a deep, basic disorder of character.* It is often a symptom of a depression or unhappiness unresolved since childhood. It has its roots in the insecurity of the individual childhood. Infidelity is more likely to occur among the neurotic than the so-called normal.

After thus tracing the probable origin of adulterous conduct, Dr. Caprio writes effectively also of its consequences:

> Men and women given to infidelity often become victims of chronic insomnia or indigestion or a host of other psychosomatic symptoms of repressed guilt.[9]

Suppose adultery is condoned by both husband and wife? Suppose they agree to experimentation with one of the so-called alternatives to marriage: mate swapping, "swinging," communal families with permissive sexual behavior, "open marriage." Hasn't our discussion of the relationship between sex and love on the highest human level already answered?

It would be foolish to deny that there are probably couples who can take one or another of these alternatives in their stride. But they are not the ones who are capable of reaching the utmost marriage can offer in ecstasy and love. The price to be paid for this kind of sexuality is the separation of sex from love, indulgence in sexual gymnastics for their own sake, a surrender of our uniquely human potential to that of the animal world. Each couple can and must make this choice; no couple can have it both ways.

Ten years as attending physician to the students at Syracuse University gave Dr. Robert J. Collins an unusual opportunity to observe numerous varieties of sexual behavior and their consequences. His conclusion is especially applicable to the choices proposed as alternatives to marriage:

> The "new morality" is a fad. It ignores history. It denies the physical and mental composition of human beings. It is intolerant, exploitative, and is oriented toward intercourse, not love. The unity and community that couples seek cannot be accomplished at the pelvic level.[10]

Nena and George O'Neill, husband and wife anthropologists, were among the earliest and most persuasive proponents of so-called "open marriage." There is much to be commended in their thinking: the ideas that husbands and wives should be honest in their communication of feelings to each other, that neither should assume a role of dominance, that the structure of sexual roles in many marriages is too rigid. Their advocacy of free sexual experimentation outside marriage, however, is a denial of everything we now know about the relationship between sex and love. Even the O'Neills seem to have backed away from this aspect of their initial suggestions. Five years after their first joint book, Nena published a second volume based on interviews with couples they had studied for their first work. Among her revised conclusions: ". . . the assurance of sexual fidelity is still an important and necessary attribute of most marriages."[11]

In a good marriage—as in life generally—the wise person tries to establish prudent lines of policy in advance of specific crises. Husbands and wives will talk about such matters freely and will reach joint decisions on the basis of what they both want out of marriage and of the long-range effects of unfaithfulness on their relationship to each other. Both will then remember that free will is a flexible commodity. Each step we take either limits or enlarges our freedom for the next. The husband who invites his secretary out for drinks and dinner, the wife who accepts the luncheon invitation of an old boyfriend, may have appreciably circumscribed their remaining freedom. The delicate balance between indiscretion and control can become so tenuous as to be imperceptibly tipped by the mildest emotional breeze. Only if each decision is made in line with overall policy, with what we earnestly desire the final outcome to be, can we be reasonably confident of success. In the perceptive words of a physician: "The path from flattery to an affair is a short crosscut." This is another instance of the oft-repeated truth that in every decision we gain something and lose something. We cannot have it both ways. No one can clip the coupons of immediate and unlimited sensual pleasure, yet at the same time build the kind of marriage investment which will in the long run yield maximum happiness.

CHAPTER NINE

"Be Fruitful and Multiply..."

Do you wish to have children? When? How many? Spaced how far apart? For reasons which must long since have become clear, I assume that you and your loved one have already discussed these questions and I hope you agree on the answers, whatever they may be.

According to the Torah, the first positive divine commandment directed to humanity was to procreate. "Be fertile and increase, fill the earth." Tradition holds that a Jewish male has met this obligation after he has fathered two children. Rabbinic authorities differed on whether this had to be two sons, or if a son and a daughter would do. There was never any doubt, however, that every married couple would, in the normal course of events, want and have children.

Today the matter is less simple. Even where the financial support and education of children is not a problem, and especially in marriages involving two careers, conception of offspring is often delayed, sometimes permanently prevented. To have or not to have a family? Couples retain the right and responsibility to answer for themselves. Eagerly prospective grandparents should desist from pressuring their married children; the decision is too intimate for anyone other than the couple to make. In approaching it, you and your mate will want to consider the following:

On a personal level, the danger of complications in childbirth increases when a woman is older than her mid-thirties.

Most of us, moreover, are better able to handle the problems of rearing children before we grow almost old enough to be their grandparents. On a social level, Jewish couples face a painful ambivalence. Their concern for overpopulation and ecology may prompt them to have few children or none. At the same time, the precariousness of Jewish survival in today's world may urge upon them a larger family. More than a few young Jewish couples have felt a personal responsibility to help replenish the population reservoir so ravished by the Holocaust. How you and your spouse decide to balance these conflicting demands is your business. I did not attempt to influence my own children in this regard; what moral right would I have to usurp your judgment?

WILLING, BUT NOT ALWAYS ABLE

How ironic it is that, while some couples utilize every known means to prevent the conception of a child, others who yearn for children desperately seem unable to conceive any. Those who are thus thwarted need two kinds of first-aid: emotional and practical.

It should help considerably to know that the problem is by no means uncommon; as many as one out of six married couples will discover themselves to be at least temporarily infertile. An apparent inability to have children is neither something of which to be ashamed nor a deficiency to be blamed on oneself or one's mate. To act as if it were a blemish to be hidden, an embarrassment never to be disclosed or discussed, is to compound one's discomfort.

What are some of the emotional dead-ends to be identified and avoided? Jealousy and/or hostility toward couples who have or are expecting a child. . . . Guilt caused by the gnawing assumption that you are yourself the cause of the problem. . . . Resentment of your spouse because you believe he or she is responsible. . . . Blaming either yourself or your mate for childlessness makes no more sense than faulting a person for being bald or short or thin.

You have probably heard of women who seemed unable

to conceive, gave up in despair, adopted a child, then became pregnant after all. On the strength of such dramatic sequences, some physicians recommend that relaxation is a good prescription to increase the probability of becoming pregnant. Aside from the extreme unlikelihood of anyone who is anxious on this score being able to relax, the evidence does not seem to support this popular fiction. As with many physical conditions, there seems to be a certain rate of spontaneous cure, of couples who finally achieve success in conceiving a child, without consulting a physician or undertaking any special effort. So far as we know, this rate doesn't vary between those who have adopted a child and those who have not.

Can anything be done by a frustrated couple other than trusting to spontaneity or luck? Fortunately, yes. A medical expert can be consulted. The proportion of infertile men and women who can be successfully diagnosed and treated is constantly increasing as new knowledge is discovered. In many communities there are groups organized for the express purpose of helping with this problem.[1]

There is no cause for despair. Even if favorable results are not forthcoming, it is possible to enjoy a richly fulfilling marriage without children. And there are other steps to be considered by couples who remain infertile.

CHOSEN CHILDREN

One such option, obviously, is adoption. Although the rearing of orphaned children was quite commonplace in Jewish circles, strangely enough there is nothing on this subject in talmudic law. Only in modern times have a number of rabbinic authorities—both in the United States and Israel—dealt with adoption in response to specific inquiries. The general tenor of their judgments is that an adopted child is considered in every sense to be fully the child of the adopting parents. This is especially true if the child is reared to fulfill the *mitzvot*, the religious duties incumbent upon all Jews, or to become a scholar. Indeed, even if children have living biological parents but other childless adults rear them as scholars, it is considered altogether proper for both parties to call each other parent and child.[2]

Are there risks involved in adopting a child? Of course there are. At best, one can't possibly know as much about the genetic heritage of someone else's offspring as about one's own. Yet there are risks in the natural process of conception and birth too, aren't there? Adoption risks can be minimized if a child is obtained through a recognized agency which thoroughly investigates both the physical and mental backgrounds of the children it places.

The agony confronted by so many would-be adopting parents today is that such agencies have very few healthy babies, if any. Not only has the more extensive use of birth control and abortion reduced the availability of infants for adoption, but an increasing number of mothers who give birth to babies out of wedlock are choosing to keep them. Whatever the explanations or reasons, the fact is that, except for babies of racially mixed couples or children with serious disabilities, the reservoir of adoptees available through reputable agencies has virtually evaporated. Understandably, most couples wish to adopt only normal, healthy infants; others find gratification and fulfillment through deliberately providing security and love to a handicapped child.

As the number of healthy babies decreases, many couples are forced to deal with the so-called black or gray markets, with physicians and attorneys who specialize in matching unwanted or orphaned babies with couples who yearn to be parents. Some of these individuals are reputable and honest; others are interested only in making money. The cost of thus adopting a child can be staggering. Rarely are the backgrounds of either the children or the prospective parents investigated as carefully as they should be. Yet often there is no other choice.

Confronted with this dilemma, what should a couple wanting to adopt a child do? By all means, consult whatever adoption agencies there are in your area; register with them, be interviewed, and check with them periodically. Let your need be known to all obstetricians and attorneys you know; they are the most likely to know of available infants. Spread the word to your family and friends. One never knows when or where they may hear of an adoptable child. The more contacts you make, the greater is the probability of success. If there are organizations of adoptive parents in your community, establish contact with them.[3] Despite the difficulties, and though there can be no guarantees, babies are being adopted every day; one of them could be yours. I know of one couple who adopted four children in the past decade.

Is it possible to love an adopted child as dearly as if you had biologically conceived it? Millions of adopting parents will enthusiastically say *yes!* One of my favorite true stories is of the mother who, when asked which of her two children had been adopted, paused for a moment, then replied, "You know, I actually have difficulty remembering."

ALL NATURAL

Only recently has medical science made so-called artificial insemination possible as an alternative to adoption for infertile couples. I have long felt the adjective to be unfortunate. The conception, gestation, and birth of a child by this method is entirely natural; the only respect in which it differs from the norm is that sperm is injected into the woman by syringe rather than by sexual intercourse. There are two types of artificial insemination: AIH refers to instances in which the sperm is obtained from the woman's husband, while in AID it comes from an unknown donor. Only an expert in fertility problems can ascertain in a given case which should be chosen.

It was estimated in 1977 that as many as a million living individuals had been conceived in the United States through AIH or AID and that this number was being increased annually by more than 20,000. The ability to deep-freeze human sperm has made it possible to establish sperm banks in at least twelve American cities. Careful tests are given in advance to the anonymous men who donate sperm. The probability of suffering genetic defects is no greater—perhaps even less—than through normal conception.

Science seems to be hovering now over the threshold of yet another alternative for the infertile couple. The world's first so-called "test-tube baby" was born in 1978. An ovum fertilized through sexual intercourse was removed from the body of a woman who had conceived and transplanted into the womb of another woman, where it developed and from which it was eventually born. Theoretically, some scientists believe it will one day be possible for a human embryo to be conceived, to gestate fully, and to be "born" in a petri-dish, a chemical receptacle in which it would be provided with essential nutrients.

I shall not enter here into the moral dilemmas involved—assuming that such a theoretical possibility becomes practical—or the equally perplexing problem of what such procedures might do to the emotional relationship between mothers and their children. Religious authorities differed widely about Louise Brown, the first known human child conceived outside the womb of her biological mother. Liberal religionists in general tended to condone; orthodox and fundamentalist leaders, to condemn. There will be much discussion and dissent on this in years to come.

What does Judaism have to say about the use of artificial insemination? It would be logical to assume—would it not?—that, since this is so new a development, Jewish law is silent on the subject. Logical . . . but wrong! Here is a classic example of how Jewish law takes as its starting point an ancient incident involving the same or a similar principle, then extrapolates to reach conclusions about a novel situation.

In this case the precedent was the belief—common in talmudic times and found among both Jewish and Moslem physicians in the Middle Ages—that a woman could be impregnated by the presence of male seed in her bath. If this occurred, was her pregnancy accepted? Was the child thus conceived legitimate? Could it claim inheritance from her husband? All modern rabbinic speculation about AIH and AID derives from such older questions as these.

While there are differences of opinion, the prevailing view among contemporary rabbis—Orthodox as well as Conservative and Reform—holds that AIH is acceptable, particularly if that seems to be the only way a woman can become pregnant. There is no such consensus, however, regarding AID. Reform rabbis are inclined to accept it;[4] with some dissent, most Orthodox rabbis disapprove. An interesting exception to prevailing Orthodox opinion is to be found in a 1977 decision of the Haifa Rabbinical Court, which reversed its own previous judgment by saying that artificial insemination with sperm from an anonymous donor does not constitute adultery if the woman's husband has consented in writing. It ruled, moreover, that the husband in that case is responsible for the child's support.[5]

Even among some of those who reject AID, there is no doubt about the fact that a child thus conceived belongs in the family; it is considered to be the child, not of the donor, but of the woman who gives birth to it. A leading American Jewish physician summarizes the Orthodox rabbinic view as follows:

> Artificial insemination using the semen of a donor other than the husband is considered by most rabbinic opinion to be an abomination and strictly prohibited. . . . Some authorities regard AID as adultery, requiring the husband to divorce his wife and her forfeiture of the *ketubah;* and even the physician and the donor are guilty when involved in this act akin to adultery. Some rabbinic opinion, however, states that, without a sexual act involved, the woman is not guilty of adultery. . . .
>
> There is near unanimity of opinion that the use of semen from the husband is permissible if no other method is possible for the wife to become pregnant.[6]

I repeat: all decisions about having children—by intercourse, by adoption, by AIH or AID, by whatever means—should be made by agreement between husband and wife. Together they will consider their mutual readiness for parenthood, their financial situation, their religious convictions, the very best medical advice they can obtain. But the decision must ultimately be theirs.

CHAPTER TEN

Miles Apart

There has been far too great a tendency in recent years to assume that all religions agree in their ethical values. While it is true that the various strands of Christianity and Judaism share much ethical aspiration in common, there are also significant differences. In no area is this truer than in their respective attitudes toward sex. It would be foolish to pretend that there is only one Christian or one Jewish point of view on sex. Yet a careful examination of what may be called the main-line historical approaches of the two traditions will disclose major divergences. The Jewish bride and groom who are aware of what their faith teaches about sex, love, and marriage, and who attempt to apply these precepts to their marital behavior, possess an asset of inestimable value. Many of the truths emphasized today by modern science were anticipated by our ancestors long centuries ago. We shall be better able to appreciate them if we attend first to the views of Christianity.

It is not our purpose here to invite odious comparisons. Neither do we intend to act, however, as if Judaism has nothing unique to contribute to the making of a good marriage. We shall call upon Christian authorities themselves to express the attitudes of their faith. The first historic truth to which they will attest is that through much of its development Christianity has been negative and suspicious in its approach to sex. It is not without significance that Jesus—unlike nearly all his contemporaries among the leaders of Judaism—was never married. According to Christian theology, moreover, both he and his mother were born to virgins. Judaism and modern science agree that this is impossible; the only way a new human life can be initiated is through the fertilization of an ovum by a spermatozoon. Today, as we have just seen, it is possible through artificial insemination for a woman who has never experienced sexual intercourse to be impregnated. No such technique was known, however, two thousand years ago.

Paul, who was the founder of Christianity, looked upon sexual desire and especially coitus as evil. He expressed the explicit wish that all men might be capable, as he was, of remaining permanently celibate. Because they were not, as a concession to human weakness he said: "It is better to marry than to burn."[1]

The disdain of Paul persisted through most of early Christian Church history. Summarizing his view and that of the New Testament generally, one Christian religious authority has written:

> In this idea of marriage as an accommodation to human weakness and a hindrance to the fullest service of God there is but little appreciation of its dignity and high calling; nor do the writers of the New Testament show much sense of the joys and privileges of family life. . . .[2]

The same writer, commenting on the preponderant Christian attitude in the centuries following completion of the New Testament, has said:

> While none denied that marriage, relatively speaking, was a good thing, it was nevertheless tolerated rather than commended. . . . Of the joys, privileges, and opportunities of home and family life we find little appreciation, while hardly more than lip service is paid to the blessing of children.[3]

From time to time a voice of protest or disagreement was raised within the Church, but for the most part sex was disparaged and intercourse even within marriage was reluctantly accepted only as a concession to human weakness and a biological necessity. Additional evidence of this attitude is to be found in the fact that in some Christian denominations to this day—most notably but not exclusively in Roman Catholicism —religious leadership is limited to those who remain celibates or virgins.

The very thought of sex was considered sinful in Christianity. Thus Jesus is quoted in the New Testament as saying: ". . . every one who looks at a woman lustfully has already committed adultery with her in his heart." In the extreme Christian view sexual desire and its fulfillment were scarcely more ethical within marriage than outside it. St. Jerome, for example, wrote: "He who loves his own wife too ardently is an adulterer." The Church Fathers condemned the use of cosmetics and other adornments by all women, whether married or not, on the ground that it might increase their sexual attraction for men. According to Tertullian, even the natural, unadorned beauty of women "ought to be obliterated by concealment and neglect, since it is dangerous to those who look upon it."[4]

No one was more immoderate or intense in the expression of such views than St. Augustine. Psychiatrists find it very significant that in his youth Augustine's sexual behavior was extremely debauched and depraved. Later in life he himself wrote, regarding his earlier years: "I boiled over in my fornications." He is alleged at one point to have intoned this prayer: "Lord, make me chaste—but not yet!" When Augustine reacted, it was from one extreme to the other, condemning all intercourse that was not directly intended to produce progeny. He said: "Intercourse even with one's legitimate wife is unlawful and wicked where the conception of offspring is prevented." He also decreed: "It is good for a man not to touch a woman." His rejection of all intercourse not intended to impregnate was described, fifteen centuries later, by Pope Pius XI as "an uninterrupted Christian tradition." Meanwhile, in the thirteenth century, St. Thomas Aquinas agreed that "every carnal act done in such a way that generation cannot follow is a vice against nature and a sin ranking next in gravity to homicide."

Many modern Catholic authorities have echoed these views. Thus a prominent Jesuit, Father William J. Gibbons of

Fordham University, has said that the church "does not wish to see sexual expression regarded as an independent good."[5] Some voices within the Roman Church have commenced to question this stand but they still appear to be much in the minority.[6]

The Protestant view was similar. So recent and eminent an authority as Soren Kierkegaard, nineteenth-century Danish philosopher and theologian who is still admired and quoted by many Christian authorities, almost seems to be echoing the views of earlier Christians when he writes:

> It is an abominable lie to say that marriage is pleasing to God. From the Christian point of view it is a crime, and what is odious about it is that by this very crime the innocent individual was introduced into that community of criminals which is human life.[7]

Augustine even attempted to read his own new view of sex back into the minds and lives of the Hebrew Patriarchs—Abraham, Isaac, and Jacob—saying that they would have preferred to fulfill God's commandment to "be fertile and increase" without indulging in intercourse, but this was manifestly impossible. Therefore, he concluded, they must have experienced coitus with their wives only reluctantly and out of duty.

This transference by Augustine of his own later contempt for sex to the Patriarchs was ridiculous. There is not the slightest shred of evidence that they actually felt as he did. Indeed, as we shall see very shortly, biblical Judaism is characterized by an honest, open, at times almost lusty acceptance of sex.

My brief resume of Christian attitudes toward sex would be neither adequate nor fair if I failed to add that in more recent times the views summarized above have been appreciably altered, if not altogether abandoned, by many Christian individuals and denominations. It is now increasingly accepted in Christian circles that an active sex life in marriage is commendable even when it is not intended to produce children. Insofar as this is true, however, it is important to recognize that these Christians have renounced their own historic approach to sex and have approximated that of Judaism. It is also essential to bear in mind that large numbers of Christians even in our own day have been educated to accept a theological stigma against sex.

A DIFFERENT VIEW

What does Jewish tradition say about marriage and sex? To begin with, it sees marriage, not as a necessary evil or a concession to human frailty, but as a primary good. The only purpose for which the sale of a Torah scroll was permitted was to make marriage possible for an orphan who would otherwise have been too poor to marry. Despite the immense importance which Judaism has always assigned to study, the Talmud is explicit in saying: "A man shall first take unto himself a wife and then study Torah." In ancient Temple times the High Priest was not permitted to perform the most sacred rites of the year, those of atonement on Yom Kippur, unless he was married.[8] It was decreed also that, if marriage and funeral processionals happened to approach an intersection simultaneously, the former was to proceed first.

Our rabbis were convinced that whatever freedom an individual had to relinquish because of marriage was more than counterbalanced by what was gained. They made this clear in their parable about the emperor who said one day to Rabbi Gamaliel: "Your God is a thief, because it is written [in Genesis]: 'The Lord God cast a deep sleep upon Adam and he slept; and He took one of his ribs. . . .' " Rabbi Gamaliel's daughter, who had overheard the conversation, asked her father to let her handle the matter. The next day she entered a complaint with the emperor that thieves had broken into her home the night before, taking a silver vessel and leaving a gold one. "Would that such a thief visited me every day!" exclaimed the emperor. The rabbi's daughter at once continued: "Was it not, then, a splendid thing for the first man when a single rib was taken from him and a wife was supplied in its stead?"[9]

Judaism looks with emphatic favor on marriage and on sex within marriage. It believes that intercourse between husbands and wives is desirable and wholesome; that God intended it, not only as a means to propagate the human species, but also to fortify and reinforce their love. There is an occasionally discordant opinion among the authentic spokespersons of Judaism, but such is clearly an exception, not the rule. That which has been the major motif in Christianity is but a minor and incidental melody in the symphony of Judaism.

Typical of normative Judaism is the following statement, attributed to Nachmanides in the thirteenth century. Some authorities doubt whether he was in fact its author. Even if not, however, the fact that he was alleged to have authored these words and that they have been cited to illustrate the authentic Jewish point of view is significant:

> The act of sexual union is holy and pure. . . . The Lord created all things in accordance with His wisdom, and whatever He created cannot possibly be shameful or ugly. . . . When a man is in union with his wife in a spirit of holiness and purity, the Divine Presence is with them.[10]

Ours may well be the only religious tradition in history to recommend that husbands recite a prayer before enjoying sexual intercourse with their wives. The following, for example, appears in an eighteenth-century collection of Jewish prayers:

> O Lord my God and God of my Fathers, ground of all the universes . . . may it be Your will that You emanate from Your spirit of power unto me and give me might and strength in my organs and my body that I might regularly fulfill the commandment pertaining to my sexual cycle; that there be not found in my organs, body, or passion any weakness or slackness; that there be no forcing, unseemly thought, confusion of mind, or weakening of power to prevent me from fulfilling my desire with my wife. Rather, now and forever, let my passion be ready for me without fail or slackness of organ, at any time that I should desire. Amen.

Both Bible and Talmud discuss matters pertaining to sex with uninhibited honesty. King David is portrayed as having indulged in adultery and being severely punished for it. One of the shorter books of the Bible is devoted in its entirety to the physical side of love. True, Jewish tradition considered Song of Songs to be an allegory depicting the mutual love between God and the Jewish people. But this was undoubtedly a later sublimation of what had originally been a beautifully poetic series of passionate love songs. The fact that such literature was included in the very canon of Holy Scripture, however it may have been reinterpreted by the rabbis, discloses much concerning the wholesome approach of ancient Judaism to sex. From Song of Songs come the very beautiful words of the modern Israel song, often engraved on wedding rings: דודי לי ואני לו (Dodi li va'ani lo)—"My beloved is mine and I am his." Here also are to be found descriptions of a woman in pursuit of her lover (3:1–4), of her physical beauty as seen by him (4:1–5), and of his physique as it impresses her (5:8–16).

The Talmud contains an interesting discussion on the best time for husband and wife to experience intercourse. Rabbinic literature recognizes that the sex urge varies from individual to individual, that consequently one man may require intercourse more frequently than another. The Shulchan Aruch states:

> . . . each man is obliged to perform his marital duty according to his strength and according to his occupation. Gentlemen of leisure should perform their marital obligation every night. Laborers who are employed in the city where they reside should perform their duty twice weekly, but, if they are employed in another city, once a week. Donkey-drivers [should have marital relations] once a week; camel-drivers, once in thirty days; sailors, once in six months. As for scholars, it is obligatory for them to have intercourse once a week, and it is customary for this to be on Friday nights.[11]

It is clear from this quotation that the frequency of intercourse was to be governed both by the basic nature and physique of the individual and by the intervals of travel imposed upon him by his vocation. Even more indicative of how Jewish tradition felt about sex is the remarkable fact that precisely the Sabbath was chosen as the night most appropriate for intercourse by a scholar and his wife!

WOMEN'S NEEDS TOO

The statement just quoted from the *Shulchan Aruch* may seem to relate the frequency of coitus only to the nature and need of the husband. Elsewhere, however, Judaism recognized that women too are active partners in the sexual relationship and that their needs must also be met. Even though, in early times, marriage was more often than not arranged for a girl by her parents, the rabbis insisted that her consent was indispensable before the nuptial contract could be executed. One of the greatest of the talmudic authorities, Rav, severely punished any man who married without first obtaining the consent of his prospective wife.[12]

This awareness of the emotional and sexual needs of women was all the more notable for having been achieved in a patriarchal society and at a time when most cultures supposed that only men have strong sexual desires. It was decreed that a husband must not leave on a long journey without first having intercourse with his wife and must do so again as soon as possible after his return. Refusal to cohabit was accepted by Jewish law as grounds for divorce at the initiative of either husband or wife. The bridegroom was bidden to be sensitive to his wife's natural timidity in their first performance of coitus: "The Torah teaches gentle manners: the bridegroom should not enter the marriage chamber until the bride gives him leave."[13] That women share in the sexual responsibilities and opportunities of marriage and should play an active role in them is implied in the following admonition by Meir of Rothenburg, the outstanding rabbi of thirteenth-century Europe. Contrary to the strictures of early Christianity against the use of cosmetics, he asserted: "Let a curse descend upon a woman who has a husband and does not strive to be attractive."[14] The *Shulchan Aruch* decrees that a married woman may enhance her appearance with cosmetics even during the thirty-day mourning period for a close relative (that is, after the first week), "so that she does not become repulsive to her husband"! A mourning bride is permitted to adorn herself even during the first week.[15]

Up to this point a cynic might protest that even the pas-

sages and injunctions which seem to address the sexual needs
and rights of women are in fact calculated for the benefit of
their husbands. The tradition, fortunately, is too explicit to
justify such doubt. The Torah itself catalogues three primary
obligations of husbands to their wives: food, clothing, and
sexual rights. Sexual rights are emphasized by the Talmud as
the most important of all in the stipulation that a woman may,
by pre-nuptial agreement, surrender her claim to food and
clothing, but not to sexual gratification! The Schools of Sham-
mai and Hillel disagreed on how long a man could deny sexual
intercourse to his wife before she could ask for a divorce.
According to the former, two weeks; according to the latter,
only one week. The astounding thing is that such instruction
was written entirely by men, who were addressing themselves
to men.

At a time when, among other peoples, women were
thought of only as receptacles for male pleasure and impregnation, the creators of Judaism revealed a most astonishing sensitivity to their wives as active sex partners. Men were even
obliged to intuit their women's sexual needs, to initiate intercourse when it was reasonable to suppose their wives wanted
or needed it. They were adjured to increase a woman's sexual
pleasure by commencing with stimulating foreplay. Here, for
example, is a paragraph from a thirteenth-century Jewish
scholar:

> . . . engage her first in conversation that puts her heart
> and mind at ease and gladdens her. . . . Speak words
> which arouse her to passion, union, love, desire, and
> eros—and words which elicit attitudes of reverence for
> God, piety, and modesty. Tell her of pious and good
> women who gave birth to fine and pure children. . . .
> Speak with her words, some of love, some of erotic
> passion, some of piety and reverence. . . . Hurry not to
> arouse passion until her mood is ready; begin in love;
> let her (orgasm) take place first. . . .[16]

The impact of this final phrase increases when we remember
that most men at that time preferred male to female children

and that the rabbis believed a son would be conceived if a woman's orgasm preceded her husband's.

Judaism looks upon intercourse in marriage, not as something sinful, not as a regrettable necessity, but as a beautifully meaningful experience which enhances the love of husband and wife. Every form of sex play which leads to that end was approved. Maimonides said:

> The sexual union should be consummated only out of desire and as the result of the joy of the husband and wife. . . . He must not approach her when he thinks of another woman and certainly not when he is under the influence of alcohol or while they are quarreling, and hatred divides them. He must not approach her against her will or force her to submit to him out of fear.[17]

The final sentence of this statement reiterates a view which the Talmud had expressed many centuries earlier: "He who coerces his wife will produce unworthy children."[18]

Another talmudic authority urged that each act of coitus in marriage be as exciting and fresh as the first.[19] Judaism acknowledged and accepted the fact that intercourse serves more than the purpose of propagation when it decreed that even the marriage of a couple incapable of producing children is legally valid.

Clearly, then, there has been a major divergence between the historic attitudes of Judaism and Christianity pertaining to sex. In most faiths the mystics were especially prone to withdraw from active sex life into monastic celibacy. In Jewish tradition even the mystics refrained from such asceticism. The biblical Nazirites, denied so many other luxuries and pleasures of normal life, were not pledged to celibacy. For a long time it was supposed by scholars that the ancient Essenes, a small mystical sect which lived in Palestine at about the time of Jesus, consisted only of men. Recent discoveries in the area of the Dead Sea lead us to suspect now that even this numerically insignificant group of mystics may have lived normal sex lives, with men and women together in the community. The eighteenth-century Jewish mystical movements—unlike similar tendencies in most other faiths—never repudiated or rejected an active sexual partnership in marriage.

Dr. Gershom Scholem has written the following in his monumental study of Jewish mysticism:

> There is, however, one important respect in which Chasidism differs from its Christian contemporaries: it does not enjoin sexual askesis; on the contrary, the greatest importance is assigned in the *Sefer Chasidim* to the establishment and maintenance of a normal and reasonable marital life. Nowhere is penitence extended to sexual abstinence in marital relations.[20]

A word of caution is in order here. Without detracting in any way from the foregoing, it must be honestly acknowledged that many contemporary Jews are unaware of what Judaism teaches about sex; many, moreover, who know these things intellectually are emotionally incapable of implementing them in their lives. People who have been preconditioned by early childhood experience to regard sex with suspicion, contempt, or fear will need more than this chapter—or indeed, many such chapters —to absorb Jewish tradition into their hearts and minds. If their antipathy to sex is deeply rooted in repressions, some form of psychotherapy may be required. For most Jewish couples, however, this will not be needed. As they approach marriage, they can gain immeasurably from understanding the wholesome maturity with which their own faith has encouraged the proper enjoyment of sex.

A PRACTICAL APPLICATION

The differences between Judaism and Christianity on the legitimacy of sexual pleasure lead inevitably to a divergence of view with regard to birth control. If sex is evil, if coitus is acceptable only for the purpose of procreation, it follows that deliberate contraception must be sinful. This has been precisely the historical logic of the Church. Originally both Catholics and Protestants were opposed to birth control. Among Protestants there has been a steady inclination to relax this opposition; many leading Protestant denominations, as they have moved closer to our Jewish point of view on sex in general, have also come to accept birth control.

Though change in the Roman Catholic Church has been much slower and less substantial, it has appeared there too. At one time the Church insisted that under no circumstances should a married couple cohabit unless they intended pregnancy as a consequence. We have already examined the views of Augustine, Aquinas, and Father William Gibbons in this respect. Later the Catholic attitude shifted to approval of the so-called rhythm method, which is extremely unreliable. This removes the stigma of sin from married couples who indulge in coitus for pleasure and love—even if they deliberately time themselves to avoid pregnancy—provided that their failure to conceive results from the incidental absence of an egg to be fertilized, not from any interference on their part with the normal processes of nature. Most Catholic theologians consider rhythm a *natural* method of family planning; as such, they accept it. All other devices for birth control they condemn as *artificial.* [21]

In very recent years there has been debate among Catholics on whether the contraceptive pill might not be approved as a natural method. Dr. John Rock, a nationally prominent gynecologist whose research contributed substantially to development of the pill, is a leading Catholic layman. He has urged upon his Church acceptance of this method. A few priests and bishops have voiced similar views. In the summer of 1968, after an exhaustive study of the entire question by a special commission he had previously appointed, Pope Paul VI vigorously reaffirmed the traditional Catholic opposition to all mechanical or chemical methods of contraception. More recently, near the close of 1979, John Paul II again rejected the practice of birth control by Catholics. Despite much discussion and even some resentment within the Church, this remains official Catholic doctrine.

There is much difference of opinion, incidentally, among medical experts on the use of "the pill." Some feel that it is the most advisable method of birth control; others fear that its side effects may outweigh its advantages.

It should go without saying that whether or not Catholicism changes its attitudes still further is the business only of Catholics themselves. The foregoing comments on the subject have been introduced only to provide a background of contrast for exposition now of our Jewish attitude on birth control. We make no distinction between *natural* and *artificial* methods. To regulate conception by either mechanical or chemical means is to us no more reprehensible than to regulate or control other automatic processes of the body through medication or surgery. We believe God wants us to use our intelligence responsibly toward learning more and more about nature and to bring healing and health upon ourselves by regulating and abetting nature's autonomous procedures.

Judaism has always believed that the noblest fulfillment of marriage is the birth and rearing of children. No marriage is deemed complete unless it produces children. Among many rabbinic sayings to this effect is the following:

> A man is not a complete man if he has no son and daughter. . . .[22] A man without children is like a piece of wood, which though kindled does not burn or give out light. . . . A man with children eats his bread in joy; a man without children eats it in sadness.[23]

Yet the emphasis our ancestors placed on parenthood did not blind them to the fact that intercourse serves functions other than just procreation. They believed that God has endowed us with sexual desires and needs because He considers these to be good. Partners in marriage, therefore, should live as full and active a sex life as they wish, utilizing their choice of birth control methods, in order that they may continue to express and enrich their love through intercourse, without producing more children than they can properly love.

Orthodox Jewish tradition has approved only those methods of contraception practiced by women, not those used by men. This is a matter now of no more than academic interest, since it happens that by the dictates of modern science the most reliable contraceptive methods in any event are those employed by women.

We find the following statement five times in the Talmud and once in Tosefta:

> There are three women who, when experiencing sex relations with their husbands, may (or must) take the precaution of using an absorbent to prevent conception: a minor, a pregnant woman, and a woman who is still nursing her baby.[24]

What were our teachers really attempting to tell us in this passage? Three things: that the prevention of pregnancy in a minor was permissible to safeguard the health of the prospective mother; that it was legitimate in the case of a woman already pregnant, for her sake as well as that of the child she carried; that it was acceptable when a mother was still nursing, for the welfare of a child already born. The explanations of Rashi and other commentators on this passage allow no room for doubt. The only area of potential disagreement is whether, under any of the foregoing circumstances, a woman *may* or *must* use a contraceptive device. It is also clear from the opinions of medieval and premodern rabbis that contraception was deemed permissible in cases where a woman had given birth to children who were mentally retarded or suffered an incurable congenital disease.

Social conditions of emergency proportion were also accepted even by the most Orthodox rabbinic authorities as justification for the practice of birth control. Thus during the Nazi persecutions Jewish women were permitted by their rabbis to live normal sex lives with their husbands while preventing pregnancy. The hazards to both mother and child were considered beyond reasonable risk. The very reverse of this reasoning is used by some Jews today. They say that—despite the permissiveness of Jewish law regarding contraception—to compensate for the brutal destruction of six million Jews by Hitler and the alarming reduction of world Jewish population due to our relatively low birth rate, we ought not restrict the size of Jewish families. While there is no doubt merit to this argument, it does not refute the fact that only a tortuous kind of logic can twist Jewish tradition into a blanket prohibition of birth control.

TURNING TO THE PRESENT

After exhaustive study of all the pertinent talmudic references, Dr. Jacob Z. Lauterbach, formerly professor of Talmud at the Hebrew Union College, summarized his own views as follows:

> . . . according to the opinion of all the teachers, it is not forbidden to use a contraceptive in cases where conception would bring harm either to the mother or to the child born or unborn. And I cannot see any difference between the protection of a minor from a conception which might prove fatal to her and the protection of a grown-up woman whose health is, according to the opinion of physicians, such that a pregnancy might be fatal to her. Neither can I see any difference between protecting a child from the danger of being deprived of the nourishment of its mother's milk, and protecting the already born children of the family from the harm which might come to them due to the competition of the larger number of sisters and brothers.[25]

A modern extension of the talmudic view is to be found in the following statement, adopted by the Biennial Assembly of the Union of American Hebrew Congregations in November of 1959:

> We fully recognize the right of all persons, for religious reasons or otherwise, to abstain from or to practice birth control as they see fit. However, the failure of large sections of our population to plan their families effectively is due neither to conscience nor to free choice, but rather to legal and official obstacles imposed upon many Americans with the result depriving them of knowledge and medical assistance in this field. . . . When government responds to the theological beliefs of any religious group by interfering with the dissemination of birth control information to all who desire it, such interference represents an improper

imposition of such religious beliefs upon the community at large. Therefore, be it resolved that:

A. We favor the elimination of all restrictions and prohibition against the dissemination of birth control information and of rendering birth control assistance by qualified physicians, clinics, and hospitals.

B. We favor the wider dissemination of birth control information and medical assistance, both by private groups, such as the Planned Parenthood Association, and health agencies of local, state, and federal government as a vital service to be rendered in the field of public health.

The pressure of population throughout the world today is such that, unless effective birth control be practiced on every continent, the consequence in a relatively short period of time will be disastrous. Our immediate concern with the Jewish point of view on contraception, however, derives from the harmful effect of unwanted children on the success of marriage and family life. The married couples who prefer not to have children are depriving themselves of inestimable happiness. By the same token, the couples who produce more children than their physical and emotional resources can decently support are jeopardizing not only their own future but equally the welfare and health of their offspring. This is the unmistakable conviction of our Jewish faith.

It would nevertheless be both misleading and unfair to leave the impression that all modern Jews are, without exception, agreed on the subject of birth control. We have already indicated that on sex in general there is often a great gap between intellectual understanding and emotional acceptance. Some Orthodox Jews, therefore, will use tradition selectively to justify a position on contraception which scarcely differs from the Catholic view. Their attitude must not be confused, however, with that of authentic Jewish tradition. Paradoxically, there are some situations in which a knowledgeable Reform or Conservative Jew may grasp the intent and spirit of Jewish tradition more accurately than an Orthodox Jew!

AFTER THE FACT

How does Judaism view abortion? Not a simple question; no simple answers. In general, the Jewish attitude is more permissive than that of most Christian authorities, less lenient than the stance of those who advocate abortion-at-will. Our tradition certainly does not accept the opinion that a woman owns her own body, hence can do with it or to it whatever she wills. We hold that a person's body is a gift from God, that each of us is responsible for the proper care of so precious a behest. No one is allowed to abuse her or his body, to treat it casually.

Yet there are circumstances under which Judaism permits abortion. Only certain dissident sects, only Philo and Josephus among ancient Jewish writers condemned it outright as a capital offense. Though it is quite probable that abortion was practiced by ancient and medieval Jews under carefully stipulated circumstances, the subject is not treated at length in our religious literature until the seventeenth century. The failure of Judaism to reject abortion as categorically as did Christian tradition springs from the fact that our authorities did not regard the unborn fetus as a human being with a soul.

A fetus which threatened an expectant mother's life could be aborted; it was legally considered in the category of a "pursuer" who could be killed if that were the only way to save the life of its potential victim. If, during pregnancy or even the initial phase of childbirth, a mother's life is in jeopardy, the unborn child may be sacrificed to insure her survival. Only after the infant's head has emerged—or according to some authorities, the greater part of its body—is its life considered as important and valuable as the mother's. Thereafter, neither life may be sacrificed to save the other.

Many modern authorities on Judaism hold, however, that the infant's life may still be sacrificed if necessary to save the mother. Since a newborn child is not deemed to be entirely viable until the thirty-first day following birth, up to that point —especially if both lives are endangered—the mother retains priority.

On the question of abortion in a case where the mother's life is not literally at stake, rabbinic scholars differ. Most Reform and many Conservative rabbis would permit it if a continuation of the pregnancy seriously threatens a woman's emotional or mental health. Even many Orthodox rabbis would agree when carrying the fetus to term might drive an expectant mother to either hysteria or suicide. They would otherwise tend to be more restrictive. A majority of non-Orthodox rabbis today allows abortion in cases of a pregnancy resulting from incest or rape, also if there is reason to fear the birth of a seriously defective child.

All authentic leaders of Judaism are agreed that human life is sacred; that conception of unwanted infants should be prevented, not aborted; that abortion should not be practiced just for reasons of expediency or convenience.[26]

CHAPTER ELEVEN

Men, Women, and God

Sexual intercourse, contraception, and abortion are by no means the only aspects of love and marriage on which Jewish tradition has spoken. Long before the advent of modern psychology and marriage counseling, the founders and expositors of Judaism had worked their way to many of the insights on love described in earlier chapters of this volume. They knew, for example, that love means a total sharing of life between husband and wife, that it provides a fulfillment together for each that would be impossible for either alone. Thus one of the ancient rabbis said: "He who has no wife remains without good, without a helper, without joy, without a blessing. . . ." To which a colleague added: "He is not a whole man." Still other rabbis proclaimed: "The unmarried man diminishes the likeness of God." In similar spirit, a medieval Jewish mystic declared: "The שכינה (*Shechinah*)—God's Presence—can rest only upon a married man, because an unmarried man is but half a man, and the שכינה does not rest upon that which is imperfect."[1]

The point should not be exaggerated. Many single men and women have lived happy and successful lives. Surely it is better to remain single than to undertake a bad marriage. Yet our rabbis were undeniably voicing a profound truth when they asserted that the right kind of marriage brings to each partner a wholeness and fulfillment which can be enjoyed in no other way.

The completeness which husband and wife bring to each

other was further emphasized by our ancient teachers in their comments on the ineffable sadness of either mate's losing the other. Thus, according to the Talmud: "The widower lives in a darkened world."[2] The Midrash adds that, when a man's wife dies, his steps are shortened, his spine becomes bent, and it is as if the Temple had been destroyed in his time. To which Rabbi Samuel bar Nachman added: "For everything there is a substitute except for the wife of one's youth."[3]

The association of love with God is of special consequence. I mentioned in Chapter 4 the legend which recounts that God creates each soul in two parts—one-half to be placed in the body of a male, the other in the body of a female. Marriage means that the two halves of a single soul—created together, originally meant for each other—are reunited in accordance with God's plan. In another rabbinic tale we are told that God thought His creation of the universe was completed after He had formed Adam. He was disturbed, however, by a note of discord which marred the harmony of the spheres. An angel whom He sent to investigate reported that the disturbing sound was Adam's sigh of loneliness. Then God created Eve as Adam's partner; the discord disappeared and the work of creation was really finished. Along the same vein, you will remember from an earlier chapter that an ancient rabbi, when asked by a Roman woman how God has occupied himself since He completed creation, replied that He spends His time matching couples for marriage!

Yet another rabbinic passage elaborates charmingly on the great concern of God with marriage:

> The wedding of the first couple was celebrated with pomp and ceremony never repeated in the whole course of history since. God himself, before presenting Eve to Adam, attired and adorned her as a bride. Then He appealed to the angels, saying: "Come, let us perform services of friendship for Adam and his helpmate, for the world rests upon friendly services, and they are more pleasing in My sight than the sacrifices Israel will offer upon the altar." The angels accordingly surrounded the marriage canopy, and God pronounced

the blessings upon the bridal couple, as the *chazan* does under the *chupah*. The angels then danced and played upon musical instruments before Adam and Eve in their ten bridal chambers of gold, pearls, and precious stones, which God had prepared for them.[4]

Does the repeated association in Jewish tradition of God with love mean that Judaism holds marriages to be made in heaven?

That depends on the specific meaning assigned to these words. If they are assumed to imply that for each man there is only one woman—and for each woman only one man—with whom either could be happy, the thought surely is one we today cannot accept. The truth is that for each of us there is no doubt a certain type of person with whom a successful marriage would be possible, but there are surely numbers of individuals who come at least reasonably close to that type. Aside from much other evidence, the fact that so many men and women, after the death of a first mate, are able to achieve happiness later with a second would dismiss the notion that God literally sets aside only one specific individual for each of us.

Yet there is valid truth to the quaint, poetic ways in which our ancestors identified love with God. They thus expressed their conviction that love is part of the very plan of the universe, not just an incidental relationship conjured up by us on our own. The mutual love of husband and wife reflects something basic and integral within the very nature of the universe and life. This truth can be observed and expressed in the lexicon of modern science too. We tend to think of nature as harsh and cruel. Often it is that. What we too frequently forget, however, is that the primal beginnings of love may be seen in nature too. For example: protons, neutrons, and electrons must all remain in the proper proportion and relationship with each other in order for atoms to exist. It can almost be said that they must serve certain purposes for each other, rather than each existing only for itself. Atoms must follow a similar pattern if there are to be molecules. Molecules, in turn, must relate to each other in a manner which could almost be called "cooperative" if there are to be cells, cells if there are to be whole organisms, individuals if there are to be tribes and nations, nations if a peaceful world is to survive.

Once the human level has been reached, all quotation marks and qualifications can be removed from the word *cooperative*. Prior to the appearance of human beings, admittedly it is only by stretching our imagination that we can use such terms. We do not mean to infer that there is any conscious or direct parallel between our behavior and that of matter's most elementary particles. Nor that love exists anywhere in prehuman forms of life. Only that nature itself provides a paradigm for the kind of relationship among components which is destined later in the evolutionary process to emerge into love.

This can be seen most dramatically in the relationship between cells. The first forms of life on earth consisted of only a single cell. That isolated cell had to perform for itself all the functions necessary for the maintenance of life: digestion, respiration, locomotion, elimination—these and many other processes had to be encompassed by each cell. In the course of evolutionary time, however, large numbers of cells "learned" to remain together as parts of a larger organism. Again quotation marks must be used for the word *learned* because there was nothing deliberate or conscious about the change; it took place automatically, as part of nature's steady development, without either knowledge or choice on the part of the cells involved.

As cells developed the capacity to form multicellular organisms, they also began to specialize. At the risk of deliberate oversimplification, it could be said that one group of cells undertook the responsibility of digestion for the entire organism, thus freeing another group to take over respiration, still another to handle locomotion, yet another to meet the needs of elimination, etc. In short, individual, hitherto isolated cells were developing the ability to perform together essential services for other groups of cells and for the whole organism. Thus each separate cell was able to realize its own potentiality to a far greater degree than any of them could have done alone.

You will observe that the language used in the last sentence comes close to that with which we defined love in an earlier chapter. Surely it would be stretching the truth to call the relationship between cells—or, for that matter, even between animals—love. Yet here, on the crudest, most elementary level of simple biology, we recognize nature's preliminary pattern for what later becomes love. The potentiality for love was inherent in nature from the beginning; evolution has moved perceptibly toward its realization. Human love developed out of these earlier relationships just as truly as the human arm and hand developed from the foreleg and paw of animals. Our Jewish ancestors were not aware of all these scientific details. Yet, by uncanny intuition they understood that the love which unites husband and wife is, at its best, a reflection of something which lies close to the very heart of reality.

MEANS TO THE END

Because they appreciated the nature and value of love, our rabbis understood also that, like everything precious, it would deteriorate if it were not cherished and tended. Therefore they pronounced a great many choice epigrams in which advice was given to husbands and wives on how to treat each other. The fact that most of their directives were addressed only to men should not mislead us. These passages were written exclusively by men, to be read almost entirely by men. But the advice they proffer is no less valid for wives. It is worth noting, incidentally, that, beneath the superficial sexism of directing their attention only to men, these ancient rabbis demonstrate remarkable concern for the welfare and needs of women. In part, we have already seen this. I shall return to it later in considering the effects of the women's movement on marriage.

Here are a few of the rabbinic recommendations addressed to married couples:

> Your wife has been given to you in order that you may realize with her life's great plan; she is not yours to vex or grieve. Vex her not, for God notes her tears.[5]

> A wife is the joy of man's heart.[6]

> A man should eat less than he can afford, and should honor his wife and children more than he can afford.[7]

A man should be careful not to irritate his wife and cause her to weep.[8]

If your wife is short, bend down and hear her whisper.[9]

He who loves his wife as himself; who honors her more than himself; who rears his children in the right path, and who arranges for them to be married near the period of their puberty, concerning him it is written: "And you will know that your home is peace." (Job 5:24)[10]

Man should ever be mindful of the honor of his wife for she is responsible for all the blessings found in his household.[11]

A man must not cause his wife to weep, for God counts her tears.[12]

Strive to fulfill your wife's wishes, for it is equivalent to doing God's will.[13]

When the husband is blessed, his wife is also blessed thereby.[14]

A wife who receives love gives love in return; if she receives anger, she returns anger in equal measure.[15]

It was recognized by these wise teachers of Judaism that in a good marriage important decisions are made by husband and wife together. The Talmud therefore decrees that the choice of a new place of residence or a new profession must be made jointly. The only circumstance, significantly enough, where this did not hold was if one mate wanted to live in Palestine and the other did not. In that event, the desire of the one who wanted to live there was given priority.

Jewish tradition also recognized many centuries ago that husband and wife must be sensitive to each other's moods and needs, must be able to perceive them even without a word from the other. Thus a chasidic rabbi related this incident:

A commander-in-chief received a message telling him that his main line of defense had been broken by the enemy. He was greatly distressed and his emotions showed plainly on his countenance. His wife heard the nature of the message and, entering her husband's room, she said: "I too at this very moment have received tidings worse than yours."

"And what are they?" inquired the commander with agitation.

"I have read discouragement on your face," replied the wife.

"Loss of courage is worse than loss of defense."[16]

Many of these ancient insights will at once be recognized to have anticipated some of the steps toward a happy marriage which were suggested in our chapter entitled "Promise Is a Seed."

NO OTHER LOVE?

Most of the foregoing quotations from Jewish tradition seem to assume monogamous marriage. Yet it would be idle to pretend that through substantial spans of Jewish history polygamy was not practiced. The fact that Adam is described in Genesis as having been given only one wife has been adduced as evidence that monogamy was always the ideal in Judaism. The prophets and virtually all the rabbis mentioned in the Talmud also had, each of them, but one wife.

Yet in this respect, as in many others, the ideal was not always realized. There are numerous biblical instances of polygamy; these include Kings David and Solomon. The most we can say is that polygamy was not practiced as widely among ancient Jews as among their contemporaries.

Talmudic law accepts the validity of polygamous marriage. One rabbi sanctioned a man's marrying as many women as he could support; a colleague countered that a woman could claim a divorce if her husband married a second wife.[17] Regardless of legal permissiveness, the fact that a Jewish husband was required, as part of the marriage ceremony, to guarantee financial support for his wife in the event of divorce deterred all but the wealthiest from undertaking multiple marriages.

It was not until the beginning of the eleventh century that Rabbi Gershom ben Yehudah, known as "the Light of the Exile," issued his famous prohibition of polygamy. Even under his decree, however, a man whose wife was either insane or rebellious was permitted to marry a second woman. Rabbi Gershom's edict was accepted only by the Ashkenazic or Western Jews; Sephardic and Oriental Jews continued to practice polygamy, though on a limited basis. In Africa the following declaration was inserted in the marriage contract: "The said bridegroom . . . hereby promises that he will not take a second wife during the lifetime of the said bride . . . except with her consent."[18]

The State of Israel has had to deal with some remnants of polygamy, especially among immigrants from North Africa. While Israeli citizens are legally restricted to monogamy, a man who brings two wives with him into the country may keep them. If either wife subsequently requests a divorce, the state will support her. I myself, while visiting the apartment of a Moroccan Jew in Ashdod, have met his two wives. The bitter enmity between them, which was immediately evident, attested to the wisdom of monogamy.

It becomes apparent, then, that although polygamy was not proscribed until about nine hundred years ago, and despite the vestigial remnants of multiple marriages today among a very small number of Jews, monogamy has long been a cherished ideal in Judaism, an ideal which is now almost universally achieved.

A FINAL DIFFERENCE

In the preceding chapter we discovered how Judaism differs from other faiths in its attitude toward love, marriage, and sex. There is one more difference to be discussed at least briefly before I can in good conscience bring this part of our consideration to its close. Throughout the centuries our faith has also evolved a unique and interesting stance on the subject of divorce. Here again, a background of contrast will be instructive. Some religions are unalterably opposed to divorce.

It is ironic that in many instances precisely those faiths which have historically looked upon marriage with jaundiced eye are the ones that have insisted that it is too sacred ever to be dissolved. And Judaism, which has always approved marriage enthusiastically, is far less rigid in recognizing the possibility of failure, in allowing room for the correction of mistakes.

There are religions which prohibit divorce altogether, others which reluctantly accept divorce but do not permit either partner to marry again. While Judaism recognizes that marriage is a sacred enterprise, not to be undertaken lightly or tentatively, it nevertheless provides for the possibility of human error. The Talmud stipulates that "a man should not marry a woman with the thought in mind that he may divorce her."[19] It further recognizes divorce to be a pathetic tragedy, in saying: "He who puts away the wife of his youth, for him God's very altar weeps."[20]

A beautifully poignant and poetic story is told in our tradition concerning one couple who contemplated divorce. It is based on the talmudic law that a husband whose wife has not conceived in a decade of married life may divorce her.

> There was a woman in Sidon who lived ten years with her husband and had borne no children. They went to Rabbi Simeon b. Yohai and asked to be divorced. He said to them: "As your coming together was with a banquet, so let your separation be with a banquet." They agreed and prepared a large banquet at which the wife made her husband drink more than enough. Before he fell asleep he said to her: "Pick out what is most precious to you in my house, and take it with you to your father's house." What did she do? When he had gone to sleep, she beckoned to her servants and said to them: "Carry him on his mattress to my father's house." In the middle of the night he awakened and said to her: "Whither have I been brought?" She said: "To my father's house." He said to her: "Why have I been brought here?" She replied: "Did you not tell me last night to take what was most precious to me in your house and go with it to my father's house? There is

nothing in the world more precious to me than you."
They went back to Rabbi Simeon b. Yohai and he
prayed for them and they had a son.[21]

There can be no doubt, then, that in Judaism marriage is
deemed to be a permanent, sacred bond, not to be terminated
for slim cause. Yet our tradition does permit divorce. It recognizes that even more tragic than the separation of husband and
wife is their living a life of pretense and deceit.

Often couples who have reached the end of the road remain nonetheless together out of consideration for their children. No one can afford to minimize the tragic consequences
of divorce on children; in order to maximize their chance for
wholesome development, they need a unified home, with discipline and love from both parents. But a home kept ostensibly
intact physically after it is already broken spiritually—which
means to say, a home which is maintained though husband and
wife no longer love each other or perhaps have even come to
hate each other—can injure children even more devastatingly
than divorce. In the 1950s a Washington State study of school-
boys revealed that intact but quarreling families were more
likely to produce delinquents than broken families.[22] Because
it understood this long centuries ago, Judaism has provided the
justification and machinery for honorably ending a marriage
that has failed.

The conditions which warrant divorce are first described
in the Bible:

> A man takes a wife and possesses her. She fails to please
> him because he finds something obnoxious about her,
> and he writes her a bill of divorcement, hands it to her,
> and sends her away from his house. . . .[23]

The matter, however, was not quite so simple or easy as it
appears to be here. As in so many other instances, a complicated garment of talmudic law was woven from a solitary biblical thread.

The rabbis were uncomfortable, to begin with, over the
fact that Deuteronomy seems to extend the right of divorce
only to husbands. They therefore provided that under certain

circumstances a wife could petition the court for a divorce and, if right were on her side, the court could pressure the husband to assent. Maimonides articulated this principle of Jewish law as follows: "If a woman says, 'My husband is distasteful to me, I cannot live with him,' the court compels the husband to divorce her, because a wife is not a captive."[24]

What were the circumstances which entitled a wife to sue for divorce? The court considered her request to be justified if her husband refused to have sexual intercourse with her, if he contracted a loathsome disease which she could not endure, or—as we have already seen—if his occupation contaminated his person with an odor she found intolerably offensive. Also if he treated her cruelly, prohibited her from visiting her parents, changed his religion, or was notoriously immoral.

A husband, in turn, could seek a divorce if his wife were guilty of adultery, insulted him or his father in his presence, was morally indecent in public, disregarded the ritual laws pertaining to women, or refused to have intercourse with him. If the two agreed mutually that they wished to terminate their marriage, no further justification was required; the court had to grant their request. No matter what the circumstances of separation, however, the financial protection promised the wife as part of the traditional wedding ceremony had to be provided.[25]

In Orthodox and Conservative Judaism it is necessary for a couple to obtain a religious as well as a civil divorce. The religious divorce, called a גט (get), is issued by a rabbi or a rabbinical court. In Reform Judaism the civil divorce is sufficient. In all branches—provided the divorce was valid—there is no objection to a second marriage. This discrepancy among the several branches of Judaism sometimes poses a perplexing problem. No Orthodox or Conservative rabbi will officiate at the marriage of a divorced person unless a גט was obtained. If, then, a divorced Reform Jew who did not receive this religious decree wishes to marry into a Conservative or Orthodox family, only a Reform rabbi will be able to oblige.

The גט is frequently a vexing matter even for those who believe in it. There have been many cases—especially if divorce proceedings have left a residue of rancor—where a husband will refuse to grant his former wife a religious divorce to facilitate her remarriage. Even unsavory instances of attempted blackmail have been known. Responsible religious authorities are eager to eliminate all such abuses.

We see, then, that Judaism accepts divorce. But only as a last resort. The most prodigious effort must first be made to mend whatever imperfection mars the couple's happiness. Indeed, reconciling a quarreling couple is adjudged a great virtue in Judaism. The story is told of Rabbi Meir, who lectured to the public each Friday evening. A certain woman attended these sessions regularly. Her husband, who was not interested in them himself, objected to the fact that she returned home every week later than he wished. Finally he banished her from the house in a temper, saying that she could not return until she had publicly spat in Rabbi Meir's eye. She spent the week with a neighbor and returned the ensuing Friday to hear the rabbi's lecture. Meanwhile, Rabbi Meir had heard of her husband's unreasonable demand. He called the woman to him before the assembled audience and said: "My eye pains me; spit into it and it will be relieved." It took considerable persuasion before the woman was willing to comply, but she finally did. When her husband heard of it, he permitted her back into their home. The *midrash* which recounts this tale concludes with the following:

> "Learn, then, that no act is disgraceful that tends to promote the happiness and peace of husband and wife."[26]

FIRST AID

The paragraphs which follow are written in the hope that you will never need them.

A simple cut on the finger—if quickly perceived and anticepticized—presents no serious problem. If the same cut is ignored, allowed to fester in filth, it could develop into a very serious infection. Similarly, some marriages which dissolve in divorce could have been salvaged if trouble had been recognized and treated when it began.

Any relationship as intimate as marriage is bound to be characterized by occasional tensions and quarrels; the mature couple will not exaggerate these into crises but will pay prompt attention to any problem which seems to persist. Often it will suffice just to face the difficulty openly, to talk about it honestly. One research study indicates that average couples talk together about their marriages less than half an hour a week. If more assistance than open communication is needed, a wise friend can sometimes help. Or a professional: your rabbi, physician, attorney, a marriage counselor. No one of these is likely to succeed, however, unless both husband and wife are willing to work at repairing a damaged marriage, to recognize—both of them—their individual mistakes and to expend, both of them, effort and time toward improvement.

Where marital tensions are related to personality quirks in either partner, a hard decision must sometimes be made: whether to seek help from a marriage counselor or a psychiatrist. The latter will concentrate on the emotional difficulties of the individual patient. If such treatment succeeds, it can greatly improve the marriage. During the months or even years of therapy, however, the marital relationship may become even more turbulent. A marriage counselor will focus on the troubles disturbing both mates rather than on each as an individual. The dilemma can be painfully complicated by the fact that these two areas of priority are seldom separable. A troubled person adds to the tension of an unsteady marriage; a marriage in jeopardy increases the psychic anxiety of an emotionally disturbed person.

Where to commence? Couples must answer for themselves. If the emotional imbalance of either partner is very serious, probably with a psychiatrist. If not—or if one is unwilling to "sweat out" the other's period of therapy—perhaps with a marriage counselor. It is encouraging to know that large numbers of troubled couples who seek professional help in time are able not only to maintain their marriages but greatly to improve them. Even where they do not succeed in their

primary objective of saving the marriage, often they are ena-
bled to dissolve it in a less destructive manner than would
otherwise have been the case.

Can marriage encounter groups help? My own impression
is that they may add a dimension of open communication to a
basically good marriage, but they will probably not cure one
which is deeply disturbed. Vitamins can augment the vigor and
strength of a person who is essentially healthy. They are no
substitute for the medications needed in serious illness.

SUMMING UP

We Jews believe that marriage is the most sacred relationship
in human experience. It should never be undertaken without
very serious contemplation; it deserves and demands a deep
sense of commitment on the part of both mates, an unswerving
determination to work hard at it, and resolutely to surmount
all obstacles to success. But so long as men and women are
fallible, mistakes will be made. If two mates discover that in the
case of their marriage such an error has in fact been compounded and that, despite the most diligent efforts of both,
there is no realistic chance for happiness together, our faith
looks upon this as a lamentable failure but accepts it as such
and recommends divorce under the most civilized conditions
possible.

CHAPTER TWELVE

New Times...
New Problems

There should be no need to argue at length that we live in a time of unprecedentedly rapid change. This is true in every area of experience; at times it is so frightening that one competent commentator has labeled our reaction to it "future shock." We would be blind not to recognize that sex and marriage cannot be immune from the radical changes we confront generally. Marriage and the family as you are likely to know them a few years from now may differ a great deal from what they have been in the past.

One important indication that this will be so may be found in the women's movement, a thrust to change the image and self-image of women in our society. Before turning in some detail to the aims of this movement, let's have a look at the status of women in Judaism. In doing so, it would not be fair to judge the attitudes and actions of our ancestors only by the standards of today. There are many respects, as we shall soon see, in which they did not give women all the credit and respect due them. Yet ancient Judaism was far superior to other cultures of the time. Aristotle, for example, called women "deficient males." All that a Moslem had to do to divorce his wife was to repeat three times before witnesses: "I hereby divorce you."

The early Christian Church also denigrated the importance and role of women. Among other choice admonitions addressed to them in the New Testament are the following:

". . . women should keep silence in the churches . . . they are not permitted to speak, but should be subordinate . . . if there is anything they desire to know, let them ask their husbands at home."[1] A menstruating woman was not allowed to receive communion or even to enter a church; according to popular Christian belief she would sour milk and kill any grass on which she walked.[2]

While the role of women in traditional Judaism was nowhere near what today's advocates of *women's liberation* would approve, it was noticeably superior to that of other contemporary civilizations. The ambivalence of the Jewish view can be traced all the way back to the story of creation in Genesis. There are two such stories, one related in Genesis 1:26–31, the other in 2:18–24. According to the first account, man and woman were created simultaneously and equally: "And God created man in His image, in the image of God He created him; *male and female He created them.*" In the second story, woman is brought into being almost as an afterthought and for the comfort and convenience of man. After observing that "it is not good for man to be alone," God decides to "make a fitting helper for him. . . . So the Lord God cast a deep sleep upon the man and he slept; and He took one of his ribs and closed up the flesh at that spot. And the Lord God fashioned into a woman the rib that He had taken from the man, and He brought her to the man." In similar vein, the first sin in the Garden of Eden is blamed primarily on woman. For this, her punishment is:

> Yet your urge shall be for your husband,
> And he shall rule over you.

Just as the two creation stories are inconsistent in their evaluation of women, so in following Jewish thought through subsequent centuries it is easy to find evidence on both sides of the question. The Talmud describes a woman who complained to Rabbi Judah that her husband had treated her abominably. The rabbi is reported to have responded: "Why are you different from a fish? You have no more right to complain against your husband's treatment than the fish has a right to object to the manner in which it has been cooked."[3]

Rabbinic law prohibits a man from marrying a woman whom he has not seen lest he later find her repulsive. No such restriction was imposed on a woman, however, for, "no matter how ugly and repelling the husband may turn out to be, she will surely be satisfied since to be married to a man, be he ever so loathsome, is better than to remain a spinster."[4]

Perhaps the most unacceptable of all such denigrations is the blessing pronounced every morning by traditionally observant Jewish males: ברוך אתה יי אלהינו, מלך העולם, שלא עשני אשה (*Baruch Atah Adonai Elohenu, Melech ha-olam, shelo asani ishah*)— "Praised be the Eternal our God, Ruling Spirit of the universe, who did not make me a woman." This blessing bothered many of our medieval commentators who proceeded to mitigate its harshness. They said that the man who thanked God for making him a male was no more downgrading women than the כהן (*kohen*), the priest, who voiced gratitude for having been made a priest, meant to disparage others.

In both cases, we are told, the concept of מצוה (*mitzvah*)— of special religious responsibility—is involved. For the faithful Jew a מצוה, while of course entailing extra obligation and burden, gives one the privilege of serving God in special ways. The priest expressed appreciation for the fact that he was permitted to perform מצוות (*mitzvot*) beyond those assigned to other Jews; this did not mean that he judged himself to be innately superior to them. Similarly, the rabbis insisted, men were grateful for the fact that they had to fulfill certain מצוות of which women were absolved because of other important responsibilities. It would be unrealistic to deny that there must have been men who misinterpreted this formula to imply male superiority. Judaism at its best, however, was almost as uncomfortable with any such notion as we are today. Evidence of our tradition's favorable attitude toward women is the fact that two books of our Hebrew Bible are named after women, that the Matriarchs and Moses' sister Miriam are assigned major roles in the biblical narrative, that the Talmud enumerates forty-eight male and seven female prophets in the early stages of Jewish history.[5]

Regarding numerous incidents in the Torah, high praise is heaped by later commentators upon women. We are told that the faith of women during the Egyptian slavery exceeded that of men and that the Exodus from Egypt was granted as a reward for their righteousness.[6] According to an ancient *midrash,* before God gave the Torah in detail to the men at Sinai, He enunciated its basic principles to the women. Another *midrash* asserts that, when Aaron was about to make the molten calf, the women of Israel refused to contribute their golden jewelry for this purpose. It was only after the men had given theirs that Aaron was able to proceed. Later the women reminded Moses of their virtue in this respect when he was reluctant to accept their gifts for the building of the wilderness sanctuary. Thus reminded, Moses acceded to their request and accepted their contributions.

When God decided in exasperation to destroy the Temple because of the people's repeated sins, tradition tells us that the Patriarchs, Moses, and the prophets all interceded in vain. It was only after Rachel implored Him that He agreed eventually to bring His people back to the land they were about to lose.

In Judaism, woman's charity is judged to be more direct than man's,[7] her prayers are answered first[8] and she exercises the dominant moral influence on the family. To illustrate the latter truth, our rabbis told the following tale:

> It is related of a pious man who was married to a pious woman that, being childless, they were divorced. He married a wicked woman and she made him wicked. She married a wicked man and made him righteous. It follows that all depends upon the woman.[9]

Women clearly suffered an inferior status in Jewish law and ritual observance. Yet, even here, much depends on the perspective and prejudice of the observer. Except for certain special cases, women were not accepted as witnesses in a trial[10] and did not inherit equally with their male siblings.[11] They were not expected to perform most of the daily religious duties or recite the many blessings assigned to men; they had to sit by themselves in a special section in the balcony of the synagogue. Here again, however, it is possible to interpret at least part of this differentiation as either discrimination or privilege. Most authorities on Judaism adopted the latter view. They agreed that it would be grossly unfair to hold women responsi-

ble for a complete schedule of duties which had to be performed at specific times during the day, thus conflicting with
the needs and demands of their children. One modern observer summarizes this approach admirably in saying: "Not
even an angel is given two missions simultaneously."[12]

If women were *prohibited* from performing the מצוות assigned to men, that would be rank discrimination. The fact is,
however, that they were *excused,* not *prohibited.* The distinction
was clear to a medieval commentator:

> We do not prevent women from reciting the blessing
> over the לולב (*lulav*) and the סוכה (*sukah*). The fact
> that the Talmud says that women are free from positive
> commandments that are fixed by time means merely to
> specify that they are not in duty bound to obey those
> commandments, but, if a woman desires to fulfill these
> commandments, she may do so and we do not prevent
> her. . . .[13]

Even so brief a summary as this should not be concluded without reviewing our discovery in an earlier chapter that Judaism
was sensitive to the sexual needs and rights of women long
before other cultures had achieved this kind of insight. In this
respect, the women's movement now is still struggling for un-
derstandings accepted by our tradition long centuries ago.

It would be foolish to pretend that Jewish tradition extended full equality to women. Much improvement is still
needed. In each period of history, however, our heritage
treated women more fairly than other cultures of the time. And
it includes insights which can still guide us as we strive for
further justice on behalf of women.

AND TODAY?

Jewish thought is dynamic on this as on most other matters
of importance. The institution of בת מצוה (*Bat Mitzvah*) ceremonies can be cited as an example. True, in some congregations, there is an implied inferiority in the fact that girls celebrate their *Bat Mitzvah* rites at a different time and with a

somewhat different format from that followed by their brothers. Elsewhere, the equality is complete; boys and girls celebrate בר מצוה (Bar Mitzvah) and בת מצוה (Bat Mitzvah) together
on Shabbat morning, observing procedures which are identical.

Along with other religions, Judaism confronts a theological difficulty in that God is always referred to as He or Him.
Where many ancient religions believed in female gods—conceived the Essence of all being, the Creative Force within all
reality, to be womanly—we in the Western world have always
assumed Divinity to be male. Almost inevitably, little children
come to feel as a result that maleness is stronger, more powerful, more estimable than femaleness. I wish I knew an adequate
solution to this dilemma.

In Reform and many Conservative congregations today
women are counted in the מנין (minyan), the quorum needed
for a public worship service, and are called to the pulpit for
עליות (aliyot) during the Torah service. A significant number of
women have been ordained rabbis, several serve as cantors,
and quite a few are currently studying for both professions. In
the early 1970s a poll conducted by the Union of American
Hebrew Congregations revealed that nineteen percent of con-
gregational board members in Reform congregations were
women, that five congregations had elected women as their
presidents, and twenty-eight had chosen them as vice presidents. While far from perfect equality, all this is evidence that
contemporary Judaism is resolving whatever ambivalence
afflicted the tradition by moving toward the aims and goals of
the women's movement.

What, in brief, are those goals and aims? Basically, to
eliminate all denigration and prejudice—both direct and subtle
—against women in our society. A moment's reflection will
show how pervasive this prejudice actually is. By and large,
women are not hired proportionately for prestigious positions
nor are they paid the same salaries as men for comparable
work. A single woman, even if she is wealthy or earns a very
high income, often has difficulty in obtaining a mortgage or
other forms of credit.

Much of the bias against women in our society can be

traced to the notion that a woman is a defective or uncompleted man. Freud and his early followers spoke of "penis envy," the resentment of even very young girls that they lack an important and visible organ which their brothers and fathers possess. Even this view is recognized by many experts today as an example of male domination and arrogance. Why should a woman be considered inferior for lack of a penis any more than a man because he doesn't have a vagina, ovaries, or fully developed breasts?

Indeed, many psychiatrists and psychologists are convinced that much that is irrational and prejudicial in male behavior can be attributed to "womb envy," to the fact that men feel inferior because they cannot become pregnant or give birth to a child. Women are not defective men. Men are not defective women. Those men and women are defective who refuse to accept themselves for what they are and to develop their unique potentialities.

Like every movement of protest, the cry for women's liberation can be extreme to the point of being ridiculous. When a prominent leader of the movement complains that "pregnancy is barbaric" or when women seem to express resentment or denial of the differences between men and themselves, one must be suspicious of their real motives. There are, after all, undeniable anatomical and physiological distinctions between females and males. In all probability, these cause emotional distinctions, too, though certainly not to the extreme degree emphasized in our culture. You will recall my earlier description of studies which indicate significant differences of inclination and interest between boys and girls even at a very early age.

Another word about unfortunate extremes which risk making a caricature of the women's movement. In early 1978 a Norwegian woman, an active feminist, refused to accept a blood transfusion from a male donor. This was scarcely less prejudiced than the bias of whites who have rejected transfusions of blood taken from blacks. A fanatical feminist has declared that all intercourse not initiated by the woman should be considered as rape. I once officiated at the wedding of a woman who was in her seventh month of pregnancy. She was in love with the baby's father, had lived with him for a long time, but refused to marry or even to announce a formal engagement, convinced that she would thereby compromise her own integrity. This, despite the fact that her lover had offered to change his last name to hers! Only the imminent arrival of their child induced her to change her mind.

Fanaticism in the women's movement is as self-defeating as it is everywhere. It distracts people of good will and sound judgment from what should be their legitimate goal: working for equal status, prestige, and rights on behalf of women. Marya Mannes spoke for more than herself when she observed that "so much has been made of women that I thought men had become a neglected race."

George Gilder is more explicit in developing the same thought. He has suggested that biologically women are by far the stronger and more important sex. The only indispensable role of the human male in procreation is impregnation of the female. It is she who carries the fetus in her womb, who gives birth to it, who nourishes it from her breasts.

> Women control not the economy of the marketplace but the economy of Eros: the life force in our society and our lives. What happens in the inner realm of women finally shapes what happens on our social surfaces, determining the level of happiness, energy, creativity, and solidarity in the nation.[14]

Gilder is convinced that man's more transparent control of society—of business, politics, and the professions—is necessary compensation for his deep-seated biological and sexual inferiority when compared to woman. To upset this precarious balance, he warns, is to threaten male stability and ultimately our entire social order. He attributes the alarming rise in male impotence—from 3 percent to as high as 30 percent in the last decade, according to some studies—precisely to this threat.

Whether or not we go all the way with Gilder, even proponents of the women's movement should acknowledge that there is nothing inferior or abnormal about a woman who prefers to follow the more traditional role which has historically characterized her sex—to be most essentially a wife, a homemaker, a mother. She has every right to make such a choice voluntarily. What we must resolutely reject is forcing women into that role, whether they want it or not.

Two examples can help here. The story is told of a nine-teenth-century chasidic rabbi who resolved to fast and stay awake a thousand nights studying Torah. His wife remained awake with him, holding a candle so that he could see his text. One wonders whether she was not just serving as a martyr, not really fulfilling herself.

On the other hand, Mrs. Albert Schweitzer—wife of the renowned physician, theologian, and musician—once said: "It has been the joy and the pride of my life to follow and assist him in all his activities, and my one regret that failing strength prevented me from keeping pace with him." It is entirely possible for a husband and wife to share so fully in their joint interests and career that both live creatively together.

THE MOVEMENT AND MARRIAGE

Wherever one stands on the women's movement, there can be no doubt of its profound effect on marriage and family life. The sharp, almost unbridgeable distinction between the roles of men and women in our homes which prevailed until recently can no longer be maintained. Increasing numbers of women will have careers. More about that in a moment. Men will share—they already do—in the tasks of diapering and otherwise caring for babies, of marketing, of cooking, of house cleaning. Parents will no longer limit the play of little boys to erector sets, of little girls to dolls. Nor will they try to condition their sons to be independent and aggressive, their daughters to be submissive and docile. Nor will they—I hope and most fervently pray—jeopardize the health of their boy-children by transmitting to them the psychological nonsense that men do not or should not cry!

Our culture has exaggerated and distorted the real differences which undoubtedly exist between the sexes. Some of us still have the foolish notion that it is inappropriate for a woman to seek a career, to enter politics, to demonstrate leadership skills outside her home; or for a man to show tenderness, to be sensitive and gentle, to cry when he is emotionally aroused. All this is nonsense. To the degree that it has helped erase such nonsense, the women's movement has helped men also to remove blinders and shackles which have prevented them from being whole human beings.

We must be careful, however, lest women do what too many men have done in the past: use ambition and career as an excuse to neglect their children. A woman who finds important work to do beyond her domestic responsibilities in order to fulfill herself and realize her potential is following a pattern which is wholesome and healthful. But one who frantically strives to be successful in public life as an escape from her husband, her children, and her home is deceiving herself, pursuing a path which will yield no more happiness than the old way which she has properly rejected.

One of the legitimate goals of the women's movement has been to help females in our society in their search for self-identity. In the past, too many women have been identified only through their husbands; each is the wife of a businessman, clergyman, physician, or public official. When such a woman is widowed or divorced, she loses her identity. Just as most men need a vocation—a business or profession—to achieve self-identity, to know who they really are, and to respect themselves, so many women sense the same requirement. The woman who is *only* a wife or mother during the early years of her marriage—however important these roles are and whatever success she attains in filling them—is inviting a painful vacuum into her life in later years when her children are grown and her husband is presumably at the height of his career.

Younger women can suffer this kind of gap in their lives too. While their mates are rising in a career, becoming better known and more successful in their outside work, if the wives remain only at home—not growing, developing, expanding their minds and interests—the compatibility which existed between the two when they married can become dangerously diminished. After a while, they may find that all they really share aside from sex are the moments of crisis which come to their children.

When I spoke of compatibility in an earlier chapter, I included this kind of compatibility. A man who will feel uncomfortable about his wife's becoming successful in her career—possibly more successful than he is in his—has no business marrying a woman who wants very much to have a career. A woman should be as sure as possible before marrying that her future spouse's feelings about women's liberation are in agreement with her own. Any person who retains the stereotype that a husband should in every instance be stronger, more assertive, more dominant and successful than his wife had better be sure that these expectations jibe with those of a prospective mate.

The kibbutz experience in Israel has been instructive in defining the proper sex roles of men and women. When the kibbutzim were first founded, an effort was made to eliminate differences in work standards between men and women. They shared equally in all tasks: kitchen and housework, rearing of children, teaching, tractor work, heavy labor, and so on. In the course of time, however, an interesting change took place. The women discovered that certain types of labor were physically too difficult for them. In addition, many menstruating women found it necessary to take a day or two off during their periods. And of course pregnant women needed a respite from work before and after delivering their babies. As a consequence, without consciously planning it so, little by little men and women began to assume the same kinds of tasks they had always performed in the past. There was, however, one exception: Some of the women were less happy than they had been before entering the kibbutz because, instead of performing a variety of household duties during the day, the organization of kibbutz life made it necessary for each to spend the entire day on one job which soon bored her.[15]

Drs. Katchadourian and Lunde summarized the kibbutz experience regarding women's liberation in these words:

> The traditional roles of wife and mother cannot simply be abolished by decree. Despite technological advances, someone must still prepare food, care for children, and so forth. It seems unfortunate that the values and rewards of such activities, particularly child rear-

ing, have been awarded low status and prestige in our society. Furthermore, the value of many of the more public achievements of men has often been overrated whereas the importance of the father's role in the raising of children has been sorely neglected. Is flying to the moon really a greater achievement than raising a child in an atmosphere of loving concern? Which requires greater skills and patience? Which, in the long run, is most rewarding to the participants?[16]

ONE MARRIAGE . . . TWO JOBS

In several different contexts I have already mentioned the increasing numbers of women who embark upon professional or business careers. Time now for closer attention to this phenomenon and its consequences for marriage.

A woman who heard me speak on this subject some years ago wrote me the following in a confidential letter. For obvious reasons, I have not used her real name or her husband's.

> Dick complained when I took singing and acting lessons, or went to rehearsals, or was in a play. He wanted me around when he was home. Rehearsals, however, are at night; lessons must be when the teacher has time. And, also, my children don't need me at home.

> There is no easy solution to that problem. I solved it with obstinancy. He had his career, and I needed my outlet. He was too busy to share going to concerts—justifiably so—and I decided to do what I had to. One thing led to another, and before I knew it I was accepted for an acting role.

> Not for anything would I give it up. It means my husband can't swim around his pool here at our apartment complex unless he wants to do it without me in the summer and he chooses not to do it. I choose to sing and act—come hell or high water—even at the expense of my marriage.

I don't find marriage humiliating or confining, but I do want to meet people with interests other than watching soap operas, attending women's luncheons, etc. My world has been expanded by my involvements.

Dick does help with the children on weekends and in the evenings *because he wants to*, and that's part of the key. It can work only if the people involved can arrive at a workable solution and in each case it is different.

The problem so poignantly described in this letter has become more commonplace as the number of working wives has increased. According to the Department of Labor, in 1960 only 30 percent of all married women in the United States had jobs or were seeking them; by early 1978 this figure had risen to nearly 48 percent. In many cases a woman works because of economic necessity; she really has no choice. Others may feel compelled for inner reasons to embark upon a career; they need a greater sense of personal fulfillment than they can find just as wife and mother.

What's the track record on double-career marriages? Do they succeed? Are the couples involved in them happy? Answer: yes . . . and no. Much depends upon the specific temperaments of husband and wife. Some women become better and more interesting wives when they feel that they are developing and expressing themselves as whole personalities. They may also understand and share more of their husband's career problems, be less disturbed when he arrives late for dinner or is suddenly called upon to travel. Where both partners in a marriage are working, they may be able to afford a higher standard of living, to give themselves and their children more in the way of luxuries and amenities.

Yet there are also complications. By the time unavoidable additional expenses are paid—extra clothing, transportation, lunches, day care for children—many women find the increase of income to be disappointing. One expert estimates that in the higher financial brackets the average working wife nets no more than 10 to 30 percent of her total salary.[17] A related problem: there are husbands whose security and masculinity are threatened by a wife who earns more than they or achieves greater success and renown. I am not trying to justify or defend such feelings—simply stating that they exist and can constitute a problem. No matter how equitably or fairly husband and wife share household and parental responsibilities, the major portion of such chores is likely to rest upon the woman. More than a few have found the resulting tensions and pressures to be intolerable.

One need not be a sexist to recognize that double careers may also increase the incidence of infidelity. Husbands and wives who come home each night too exhausted for romance and sex, who come into close daily contact with attractive women or men at work, may be more likely to indulge in extramarital affairs. It can be argued that men have always been exposed to such temptation or that women who are alone at home during the day are no less vulnerable. Most of the marriage counselors I know, however, seem agreed that, as the number of wives with careers goes up, sexual infidelity rises also.

INNOCENT VICTIMS?

What happens to children when both parents are busy with careers? No responsible couple can afford to ignore this question. Everything we have learned about the needs of little children points to their almost desperate dependence upon reliable love from parents. The source or sources of that love must be steady; a series of changing surrogates, even if all are affectionate and efficient, will not suffice. And there is danger —if such a dependable person be found—that the child's primary love attachment will be to that person rather than to either parent.

Selma Fraiberg, a child psychoanalyst who has done extensive research in this field, tells us:

> A child cannot feel valued when he is left in the care of a succession of anonymous sitters. And in the population of under-fives, there are large numbers of babies and small children who show excessive anxieties about

separation and loss which can be attributed in some measure to experiences in which separation from the mother has brought a series of strangers into their lives.

Instead of love, trust, and self-worth, millions of small children in our country may be learning harsher values in our baby banks and communal playpens. They may learn that the world outside the home is an indifferent or even hostile one. Or they may learn that all adults are exchangeable, that love is capricious, that human attachment is a risky investment, and that affection should be hoarded for the self in the interest of survival. . . .

Today we are seeing an alarming number of babies from this environment who are showing signs of emotional starvation, who rarely smile or vocalize, who are already developmentally retarded, or who do not recognize their mothers at an age when normal babies show preference for Mother.[18]

Does this preclude double careers for all wise and loving parents? Not necessarily. There are positive aspects to day care centers and nursery schools too. All else being equal, a child who is exposed to other children under the supervision of a caring, knowledgeable adult learns to socialize earlier and better than one whose youngest years are spent almost exclusively with the parents. The dangers described by Dr. Fraiberg result from virtual abandonment of such a child to the care only of others. Two-career parents who are aware of this can take positive steps to spend as much time as possible with their children and to make every hour they have together count.

It is sometimes, though rarely, possible for husband and wife so to stagger their working hours that one or the other of them is with their children most of the day. This obviously is more likely if one works at home. Studies done at Columbia University indicate, moreover, that the quality of time spent with children is more significant than the quantity; working wives may actually spend more meaningful time with their children than some wives who do not work.[19] A woman who is gratified and fulfilled as a person may be better able to cope with her family, to give them the understanding and love they require, than one who feels frustrated and confined. The important thing is for neither parent to express and develop self at the expense of the children. Even in marriages involving only one career, husbands must remember that children need both parents, that they are entitled to at least as much attention and concern as one's vocation.

Where both parents pursue careers, compromises and adjustments become imperative. The home may not always be as impeccably clean as might otherwise be the case; meals may have to be less elaborate or gourmet, though no less nutritious. The preparation of these meals, as well as marketing, laundry, cleaning, and similar chores which were once considered to be the wife's responsibilities must now be shared.

The problems inherent in two-career marriages are exaggerated disastrously when husband and wife must live in different communities. So much so that I must question whether—except as an unavoidable temporary device and for exceptional individuals in long-standing and highly successful marriages—an arrangement of this kind is even viable. A woman participating in such a "commuterized marriage" says: "There's a lot more sacrifice involved than you'd ever imagine. It's not a relationship. It's a weekend romance. It's not a marriage." A marriage counselor is even more emphatic: "I think it's crazy. . . . The idea of living apart in separate cities for more than just a temporary period is a decision for career and not for marriage."

Not every wife (or, for that matter, every husband) who opts for fulfillment via career finds it. Many learn that there are as many dull and boring hours in even the most exciting enterprise as in housework. Some reach the same conclusion as Traute Maria Moore:

> Like so many of my friends in their late thirties with children in high school, I decided to liberate myself and go back to work. My family agreed that it would be good for me. They'd grin and bear it, and even help out.

It was exciting to have to leave the house at a certain time every day, entering the world of new ideas, new faces. My job made me feel that I'd become a person in my own right. . . .

After five years of this routine, I felt frazzled. I was doing poorly at work, was becoming a rotten mother and an even worse wife. Was this liberation? I had to either cut down or quit. Since part-time jobs in industry are rare, I quit.

A month later a friend said to Ms. Moore, ". . . now you're truly a liberated woman." Here's what Ms. Moore had to say about it:

It hit home. Yes, I miss the sense of being part of something big and important. I miss having a place to go every day. But that turned out to be less important than having time for family and friends. True liberation, I suppose, means experiencing both worlds and knowing that you can choose. But living with the choice is always bittersweet.[20]

The choice between career and family is not an easy one. Betty Friedan—a leading feminist, a founder of the National Organization for Women—quotes a successful career woman:

I was the first woman manager here. I gave everything to the job. It was exciting at first, breaking in where women never were before. Now, it's just a job. But it's the devastating loneliness that's the worst. I can't stand coming back to this apartment alone every night. I'd like a house, maybe a garden. Maybe I should have a kid, even without a father. At least then I'd have a family. There has to be some better way to live. A woman alone. . . .

Without in any way renouncing her support of the women's movement, Ms. Friedan calls our attention to the fact that, as women have turned increasingly to executive careers, they have also succumbed in larger numbers to some of the stress-induced illnesses which previously afflicted mostly men, especially to heart attacks and strokes. She warns:

> Women's equality will have been for nothing if its beneficiaries, by trying to beat men at their own old power games and aping their strenuous climb onto and up the corporate ladder, fall into the traps men are beginning to escape.

> The young men of the "counter culture" of the 1960s and seventies were rebelling against the great pressures to devote their whole lives to money-making careers— just as women in the feminist movement rebelled against the great pressures to devote their whole lives to husbands and children and to forego personal advancement. But to substitute one half of a loaf for the other is not an improvement. Why should women simply replace the glorification of domesticity with the glorification of work as their life and identity? Simply to reverse the roles of breadwinner and homemaker is no progress at all, not for women and not for men.[21]

So where do we stand on two-career marriages? Can they succeed? Of course they can—*if* husband and wife are aware of all the complications they must confront—*if* their temperaments are suited to it—*if* both are willing and able to expend the extra effort required—*if* they don't make their children pay an exorbitant price—*if* they assign at least as high a priority to their marriage as to their careers.

SECOND CHANCE

When I wrote my first book on this subject, a short, almost parenthetical paragraph on second marriages sufficed. No longer so. Though less than two decades have intervened, the incidence of second, even of third, marriages has reached the point of justifying—better yet, requiring more extended discussion. The dramatic rise in divorce rates, of course, has much to do with this. No less than 80 percent of divorced individuals in this country marry again. Incidentally—or perhaps not so incidentally—three-fourths of these second marriages are permanent.

No one chapter—far less a section of a chapter—can cover the entire matter. There are too many different kinds of second marriages for that: the widowed and divorced . . . the young, middle-aged, and old . . . the childless and those with children . . . offspring young enough still to be living at home and those already on their own. The problems and needs of each group are unique; the best I can hope to accomplish is to state certain general principles which must then be adapted to meet specific circumstances.

The initial question confronting one whose first marriage has ended, obviously, is whether to marry again at all. Despite the rapidly changing sexual attitudes of our society, men are still more likely to have this choice than women. Some of both sexes, even some whose earlier marriages were happy, opt to remain single. Their reasons are varied. They may prefer the independence to which they have again become accustomed . . . fear another disappointment if their first marital experience failed . . . suspect that a prospective partner is really more interested in their money than themselves . . . be wary, if they have reached a certain age, of having to nurse an invalid mate . . . feel that there can be no replacement for a spouse who has died. One woman, whose husband had died when she was in her fifties and who had since established a durable relationship with another man, said: "I'll never get married again. I like my life. I like my own apartment, I travel with my friend, we're invited to the same parties, we enjoy the same things, but marriage wouldn't give me anything I need." No person has either the ability or the right to make this kind of decision for another. The words which follow, obviously, are meant for those who have already made it affirmatively.

What does Judaism have to say about second marriages, particularly in the case of a man whose first mate has died? As might be expected from a tradition which favors marriage in general so enthusiastically, it encourages those who seek a second chance. Talmudic law commences by stating that a widower may marry again, after the death of his first wife, as soon as the three festivals have passed. The length of time, then, that he would be expected to remain single, depended upon the time of year that he was bereaved. The principle involved is that he should not marry a second woman while his heart is still suffused with memories of the first.

As so frequently happened, however, the Talmud immediately made room for exceptions. It decreed that under two circumstances—if the man in question had not yet fathered at least two children, or if he had young children who needed someone to take care of them—he could marry again as soon as the *sheloshim* (thirty-day period of deep mourning) for his first wife had ended. As a matter of honest fact, he was allowed to remarry even after the initial mourning of seven days had expired, but not to have sexual relations with his new wife until the end of *sheloshim*. A later authority was even more lenient— he added to the two extenuating circumstances which justify an early second marriage a man who needed someone to take care of him! Clearly, then, Judaism is permissive on the subject. Not because it would in any way disparage the memory of a man's first wife, but because it recognizes, in the words of Genesis, that "it is not good for man (read: anyone) to be alone."[22]

A TRUE TEST

Reading extensively and drawing upon a general knowledge of marriage do not reveal the full extent of what could be involved in a second marriage. I therefore devised a form for interviewing couples who had married a second time. The couples thus questioned represented varying ages and conditions; some had been widowed, others divorced. Their numbers were not sufficient to constitute anything like a scientific sampling, yet their responses opened new insights for me and confirmed many of my own observations.

What did my conversations with these couples reveal about the very special problems to be anticipated? First and foremost is the matter of children, one's own and the children of one's prospective mate. It is self-evident that this is especially serious where children are young enough to be included in the new household. You may have seen the cartoon depicting a harassed wife, desperately pleading with her new husband on the phone to come home at once because "your children and my children are ganging up on our children." Not so funny when it happens in real life. And it does happen.

Children of almost any age can resent what they perceive as the intrusion of a stranger seeking to usurp the position of an absent or deceased parent. They may reject the criticisms of such an "imposter," however objective or well-intentioned such criticisms are. Older children who have been playing a supportive role in the life of a lonely parent often are threatened—even if just unconsciously—by a new partner who seems to supplant them. And of course there is always the difficulty of integrating two sets of children—his and hers—coming from different backgrounds, harboring disparate anxieties and tensions, each set—indeed, each individual—vying with the other for attention and love.

The problems of step-parenting can be complicated. How does one avoid playing favorites, or bending over backward to avoid doing so? Cope with children who feel that loving a new "mother" or "father" implies betrayal of their biological parent? Deal with the ambivalence of a child who returns from each visit to the "other family" with aggravated hostility? Recognize and handle jealousy caused by the suspicion that a stepchild's primary love is still for the original parent who is visited now only occasionally? How, indeed?

Because such questions are so very difficult to answer, many family counselors recommend that they be approached even before a second marriage takes place. At the very least, parents who have actually confronted this situation should be consulted. Some communities have begun to set up professional agencies that can help.[23] Books are now being published to provide guidance in this area.[24] Preparation and patience are the best preventive prescriptions.

One would have to be wiser and more presumptuous than Solomon to proffer comprehensive advice to the couple confronting such a prospect. Beyond simply saying that they must be aware of reality, communicate with each other openly about it, and—consistent with their children's ages and levels of understanding—try to help them also become aware of the dynamics by which they are being moved. At least in the beginning each partner should minimize direct criticism of the other's children, conveying such comments as objectively as possible through the spouse. Long before the marriage occurs, each partner should acquaint the other with the specific nature and needs of all the children who will be members of their new family.

Is it necessary to add here that relationships with former spouses, if they are living, and with the parents of such former spouses can greatly complicate what is innately a confusing situation at best? Like so many of my colleagues, during the past decade I have faced an entire syndrome of situations I never knew in the earlier years of my rabbinic career: who stands with a child during a *Bar/Bat Mitzvah* service, the father or the mother's second husband? What if mother is so embittered toward her former spouse that she refuses even to invite him as a guest? Which "father" walks down the aisle with a bride in her wedding processional? To know that such difficulties can, and most probably will, occur is the first step toward solving them.[25]

There are other situations of which couples need to be aware as they approach the altar a second time. They're older than they were the first time, hence presumably more firmly set in character and disposition. The margin of probable change is appreciably narrower than when marriage number one took place. If either prospective partner has been divorced, there may be a fear of repeated failure or an unconscious urge to repeat one's mistake by marrying the same kind of person again. Two previously independent financial "managements" must be integrated in a manner satisfactory and fair to both parties. A widow or widower must deal with possible guilt toward a first mate as well as children, must also avoid the temptation to compare an idealized image of spouse number one to the real substance of spouse number two. In short, all the considerations which are important in choosing a first mate apply also to the second, with significant additions.

One more caveat: my earlier warning against marrying

"on the rebound" applies at least as much to a second marriage as to a first. To court another potential spouse because one is in love again, because one has found a partner to alleviate loneliness and bring a renewed fulfillment to life—this can be a most beautiful experience. To contemplate marriage, on the other hand, as a means of spiting a divorced mate or because loneliness is so gnawing one can't bear it or to restore social prestige—these are questionable motives which provide less than firm foundations for a new life. In this as in so many other human choices, it isn't always easy to distinguish wholesome from neurotic urgings; the effort must at least be made.

Do these potential problems make a second marriage seem like a fearsome prospect? They shouldn't. With no exceptions, every one of the individuals I interviewed rated the second experience as *excellent* or *very good.* There are advantages too in a second marriage; for most couples, they would seem to outweigh the disadvantages by far.

My contacts were explicit and decisive in describing these plusses: "We're both more mature than either of us was the first time. . . . I'm better able to understand myself as well as my mate. . . . I have learned how to compromise. . . . Now that the worst tensions of rearing little children are over, we can concentrate more attention and time on each other. . . . I took my first wife for granted; I'm so grateful for this second chance that I don't take a single second as ordinary or due me. . . . I'm willing to work harder at it because I have learned how fragile a marriage is and how badly it can be ruined unless both partners do their best. . . . I have learned what my mistakes were the first time and am determined not to repeat them. . . . My parents, who were a major obstacle to success in my earlier marriage, are much more relaxed about this one, besides which I am better able to resist their pressure when they occasionally forget. . . . I don't have anywhere near my former need to dominate or control my husband. . . . We have more leisure time now to spend and enjoy together." And so it goes, on and on, often with excited enthusiasm.

There are no guarantees of happiness in any marriage; yet there is every reason for confidence that a second marriage can be as successful as a first, sometimes even more so.

John Ciardi was far too flippant when he defined love as "the sexual excitement of the young, the habituation of the middle-aged, and the mutual dependence of the old." True, love changes, but it need not deteriorate into either habituation or weary dependence. As one matures with the years— refines values and goals, endures more trauma, suffers more pain and loss—one can also gain greater appreciation of a loving spouse. Every moment together becomes more precious. Of course such growth toward the deeper dimensions of love can and often does occur in a good first marriage. But, if, through divorce or death, the first marriage has ended, the future can be bright with promise for the man and woman who are fortunate enough to have another chance.

SEX AGAIN

The sexual relationship between spouses in a second marriage will obviously depend upon their ages as well as their earlier experiences. Even in an unbroken first marriage, sex in middle and advanced ages most probably differs from what it was when husband and wife were younger. We know now what was either not known or wilfully denied in the past: sexual urges and desires persist far beyond what was once mistakenly believed to be their terminal point—for most of us, into our sixties and seventies; for some, even into our eighties. But the frequency and manner, as well as the meaning of our sexual expression, alter as we age. Masters and Johnson, whom I quoted more than once previously on sex in marriage, are worth citing here again:

> Sex in a warm, emotionally committed relationship may change in character, and sexual response may become diffused after a while. It may not always reach the peaks of excitement that are sometimes experienced by a man and woman in their early, experimental encounters. But other dimensions of sexual pleasure may be discovered —the familiarity that is comforting, the safety that allows complete vulnerability, and the deepening sense of emotional intimacy, among other pleasures.[26]

In only one-fourth of the couples I interviewed was sexual adjustment labelled a serious problem. My suspicion is that this may understate the case in second marriages generally. Sex is far too intimate a relationship for patterns of adjustment, however successful, to be automatically transferred from one marriage to another. Husbands and wives, each with a heritage of sexual experience—good and bad—may have to make new adjustments, learn new patterns of expression, in their second marriages. Everything that was said earlier about establishing such patterns in first marriages, about patient trial and error, about openness and honesty and striving for mutual gratification as an expression of love both physical and spiritual—everything applies equally here.

In my marital counseling, I have discovered an intriguing analogue. Adolescent boys and girls are frequently competitive and jealous regarding sex. Because some of them develop sexually at an earlier age than others, the others may worry and fret over their eventual capabilities. This kind of false rivalry can carry over into adult life and marriage. I have already tried to discredit the notion that there are such things as universal standards of sexual performance, to be sought and achieved by everyone. In a fascinating and compelling way, a sexual anxiety not unlike that of adolescents can upset older people in a second marriage. I might add—not too cynically, I hope—that some individuals of relatively advanced age may be just as susceptible as younger persons to compensate for their fears of sexual inadequacy by inordinate boasting.

Just as not everyone becomes sexually alert or aroused at the same age, so not everyone finds the sexual urges diminishing at the same time. There is no set schedule for all of us at either the beginning or the end of our active sex lives. To assume such a schedule, to feel deficient in comparison to the sexual prowess of others, real or feigned, is to do oneself an unforgivable injustice. Couples contemplating a second marriage should communicate with each other honestly about sex, as about every other aspect of their future relationship.

Even when a man can no longer achieve or maintain an erection, it is possible for him and his wife to enjoy sexual pleasure together. I mentioned earlier the importance of man-

ual caresses in arousing a woman sexually and referred to the
fact that some women reach a higher peak of orgasm this way
than through penile contact. Men, moreover, can be capable of
reaching orgasm even when an erection is impossible.

Dr. Aaron L. Rutledge is one of many marriage counselors
who have learned that mutual sexual satisfaction is achievable
even without "direct sexual intercourse." He writes:

> . . . there are many other forms of sexual arousal and
> gratification. There are a number of oral and manual
> techniques which are as effective as penile intercourse
> —and for many women more effective—in bringing
> complete satisfaction to the wife, even though the hus-
> band is not sufficiently potent for coitus. This requires
> that the husband knows what types of caress she re-
> sponds to with most excitement, is aware of all the
> eroticised parts of the female body, and recognizes the
> role of stimulation of the clitoral area and the vulva in
> the attainment of a climax.[27]

Two conditions, prerequisite for sexual success at all ages, are
no less essential when husband and wife are older: lines of
communication between them must always be open and honest; the physical excitement they share must express a many-
dimensioned love which is spiritual too.

Should such couples live together before marriage? Especially if circumstances prevent them from marrying? Should
they test their sexual compatibility in advance? Fools will rush
in with easy answers where responsible counselors fear to
tread. The answer will not in all respects be the same for a
middle-aged or older couple as for youngsters approaching
their first marriage. Yet there are abiding principles which
should still apply. Everything we have said throughout these
pages about the proper relationship between sex and love,
about the vast difference between animal and human sexuality,
is relevant at all ages. Whatever two people do together sexually should enhance rather than cheapen their capacity to love
each other. To act promiscuously is, in my judgment, reprehensible at every stage of life. For a man and woman who
contemplate a second marriage because they love each other,

who feel permanently committed to each other, who are prevented by unavoidable circumstance from entering upon a legally endorsed marital relationship which they both want and hope to have—for such a couple to become intimate only with each other may not always be wrong. Each of us must make that kind of choice, guided by conscience, by values, by religious and moral principles. And each must be comfortable with the decision. Neither partner in such a relationship ever has the right to impose his or her will on the other.

CHAPTER THIRTEEN

"You Shall Teach Them..."

Sociologists have long marveled over the virtues of Jewish family life. Both formal studies and informal observation testify that family ties are stronger among Jews, that divorce, infidelity, and juvenile delinquency are rarer. Studies pursued well into the 1970s showed that Jews married at an older age than non-Jews and that their marriages are on the average more stable.[1] Some scholars are convinced that this superiority is a compensatory device, resulting from the fact that for centuries Jews were denied many of the satisfactions and pleasures which others received from their larger social life; therefore Jews concentrated on their families. Although there is probably a measure of truth to this claim, it would be superficial to attribute the whole of Jewish family strength to hostile external pressure.

Even as we have already discovered in our tradition unique insights on sex, love, and marriage, there is also a large body of Jewish teaching on the family. What we know today as Judaism is the result both of external and internal factors. It has been shaped in part by discrimination, but in large part also by the inner direction of our ideals. In a sense each newly-wed couple forms a bridge between the generations of past and future. Bride and groom are products of family syndromes, while at the same time they establish together a new family of their own. Our Jewish ideals of family life can help them in two ways: in understanding their respective pasts and in commencing to build a happy future.

One of the most idyllic descriptions of wholesome family

life encompassing three generations to be found anywhere in literature is that of Psalm 128.

> Happy are all who revere the Lord,
>   who follow His ways.
> You shall enjoy the fruit of your labors;
>   you shall be happy and you shall prosper.
> Your wife shall be like a fruitful vine within your house;
>   your sons, like olive saplings around your table.
> So shall the man who reveres the Lord be blessed.
>
> May the Lord bless you from Zion;
>   may you share the prosperity of Jerusalem
>   all the days of your life,
>   and live to see your children's children.

For countless generations this noble ideal was the goal of most Jewish families and was in fact realized by many of them.

The fact that this is not always true was made apparent some years ago when a student in my confirmation class asked to discuss some personal problems with me. "We don't really have a home," he said with great emotion, "just a group of people living in the same house." He proceeded to tell me that his parents paid very little attention to his wishes or his younger sisters', that he had to go home each Sunday from religious school to get lunch for himself and the girls because his mother and father always spent the whole day at their club. During the week too they were generally too busy to spend much time with the children; their concern was limited to issuing rules, followed by grim scoldings when these were violated.

This was obviously not a very attractive or desirable pattern of family life. It could scarcely be said to square with our traditional Jewish ideals. The probability is that this boy's parents weren't even aware of what Judaism teaches about the ideal family.

OBLIGATIONS OF PARENTS

It is a source of continual astonishment to discover how many of the principles of modern pedagogy were apparently known to the ancient rabbis. They were acutely aware, for example, of how important it is for parents to agree on major matters pertaining to the rearing of their children. A chasidic rabbi said: "If husband and wife quarrel, they cannot raise good children."[2] It is possible to carry this injunction to the unhealthy extreme of insisting that husband and wife must agree on all things in the presence of their children. The consequence of this can be to arouse in youngsters the suspicion that the adult world is engaged in a massive conspiracy against them. Voicing honest differences in the presence of children can be an intelligent way for parents to demonstrate how divergent opinions can be lovingly accommodated. But total agreement is imperative on all important aspects of child rearing itself. If mother and father argue, for example, on discipline, they openly invite indecision and instability into the lives of their children. This is why I suggested, in an earlier chapter, that an engaged couple should discuss their respective ideas on disciplining children. Too wide a difference may disclose fundamental incompatibilities of personality and presage later trouble both for the couple and the offspring.

The ancient and medieval teachers of our faith also knew how dangerous and destructive it is for parents to play favorites among their children. Several of them attributed the strong animosity Joseph's brothers bore him to the fact that he was the recipient of special attention from their father. The Talmud states explicitly: "Show no partiality among your sons. Treat all of them alike."[3]

Many modern parents are confused with regard to discipline. Reacting against what may have been excessive discipline in their own childhood, they have attempted to exercise none toward their children. They make a grievous mistake. A total absence of regulations and rules can be as harmful as rules which are too restrictive. For one thing, psychiatry has helped us understand that children are often frightened by some of their own impulses and desires. If these are not controlled by teachers and parents, a corrosive accumulation of guilt may accrue. There is also the fact that life itself imposes disciplines. Nature and human nature are such that immoral conduct very often carries its own punitive consequences. Children who are led to believe, early in life, that they can do whatever they want, without fear of being disciplined, are inadequately prepared for the realities of life. So far as possible discipline should be fair, should grow out of the offense committed, and be proportionate to it in severity. But the absence of all discipline is no favor to the child.

As long ago as Bible times our ancestors understood this. In the Book of Proverbs they urged:

> Train up a child in the way he should go.
> And, even when he is old, he will not depart from it.
> Withhold not correction from the child;
> For, though you beat him with the rod, he will not
> die.

In similar vein the Midrash says:

> He who rebukes not his son leads him into delinquency.[4]

Notwithstanding the recommendation of corporal punishment just quoted, it was not an unreasoning or unloving discipline which Judaism approved. It was implicitly assumed that the love and tenderness which prevailed between husband and wife would pervade their relationship to their children too. Thus rabbinic literature tells us that when God spoke to Moses from the burning bush, fearing lest he be frightened, He spoke in the voice of his father. We are also enjoined by the rabbis never to promise either punishment or reward to a child unless we truly mean to follow through.

The greatest responsibility of Jewish parents by far was to teach their children Torah, which means to say, the history, literature, theology, liturgy, and ethics of the Jewish people. Countless are the aphorisms and epigrams establishing this obligation:

> A home where Torah is not heard will not endure.[5]

> If a man does not teach his son Torah, it is as if he had merely created an image.[6]

> He who teaches his sons and grandsons Torah is as if he had received it himself at Mount Sinai.[7]

Rabbi Hiyya ben Abba saw Rabbi Joshua ben Levi hurrying one morning to take his grandson to school. He asked him: "Why the haste?" and Rabbi Joshua answered: "Is it a small thing to stand at Mount Sinai?"[8]

He who teaches Torah to children abides with the שכינה (*Shechinah*)—God's Presence.[9]

Rabbah, son of Rabbi Huna, ate no breakfast until he had taken a boy to school.[10]

Jerusalem was destroyed only because the children did not attend school, and loitered in the streets.[11]

One is immortal if his descendants study the Torah.[12]

It must not be assumed—merely because all these admonitions speak either to or concerning men—that only fathers were responsible for the education of their children. While it is true that formal education was deemed by our tradition to be within the purview of the male parent, Judaism nevertheless recognized that the religious tone of the home is set primarily by the mother's influence. This was affirmed explicitly by the *Zohar*, principal medieval sourcebook of Jewish mysticism:

> The chief influence transforming a man's house into his home is his wife. The שכינה (*Shechinah*) will not forsake his house if his wife keeps it according to the ways of Israel.[13]

The responsibilities of Jewish education, then, were clearly assigned to both parents.

ACTIONS SPEAK LOUDER

As impressive as the foregoing quotations are, they constitute but the beginning of parental obligation for education. Not only can scores of similar statements be cited for each one given here, Judaism also recognizes that the example set by parental conduct is a much more effective instructor than even the most eloquent of words. Therefore fathers and mothers were urged so to order their deeds that they would offer the right example to their children.

> Every Jew should so conduct himself that his sons will rejoice to say: "The God of my father."

A chasidic rabbi expressed this truth with exceptional eloquence:

> The Belzer Rabbi commented on the verse in Exodus 10:2, "And that you may recount in the hearing of your sons and your sons' sons how I made a mockery of the Egyptians and how I displayed My signs among them—in order that you may know that I am the Lord." It may be remarked that the end of the verse would have seemed more correct if it had been expressed thus: ". . . in order that *they* may know that I am the Lord." But the verse was intentionally worded "you" instead of "they" in order to furnish us a lesson. Recount to your sons the wonders of the Lord, but remember that this will have a beneficent influence upon them only if you yourselves recognize that He is the Lord.[14]

Another chasidic rabbi addressed himself to the same point:

> A man asked the Kotzker Rabbi to pray for him in order that his sons might study the Torah diligently. He replied: "If your sons will see that you are a diligent student, they will imitate you. But if you neglect your own studies, and merely wish your sons to study, the result will be that they will do likewise when they grow up. They will neglect the Torah themselves and desire that their sons do the studying."[15]

A third rabbi of the same group demonstrated an admirable and effective sense of humor in this direction. He is reported to have seen a man and his son, both drunk, reeling together in the gutter. Turning to his own son, who was with him, he said:

> I envy that father. He has succeeded in his ambition to have a son like himself. But I do not yet know whether you will be like me. See to it that the drunkard does not have better success with his son than I with you.[16]

We shall shortly consider the responsibilities of children to their parents. First, however, it is imperative to recognize that all of them were contingent upon the ethical teaching and conduct of the parents themselves. The Talmud is unmistakably clear on this point:

> It is possible to think that, even if the father ordered his son to defile himself or not to restore a lost article which he had found, he is to obey him; consequently there is a text to teach, "You shall each revere his mother and his father, and keep My sabbaths." (Lev. 19:3) All of you alike are bound to honor Me.[17]

It would be impossible to exaggerate the emphasis of Judaism on the moral responsibilities of parents toward their children. Only if they met these obligations—by deed even more than in word—did their children have to assume similar responsibilities toward them.

Too many parents in our own time have failed to match the understanding of our ancient teachers that the example of parental conduct is a far more effective instructor than the eloquence of parental words. Thus they urge restraint on their children while indulging in gluttonous exhibitionism themselves; they stress the virtues of ethical behavior in their homes while behaving with gross immorality in their business or professional lives; they insist that their children tell the truth while they themselves consistently lie to the government on their tax returns; they force their sons and daughters to attend religious school while they attend religious services only on the High Holy Days. Judaism emphasizes today, as it always has, that the primary obligation parents owe their children is a living model of the conduct they want them to follow.

This chapter had already been concluded, I thought, when a vivid example came to me. My son-in-law—my daughter's second husband—has training and experience as an engineer. When the energy crunch became critical early in the winter of 1979–80, he decided to seek out poor families who couldn't afford to weather-strip their homes and to do this work for them. Ray was too modest to tell us of such a decision. But my adolescent grandson—his step-son—related it to us with such joy and pride that my wife and I were moved almost to tears. A young man had been given a living model of human brother-hood worth more than tons of preachment!

Since this is not essentially a book on the rearing of children, I desist from further detail. It is, however, a book on marriage and the family. As such, it requires at least some instruction on the precepts of our faith concerning the duties of parents toward their children, duties which you yourself assume from the moment you contemplate having a family.

If I have discussed the familial responsibilities of parents before those of children, this is because, chronologically and psychologically, they come first. It might have been more pro-ductive had Moses phrased the fifth commandment, not as "Honor your father and your mother," but rather as "Honor your daughter and your son." All things being equal, parents who properly and lovingly respect their children will elicit simi-lar respect from them. They stand a good chance of their children's fulfilling the obligations which Judaism has long enjoined upon the younger generation in a household.

OBLIGATIONS OF CHILDREN

The same Book of Proverbs which stipulated the respon-sibilities of parents was equally explicit on those of children. Thus:

> A son who deals shamefully and reproachfully
> Will despoil his father, and chase away his mother.
> Hearken to your father who begot you,
> And despise not your mother when she is old.

The Torah even went so far as to order that a son who is contemptuous of his parents is to be publicly stoned. While we can scarcely accept the undue harshness of the prescribed pun-ishment, it is impressive nonetheless to perceive the impor-tance our tradition has assigned to filial respect.

The Talmud expands the emphases of the Bible. It asks, for example: "In what does reverence for a father consist?" And immediately it answers:

> In not sitting in his presence, and in not speaking in his presence, and in not contradicting him. Of what does honor for parents consist? In providing for them food and drink, in clothing them, in giving them shoes for their feet, in helping them to enter or leave the house. R. Eliezer said: "Even if his father ordered him to throw a purse of gold into the sea, he should obey him."[18]

Here again, we cannot accept literally every ancient or medieval prescription for behavior toward parents. We today would be inclined to doubt either the desirability or wholesomeness of forbidding a child ever to sit in his father's presence or to disagree with him. But we can learn from tradition that disagreement merely for its own sake is not valid and that the spirit in which a child acts toward parents is the all-important consideration.

Are we stretching talmudic truth in saying this? Not if we understand the intent of the passage which tells us that, if a father errs on a point of law, his son should not directly or bluntly charge him with having made a mistake. Instead, he should more subtly suggest: "Father, in the law it is written thus"—proceeding to quote the proper biblical passage in order to spare his father avoidable embarrassment.[19]

Another talmudic passage underscores more explicitly that the spirit of one's actions toward the parents is even more important than the actions themselves. We are told that a man who feeds his father on fattened chickens may be treating him abominably, while one who orders his father to do the heavy work of treading the mill may be acting with admirable affection. How is this possible? In the first instance, if the father asks whence the chickens were obtained, the son may impatiently reply: "Eat, old man, eat and be silent!" In the second case, the government may have issued a decree that all millers report to the capital at once. The son, fearing that this presages a period of dangerous military duty for all who respond, directs his father to remain at home, doing the relatively safe work there, while exposing himself to the greater risk.[20]

The devotion and love due one's parents are manifest further in the comment that father and mother are partners of

God in the proper rearing of their child.[21] It was said also that, because God knew He would be unable to attend himself to the needs of every child, He created parents to act in His stead. One rabbi even proposed that parents are entitled to more honor than God. This he deduced, in typical rabbinic style, from two biblical verses. One states: "Honor God with your substance" (Prov. 3:9) which he interpreted to mean that only if we possess substance are we obligated to honor God. A different verse, however, reads: "Honor your father and your mother." (Exod. 20:12) Here there is no qualifying condition; we are to honor our parents regardless of whether or not we have possessions.[22]

With reference to children no less than to parents, the fulfillment of obligation is judged by Jewish tradition more on the basis of deed than of word. Rabbinic literature contains numerous illustrations of famous men whose behavior toward their parents is considered exemplary. One such man was Abimi who was said to have had five sons, all of them ordained rabbis. Yet, whenever this man's father would summon him, he would run to open the door and exclaim: "Yes, yes, I am coming to you!" One day his father asked him for some water. By the time Abimi had come with it, his father had fallen asleep. So he stood there patiently until he awakened, then gave him the water.[23]

The mother of Rabbi Tarfon broke her sandal one day as she walked through a courtyard. In order to spare her from walking barefoot on the rough stones, Rabbi Tarfon bent down, putting his hands on the pavement ahead of each step. When he later fell ill, his mother asked the other rabbis to pray for him, saying: "Pray for my son, Tarfon, for he honors me more than I deserve." When she told them what he had done for her, they responded: "If he had done a thousand times more for you, he would not have shown half the honor for a parent which is commanded in the law!"[24]

A chasidic student is said one day to have observed in the midst of class that his rabbi was deeply engrossed in trying to unravel a certain verse. Knowing from past experience that such concentration was usually of long duration, the student ran home for lunch, assuming that he could easily return before his rabbi would be ready to resume the lesson. As he finished eating, his mother asked him to run an errand for her. He refused, giving as an excuse the fact that he had to hurry back to his studies. On the way back, however, it occurred to him that the chief purpose of studying was to perform good deeds, that helping his mother in fulfillment of a lesson he had already learned was more important than hastening to learn a new one. So he retraced his steps, did the errand for his mother, then returned to the classroom. As he entered, the rabbi looked up from his concentration and said: "You must have done a good deed for, the moment you entered, a complicated matter I had not previously understood became clear to me."[25]

Finally, the Talmud describes a Gentile whose respect for his mother was all the more noteworthy by virtue of the fact that she had apparently become demented. Once, while he was conducting a public meeting, for no reason at all she took off her slipper and hit him in the face. When her slipper fell to the ground, he bent down to pick it up for her. On another occasion she tore his silk robe, hit him on the head, and spat in his face—all in the presence of others. But he refrained from retaliation in order to spare her shame.[26]

It is clear, then, that in the eyes of Jewish tradition parents and children were mutually obligated to each other. Only if honor, respect, and love were abundantly demonstrated in both directions, could the full promise of marriage and the family be realized. This is no less true today than it was during the centuries when the Bible and Talmud were being recorded. The couple who understands our Jewish ideals of family conduct and who conscientiously strives toward the attainment of these ideals has a head start in the pursuit of marital happiness.

THE FAMILY TODAY

Did some of the injunctions and prescriptions of Jewish tradition on the family, as you perused them these past few minutes, seem archaic? As if they were faint echoes from a time which once was but is now forever gone? Surely there is no need to argue at length that the institution of the family has changed radically in our time. More than a few competent observers doubt whether it can even survive.

Thus, Prof. Urie Bronfenbrenner of Cornell University laments: "The family is falling apart. Since World War II, the extended family of several generations . . . has practically disappeared in this country. Even the small nuclear family of father, mother, and the kids is in decline."[27]

The verdict is not unanimous. Prof. Mary Jo Bane of Wellesley College has written a book on marriage under the revealing title, *Here to Stay.*[28] And Rollo May, an eminent psychoanalyst, says: "If we do away with the family, we would have to invent it by another name."[29]

There is no secret as to why the family is in trouble. We have become a nation of movers; very few of us live out our lives in the community where we were born. Members of the same family sometimes live as far apart as the Atlantic is from the Pacific. Part of the same picture is the frequency with which large corporations require their employees to move from city to city. And, of course, the women's movement, with all its positive achievements, has had a severe impact on the family.

Many of the innovations and aberrations in society today are due to the fact that individuals are bereft of the support formerly received from their families. The cults are without doubt at least partly an attempt to fill this gap. So are the various experiments in communal living, "group marriage," "open marriage," etc. Whether we call it family or not, most of us need the support and strength of others who are close to us and on whom we can depend, whatever the circumstances. The family, in short, is not an artificial invention, but a natural response to deep-seated human needs. Prof. Bane puts it well: "Family ties, it seems clear, are not archaic remnants of a disappearing traditionalism, but persistent manifestations of human needs for stability, continuity, and a non-conditional affection."[30] Dr. Herbert Hendin, a prominent psychiatrist, underscores the same truth: "The evidence is overwhelming that the family is not disposable, that even the best alternatives do not equal a reasonably good family's power to raise responsive people."[31]

Here again, Jewish tradition perceptively anticipated the insights of modern psychology. Our ancestors realized that the family is the best environment in which young children can negotiate their growth from narcissism to altruism, the best ground on which to develop that sense of mutuality and commitment which is indispensable to the success of marriage.

MORE TO THE PRESENT POINT

As important and impressive as the traditions of Judaism are on family responsibilities, they will be of doubtful value in your marriage unless we undertake now at least briefly to apply them to a few of the major familial problems you are likely to encounter. In reading the preceding paragraphs, you may have been able to recognize some of your parents' virtues and failings. It is imperative in this connection to be aware of how frequently a generation in a given family repeats the pattern of mistakes perpetrated by its predecessors. Often the very person who has consistently complained about having been treated too severely by parents becomes in turn an overly severe parent. Or, in the understandable effort to prevent such repetition, one may react to the opposite and equally damaging extreme of exercising no discipline in the home at all.

As you establish your own home, and in it start from the beginning to build foundations for your own family, a conscious effort should be made to avoid the mistakes of your parents both directly and by "over-reaction." You and your mate will be part of a continuing stream, flowing unbrokenly from the past to the future. Neither of you can altogether escape the consequences of the home in which you grew. By the same token, you will in due course have it in your power to shape the welfare of your own children. The more accurately and honestly you understand and appraise your feelings toward your parents, the greater will be the probability of working out a wholesome relationship with your children.

Whatever the emotional bonds have been between you and your parents, a transition will be required from the moment of your marriage. If your parents have gradually and gracefully loosened their hold on you already, treating you in recent years more as an adult than still a child, the difference now will be one of degree rather than of kind. But, if the emotional umbilical cord has not yet been completely severed, the change will be more radical and difficult.

The bond between each partner in a marriage and his or her parents is bound to affect profoundly the quality of the new marital relationship. The bride or groom whose parents have demanded a submissive child—never asserting an adult self, always submerged by their will—will carry this stunted self-image into marriage. He or she is likely either to act as a thwarted, indecisive child or to react so violently as to become an insufferable dictator. Neither attitude is calculated to enhance one's posture as a spouse. The young person whose only personal experience with "love" has been at the hand of a martyr-mother who catered to every desire may find it painfully difficult to realize that adult love sometimes means denial. In short, the success of your marriage will hinge substantially on whether both sets of parents grant you freedom to make your own mistakes, as they have undoubtedly made theirs. It is no less essential, however, that you and your mate be ready to assume such freedom and to transfer your major love relationship from parents to each other.

Jewish tradition has long been aware of this. Immediately after the Bible tells of Eve's creation it adds: "Hence a man leaves his father and mother and clings to his wife, so that they become one flesh." To which one of the postbiblical rabbis added: "Before a man marries, his love goes to his parents; after he marries, his love goes to his wife."[32]

This statement should not be misinterpreted to mean that you face here a choice of "either-or." I do not stop loving my parents in order to love my wife. To the contrary, unless I am able to continue loving them—on a level appropriate to my age and my marital status—there is little chance that I shall love my wife healthily. We saw long ago that my love for my wife is qualitatively different in some respects from the love I bear all others, that it achieves a dimension beyond that which I continue to feel and express for my parents. To the degree that they coincide, however, and in the measure that life may from time to time force me to establish priorities, on or before the day of my wedding my wife became the number one object of my love. My parents had to be satisfied—indeed, satisfied and happy—to assume second place. The final successful consummation of the process came when, at the time of my daughter's wedding, and later my son's, my wife and I rejoiced to witness the new member of our family taking precedence over us. Fortunate is the person who never has to choose between parents and mate. But if such a choice becomes unavoidable, marriage can succeed only when one's wife or husband comes first.

This truth too was anticipated by Judaism centuries ago. A thirteenth-century rabbi, Judah ben Samuel of Regensburg, wrote:

> If a father knows his married daughter to be busy and occupied with her husband's affairs, let him not suggest or order her to attend to his own, unless the husband allow of it, postponing his own interests for a while.[33]

But marriage obviously involves the relationship of each partner not only to one's parents but also to a new set of parents, the in-laws. I alluded briefly to this problem at an earlier point in urging, as a dimension of compatibility, that one give serious consideration to the probable future relationship with in-laws. It remains now to add that this can be an excitingly enriching experience or a depressively degrading one. Much depends on the maturity of the individuals involved, as well as their respective capacities to love.

The alertness of Jewish tradition to this problem is attested by the following talmudic extract:

> Three years had passed since the day that Abraham had sent Ishmael away. He longed to see him, and sought out his camp in the pasture-country of Paran. When Abraham came to his son's tent, he found Ishmael absent from home. He asked Ishmael's wife for a little water, but the ill-natured woman refused to give it to

him. Abraham said: "When your husband returns, pray tell him that an old man from Philistia came to visit him and, not finding him home, offered this advice: the pegs of your tent should be changed." Ishmael understood this allusion to his wicked wife and divorced her. He wedded another woman, named Fatima. The following year Abraham again wished to visit his son and again found him away from home. Without waiting for a request, Fatima offered him hospitality, and urged him to partake of food and drink. Abraham said: "When your husband returns, tell him: his pegs are excellent and he should retain them." Ishmael thanked his gracious wife, and blessed the Lord who had sent him so admirable a mate.[34]

Not every instance of in-law interference works out so well. Apparently Abraham was right in his evaluation of Ishmael's wives, and fortunately Ishmael seems to have agreed with him.

In the ideal situation both husband and wife come in the course of time to feel about each other's parents as if they were their own, and this affection is reciprocated. To achieve or even approach this ideal, the young married couple must conscientiously work toward such a relationship and the parents on both sides must strive to avoid anything remotely resembling interference. Couples old enough to marry must be presumed to be old enough to manage their own affairs. This does not mean that parents have no right to offer suggestions or advice. But the couples themselves are the ones to evaluate all such advice and to accept or reject it according to their own wisdom.

UNDER ONE ROOF?

Should a newly married couple live with either set of parents? The Talmud leaves no room for doubt. It asserts without equivocation:

Can a goat live in the same barn as a tiger? In the same fashion, a daughter-in-law cannot live with her mother-in-law under the same roof.

There is seldom room for two adult generations in one household. Rare indeed are the parents who will not at least subtly take sides in any tension between married children with whom they live; or the young husband or wife who will refrain from enlisting a parent on his or her side of an argument. Even if it means settling for a lower standard of living, the wisest course for most couples is not to live with parents. Where such doubling up cannot be avoided, every effort must be made on both sides to maintain a maximum of privacy and to eschew interference in each other's business.

The husband and wife who preserve their own integrity are precisely the ones most likely to maintain love and respect for parents and in-laws. A recognition of this apparent paradox is implicit in two statements from the Apocrypha which may at first blush seem contradictory. The first reads: "I have carried iron and removed stones, and they were not heavier than for a man to settle in his father-in-law's house." The second statement: "Honor your father-in-law and mother-in-law, because henceforth they are your parents."

Judaism recognizes realistically that often life imposes on us a necessity for compromise. On the relationship with in-laws the *Shulchan Aruch* stipulates that, if either husband or wife finds the visits of the other's family disturbing to the peace of their household, such visits are to be prohibited. Neither mate, however, has the right to deny the other visits with his or her parents in *their* home.[35] Needless to say, the very need for this kind of compromise would indicate that a sorry state of affairs had already developed.

So far we have had in mind the problem of couples living with parents immediately after their marriage. And we have without hesitation recommended that wherever possible this kind of arrangement be avoided. It occasionally happens, however, that many years later one parent dies and the survivor then wishes to move in with the children. There are, of course, situations in which either financial or emotional compulsions make it necessary for the couple to accede. Yet here too every alternative should be explored first. True, there are very rare persons who can, by their presence, enrich the lives of their children and grandchildren. But such enrichment is more likely to take place when the grandparents do not actually live in the same house. Aside from everything that has already been said, there is grave danger that children will come to feel they have two fathers or mothers, and will bitterly resent both. This is often true regardless of whether the two generations differ or agree in the discipline they exert on growing children.

LOOKING AHEAD

Everything you do from the beginning of your marriage will be setting the stage for decisions to be made in the future. Mistaken or misguided policies at the start can prejudge the choices you will want later. They can so corrupt the atmosphere of your home that in point of fact you may no longer have a truly free choice when the time for decision comes.

One altogether human danger to which attention should be called is the tendency to recognize our own faults more clearly in others than we do in ourselves. This applies especially to parents. When my son was a small boy, each time I became irrationally angry with him I knew I must have unconsciously discovered in him a failing I had not yet been able consciously to acknowledge in myself. Sometimes upon due reflection I was able to identify it, at other times not. But I knew that, in every instance where my anger was disproportionate to whatever he had in fact said or done, it was probable that I was actually the target of my own resentment. This projection of one's own defects onto others can exist in the relationship between husband and wife too, though it is probably more common in the attitudes of parents toward their offspring. In either case, to be forewarned of the possibility is to be prepared to fend successfully against it.

Parents can also at times use each other as punching bags when their real resentment is against one of their children. I recall a couple who illustrated this painfully. There was much tension between mother and son, so much, as a matter of fact, that she was irritable whenever he visited. Her conscience dictated that she act politely in the young man's presence. It never failed, however, that for hours, or even days following each visit, she was viciously argumentative with her husband.

How about the general organization and structure of the family? Who should make major decisions? Whose word should prevail when there is vigorous disagreement? No one answer to these questions will satisfy every couple. We can say in general, however, that the patterns established from the outset of your marriage will probably become permanent. If you and your mate unite at the beginning to make important decisions together, with loving consideration for each other, when your children reach the age even of minimum understanding you will want to give them a voice too in matters which deeply concern them. If, on the other hand, one of you imposes his or her decisions on the other—which means to say, if your home from the start is an autocracy in miniature—your children too will eventually be dominated by a domestic dictator. The choice is yours. The quality of your marriage and family life will depend upon it.

The appearance of a first child necessarily poses a whole new complex of problems for husband and wife. If they have already established a solid, loving relationship, these problems will be easily resolved. If the one-to-one involvement itself has never been satisfactorily resolved, the first baby can cause serious difficulties. Where parents are secure in their love for each other, a child will strengthen the ties which already unite them. Where the relationship between husband and wife is unstable, the child can be an intolerable threat. I know of one lamentable instance in which a husband was so threatened by the appearance of his first child that he actually reverted to infantile forms of behavior himself in an unconscious but clearly discernible effort to compete with the newborn infant for his wife's attention. Each time the baby became ill, the father also took to bed. This, to be sure, was an extreme, psychopathic example. More often the competition between an infant and an insecure parent is subtler, though no less harmful.

Several chapters back I stressed the importance of spending much leisure time together if husband and wife are to deepen the ties that unite them. Here again, the same emphasis applies to the entire family after children have reached the age of doing even simple little things together with their parents. I remember a man who attributed an emotional illness of long duration in his adult life to his feeling as a child that his parents loved each other with such exclusive concentration as to leave no room for him. He always felt pushed out to the fringe of their concern. Whether he was right or wrong with reference to his particular grievance is not the point at issue. The disastrous thing was that he *felt* that way. Wise parents will try to avoid even giving the appearance of shutting their children out of their lives. They will discover that time spent constructively or creatively with their children can be as enriching to themselves as to the youngsters. Two authorities on marriage have written wisely on this matter:

> If most contemporary families no longer work together in the common task of operating a farm or small business, there are many leisure time projects in which they may engage as family groups. . . . The list of such projects is endless—building a vacation shack, a family orchestra, a trailer or camping trip in summer, a family basketball team, a vacant lot garden, a family art exhibit, barber shop harmony around the piano, father-son workshops in the basement, a family reading circle, the breeding of dogs or other animals, church activity, a golfing foursome, family games, a flower garden, or a small business as a side issue. . . . What the particular project may be depends naturally on the abilities, circumstances, and interests of the particular family, and in this connection is of somewhat incidental importance. What is important is that the family plans, works, thinks, laughs, succeeds, or even fails together. It is the family in action as a group.[36]

The celebration of our Jewish holidays in the home, including joint family preparation for such observances, can serve an invaluable function in giving both parents and children a feeling of comradeship and companionship which is the most essential ingredient of family loyalty. I shall have more to say about such celebrations later.

This chapter cannot be concluded without at least a brief word concerning the sex education of your children. Remember what was said earlier about such education's commencing even before a child is actually born. Your own attitudes toward sex and especially the sexual success of your marriage will vitally affect your child. Information about sex should be given at the proper time as freely and unself-consciously as information about any other matter. Your children's interest in their own body and experimentation with it should not be frowned upon as something unnatural or dirty. Both boys and girls should be told about menstruation, wet dreams, and masturbation in a manner calculated to prevent undue apprehension or fear.

The most important principle governing sex education—indeed, all education—is truth. No child of any age should ever be told that storks bring babies. Nothing should be taught as truth that will later have to be unlearned. It is often impossible to tell young children *the whole truth;* but whatever is taught must be *nothing but the truth!* And it must be taught with wholesome attitude. A father who thinks all females are fit objects of conquest by males can truthfully transmit all the necessary facts about sex to his son, but only in a way which will lead to imbalance and distortion. A mother to whom intercourse is repulsive, who *feels* that all men are beasts, can be honest in relating information to her daughter but will probably also lead her perilously close to frigidity. Healthy attitudes are at least as important as accurate facts.

To the outer limit of comprehension, a child at each age should be supplied with all the sex information wanted or needed. If the proper kind of parent-child relationship prevails, questions will be asked freely. If not, parents may have to take the initiative in extending openings which will encourage the asking of questions. Care must be exercised, however, not to inundate children with more than they want and are able at the moment to handle. You may have heard the classic story of a child who asked one day: "Mommy, where did I come from?" The mother, elated at finally hearing the question for which she had long been waiting and was so well prepared, proceeded to give her little daughter a forty-five minute lecture on the "facts of life." Upon reaching her nearly breathless conclusion, she inquired: "Tell me, honey, what made you ask this question today?" To which the child innocently responded: "Well, Francie told me this morning that she comes from Philadelphia, so I wondered where I came from." It's always a good idea to be sure of the real question before attempting an answer.

Parents must never lose sight of the difference between true sex education and just education for reproduction. A child who is old enough to learn the anatomical and physiological facts involved is also old enough to know the role of sex in the lives and love of the parents. It should come, not as a rude shock, but as the revelation of beautiful truth, to learn how he or she was conceived. And when the time comes for discussions of premarital sex, the emphasis should be not on the dangers of promiscuity—though these cannot be entirely neglected— but rather on the advantages which can accrue to a marriage which is based on the chastity of both spouses.[37] In no area do parents have a more priceless opportunity to influence the future happiness and welfare of their children.

CHAPTER FOURTEEN

Mixed Marriage

*The hour was late—almost midnight. I had sat since 8:30 counsel-*ing with a husband and wife who had been married sixteen years and were the parents of five children. We were standing at the door of my study, about to terminate a far from satisfactory evening, when something prompted me to ask a final question. Turning to the wife, I began: "If you had known sixteen years ago what you know now. . . ."

I never finished the question. Misreading my intention entirely, the woman looked viciously at her husband and almost hissed: "If I had known then even half of what I know tonight, I would never have married him!" I am still uncertain who was more acutely embarrassed, the startled spouse or I. We both were aware, however, that the problem of mixed marriage, which had been minimized or denied through so many years, had explosively ruptured their relationship. She was Protestant and he, Jewish. Neither had converted to the religion of the other. At the time of their marriage they had agreed their children would be sent in alternate years to a Reform Jewish religious school and a Protestant Sunday school. It was the breakdown of this Solomonic "solution" that had brought them to me.

Though the wife's vehemence was certainly exceptional, there was nothing rare about their problem. No kind of anxiety appears more frequently in the average American rabbi's study than that of mixed marriage, either contemplated or already consummated. Whether rabbis will it so or not, they soon become experts. The sharing of my own experience in this area will naturally be most immediately compelling for those couples who are themselves of mixed religious background. Yet their specific situation illustrates so many of the considerations pertinent to all marriages that other couples too should find benefit in this chapter.

In all fairness, I would not want to give the impression that the unhappy episode just related is typical of all mixed marriages. I think at the moment of an extremely intelligent Jewish woman who was miserable during her marriage to a devout, observant Jew. For some years after their divorce she remained single. Finally she married a gentile man whose first marriage had been as unhappy as hers. Though neither converted to the faith of the other, in religious observance they are virtually Jewish. Her children remain loyal Jews, his child—now living with his former wife—is Christian. They do not plan to have additional children. Together, this woman and her second husband are about as happy as any married couple I know.

Where are most intermarried couples, on a spectrum joining the two I have described? This question has never been answered, perhaps never will be. My educated guess is that few are as unhappy as the first or as happy as the second, that nearly all have had to confront very serious problems.

No one is entitled to play God in another person's life. This is why I have never deliberately advised a given couple not to marry. Such attempts would in any event almost always be doomed to fail. Not even the most persuasive combination of logic and fact is likely to triumph over the physical and emotional compulsions which bring two people to the point of marriage. Yet even if the rabbi has no right directly to dissuade them, he or she retains both the right and the responsibility to explore with them three crucial areas they may either have neglected or touched upon only casually.

The first of these is their motivation for having fallen in love with someone outside their own faith group. Our generation is so psychiatrically oriented that we look for ulterior motives and dynamics for every decision—especially for those of which we disapprove. Let it be honestly acknowledged, therefore, that it is possible for a Jew and a Christian to fall in love for no more complicated reason than that they are in most respects an uncommonly good match for one another and would like to live the rest of their lives together. Part of the price we pay for living in a democracy is that our young people of high school and college age will enjoy increasing opportunities for social contact across religious and racial lines. This, in turn, is bound to increase the incidence of romance and love between Christians and Jews, between whites and blacks.

Having said this much, however, it must also be added that a devious dynamic of some kind is more likely to prevail in a mixed marriage than in one within a given group. I have already had occasion to refer to the fact that one's choice of mate can be indirect rebellion against the parents. This is especially so when the proposed mate is of another faith. Nor is this a probability only in cases where the parents are intensely devoted to Judaism. By an odd paradox, sometimes those who have been most negligent in their own practice of Jewish life become most apoplectic at the prospect of their child's marrying out of the faith. So the threat of such a match can be a devastating weapon in the hand of those who have need to reject their parents. When the motivation is unconscious, it becomes all the more difficult to resist; the probabilities of success for the marriage are correspondingly remote.

But it is not only parents against whom young people are sometimes in rebellion when they propose marrying outside their faith. It can also be the very idea of being a Jew. Despite the many advances of recent decades in the status of American Jews, the fact remains that we are a minority group and in some respects still an underprivileged one. Particularly for Jews who have never experienced the joyous and fulfilling aspects of modern Judaism, assimilation appears to be an attractive option. They may—consciously or unconsciously—crave a social prestige or status which can be achieved, they think, only by admission to the allegedly superior majority class. And mixed marriage often seems to such people to be a one-way ticket in the direction they want to travel.

Two Christian authorities on marriage have written convincingly on this point:

If you belong to a group which as such has low social status . . . you can escape, both for yourself and your children, by marrying a person who belongs to a higher status group. Particularly is this true of minority group members who are rebellious or have moved somewhat above the social station of their group. This is shown rather clearly in a study of Gentile-Jewish intermarriages, made some years ago by J. S. Slotkin, of the University of Chicago. He speaks of the rebellious and marginal as two personality types who "amalgamate with members of the dominant group in order to raise their own status."[1]

Other studies corroborate this conclusion. They show that among those who marry outside their own racial or religious groups is to be found a disproportionate number who are "unorganized or demoralized . . . detached . . . rebellious . . . marginal. . . ."[2] A rather curious fact should be noted before we move on. As Jews in America move up the ladder of economic success, it is possible for the restiveness and ambition which often stimulate mixed marriage to operate in either direction. That is to say, a non-Jew of a lower socio-economic category may unconsciously interpret marriage to a Jew to be the same kind of improvement that a Jew desires through marriage to a socially superior Gentile.

Since such personality disorders and social ambitions are probably but not necessarily among the dynamics of mixed marriage, how can couples contemplating such a match discover the truth in their own cases? There is no easy or certain answer. They face the excruciating difficulty confronted by persons who struggle to uncover their own unconscious motivations. Certain clues, however, may be helpful. A person who feels generally inferior or insecure, who has had persistent difficulty getting along with parents, who has been generally uncomfortable or unhappy in Jewish surroundings, who has followed a pattern of dating more non-Jews than Jews, who doesn't see any point to Jewish survival—such people should indeed be wary of mixed marriage. They should at the very least postpone it, pending a most conscientious effort to examine their real motives.

NOT A NEW STORY

A second legitimate area of exploration as the rabbi counsels couples contemplating mixed marriage is the probable effect of matches such as theirs on Jewish survival. Admittedly, this will be an item of major concern only to those who really care about the perpetuation of the Jewish people and their unique civilization. It may even be—in cases where unconscious rejection of Judaism has been a dynamic from the start—that introduction of this factor may strengthen the thrust toward immediate marriage. But in such instances it is doubtful whether any argument or tactic would make a difference.

Those to whom Jewish survival is important should be made aware of the fact that historically this has always been the basis for Jewish opposition to mixed marriages. The first biblical reference to the subject is to be found in Abraham's admonition to his servant when he sent him to find a wife for his son, Isaac: ". . . I will make you swear that you will not take a wife for my son from the daughters of the Canaanites among whom I dwell, but will go to the land of my birth and get a wife for my son. . . ." (Gen. 24:3)

If Abraham was less than explicit in identifying his reason for this instruction, no room is left for guesswork when Deuteronomy restates the matter in terms of legal directives. There our ancestors were warned that when they come to the land which God has promised them and become acquainted with its inhabitants—"you shall not intermarry with them: do not give your daughters to their sons or take their daughters for your sons; for they will turn your children away from Me to worship other gods." Clearly, then, it was the manifest threat to Jewish integrity and survival—not any foolish doctrine of inherent ethnic superiority—which prompted our ancestors to oppose the practice of mixed marriage. They were aware of the fact—as true then as it is now—that, when members of a numerically small group intermarry with those of the predominant majority, the direction of assimilation will be overwhelmingly from the smaller to the larger.

Any doubt as to the motivation of ancient Jews is dispelled by two additional biblical books dealing with the subject of mixed marriage. Perhaps the strongest denunciation of this practice anywhere in Jewish literature is to be found in the Book of Ezra, written soon after the Jewish people had returned to their own land from Babylonian exile. The practice of mixed marriage had become quite common during the exile. Not only did Ezra speak against it in unequivocal language, he even went so far as to order that his Jewish contemporaries divorce their gentile wives. The danger of dissolution was grave; only extremely stringent steps could avert it. In Ezra's view, collective survival was entitled to priority over individual happiness.

Another biblical book, Ruth, speaks directly to the opposite side of the question. Here we read of a Moabite girl who becomes a heroine by virtue of her marriage to a Jew. Their marriage is described approvingly. No opposition or resentment is voiced. In fact, Ruth becomes in Jewish tradition a progenitor of King David himself! The apparent contradiction between these biblical views can be understood only in terms of the difference in historic context. First, Ruth represented a single instance of mixed marriage, not a wave which threatened to engulf the entire Jewish people. Second, she adopted Judaism as her own faith, living a dedicated Jewish life and even marrying a second Jew after her first husband had died. In short, it is not mixed marriage *per se* which Jewish tradition opposes, but mixed marriage which jeopardizes Jewish survival.

In order to arrive at an intelligent attitude toward mixed marriage in our own time, then, we must undertake to ascertain whether the historic setting today resembles that of Ezra's time or of Ruth's. There can be little doubt. The threat posed by mixed marriage today may not be quite so dramatic as it was for Ezra, but the ultimate consequences are of the same order. Our earlier speculation that in theory the freedom of democratic society would increase the incidence of such marriages has been verified in fact.

Research in the area of Washington, D.C., shows that the rate of such marriages among Jews in the latter 1950s was 13.1 percent. The true significance of these statistics rests in the fact that this was an average for the entire community. Among first-generation Jews in Greater Washington the rate was only 1.4 percent; among second-generation Jews it was 10.2 percent; by the third generation it had reached 17.9 percent.[3] More recent studies reveal that one-third or more of all marriages in the United States involving a Jew are mixed. The specific figures will vary from community to community, but there is no doubt that the general trend prevails throughout the country. The rate of mixed marriage a generation hence will most probably be even higher than it is now.

A further statistic compounds the danger to Jewish survival. There is every reason to believe that the vast majority of the children born to mixed couples are reared outside the fold of Judaism. More than just logic or common sense supports this assertion. The Washington survey disclosed that, in at least 70 percent of the mixed marriage families, the children were not identified in any way with the Jewish people. This does not justify the assumption that close to 30 percent of these families were taking positive steps to educate their children Jewishly. Just telling the children they were Jews—without in any way reinforcing the statement—sufficed as Jewish identification for the purpose of this study. Other investigations verify the fact that at best less than a fourth of the children born to mixed couples are in any way identified as Jews.[4]

These figures assume their true significance only in light of the fact that the Jewish proportion of the total population in the United States has been steadily declining. In 1937 we were 3.7 percent of the whole, in 1963 only 2.9 percent. If current trends continue, it has been estimated that by the year 2000 no more than 1.6 percent of the American population will be Jewish. We do not mean to attribute all of this to mixed marriage. Other factors, such as a lower birth rate among Jews, are of great importance. But mixed marriage is undeniably an alarming part of the problem. The individual Jew who desires Jewish survival and feels a sense of personal responsibility for it cannot enter into a mixed marriage lightly.

ANY REAL DIFFERENCE?

Is Jewish survival really important enough to constitute a valid argument against mixed marriage? To answer this question we must recognize that national and religious groups— like individuals—possess unique personalities. Each results from a whole complex of environmental circumstances and historic experiences which have shaped its attitudes and capacities. This is why French music differs from Italian music and German thought is by no means the same as Russian thought.

Civilization is an elaborate tapestry, into which each people has woven its own patterns and colors. If any major component were to be removed, the sum total would be diminished. This is as true of our Jewish people as of any other. We have made our own special kind of contribution to world thought, a contribution which no other group has made in exactly the same way. More persistently and successfully than any other historic culture, we have inquired into the essential meaning of human life and have probed the moral imperatives imposed upon us by the very nature of reality.

No knowledgeable person could doubt that this has been true in the past. Where some of us err, however, is in forgetting that it can be equally true in the future. Again, a comparison between individuals and groups is instructive. Mozart died at the age of thirty-five. Nothing less than the extinction of all civilization could ever impair his prodigious musical accomplishment. But how many works of incomparable genius remained uncomposed at the moment of his death? How much more might he have given us had he lived another decade? The well-spring of his creativity had not yet run dry, yet its flow was irretrievably stopped the moment he died.

Similarly, were the Jewish people as such to expire, the threads we have already woven into the fabric of civilization would remain, but the loom would henceforth be deprived of

our future potential. No one who believes—as I do most profoundly!—that we Jews have even more to offer human kind in
the future than we have given it in the past can view our possible disappearance with anything less than raw dismay.

What is the singular pattern which history has equipped us
to weave into the total tapestry? Within the context of a book
about marriage, my description of Judaic uniqueness will of
necessity be brief. Yet it must be attempted. For what, then,
does Judaism stand—especially, uniquely?

First, that the heart of all reality is spiritual, not physical.
It follows from this that if we are to be truly human, not just
the most complex of all animals, our primary pursuit must be
after truth, after beauty, after moral goodness—not merely
after pleasure and material wealth.

Second, there is a oneness about the universe and human-
kind. A physical oneness in the sense that everything emanated
from the same creative beginning and that the same chemical
components and natural laws are operative throughout all exis-
tence—from the remotest reaches of outer space to the minut-
est molecule within my body. There is also a spiritual oneness
which inextricably binds each person on earth to every other
person, each nation or religion or race to all others.

Third, our noblest ethical aspirations, which derive from
the very nature of reality itself, must be applied to every seg-
ment of life. There can be no asceticism, no withdrawal, no
denial. All of our experience is susceptible to sanctification.
Life is to be divided, as Martin Buber put it, not into the sacred
versus the profane, but into the sacred and the not-yet-sacred.

Fourth, all human beings on earth are my brothers and
sisters. The same ethic by which my family life should be governed must be extended to the stranger whose language I don't
understand, whose mores may even be entirely beyond my
comprehension. I who am descended from oppressed strangers must be forever compassionate to all who are either strangers or oppressed.

Fifth, religion is not a separate compartment of life but is
rather a lyric melody which recurs through all the movements
of life's symphony, enriching and enhancing the whole. Which
means to say: whatever I do as a political or civic or biological

being must be influenced by what I am as a religious person.

Sixth, our greatest need today, if humanity is to survive, is a synthesis of the particular and the universal. We must learn to live as citizens of our respective nations, yet simultaneously as citizens of the world. No one is in a better position to succeed at this excruciatingly difficult task than we. For only we Jews on the world scene today exist in part as a separate nation, living on a soil of its own, yet also as a universal people, scattered over most of the planet. In humanity's ineluctable, urgent, desperate pursuit of peace, we Jews constitute—whether we deliberately will it so or not—as we have in other contexts so many times in the past—an experimental human laboratory, testing for the whole human race concepts and ideals calculated to achieve salvation.

Are we Jews the only ones dedicated to the foregoing emphases? It would be foolish to reply affirmatively. One or another of these values may, of course, by now be found elsewhere, in other cultures and among other individuals. But Judaism originated them as a comprehensive, cohesive pattern. Judaism holds them bound closely together in an integrated, organic whole which issues out of our collective historic experience. Judaism at its best expresses and reinforces them, without destructive reservations and without adulteration by other insights which are less than faithful to the spirit of these. Judaism, therefore, can best develop them as a pattern for the future. It can, that is, if it survives.

Even with reference to ideals which are universal, Judaism possesses its unique modes of expression. Take, for example, the ideal of freedom—certainly by no means restricted just to Jews. Freedom means something in Judaism that it means nowhere else. No event has been rehearsed more frequently in the telling of our people's history than the Exodus from Egyptian slavery. This could almost be called the seminal episode of our entire past. Out of it grows the ceremonial syndrome of the Passover seder and the intense preoccupation of Jews as such with the struggle of all minorities for emancipation. From this source also emerges the obsession of the Jewish people to retain its freedom in Israel. If the Jewish people and culture were to vanish, the universal cause of freedom—celebration of its past accomplishment and encouragement for its future struggle—would thereby be diminished.

There is much, then, to be lost by assimilation. Civilization would be bereft of Jewish music, Jewish literature, Jewish art, and—above all—of the rich continuing possibilities of Jewish spiritual insight. Is it too much to ask the young Jew who is enamored of a Gentile to think of this? I hope not.

A THIRD CONSIDERATION

The rabbi who spurs young couples to examine their own motives for desiring mixed marriage may be expecting more than most will be capable of achieving. The rabbi's argument for Jewish survival will probably touch only those to whom this survival has already assumed importance. But a third proper area of concern—the prospect for happiness in marriage—will be minimized or ignored by any prospective bride and groom only at their own peril.

The plain, unvarnished, inescapable fact is that couples of mixed religious background have a substantially lower prospect for success than do couples within a given group. This is true both religiously and racially. Everything we have said about interreligious marriages, as a matter of fact, applies with added emphasis to interracial marital partnerships. As our society is currently constituted and is likely to be for a long time to come, the odds faced by a black/white couple are even more formidable than those confronting a Gentile/Jewish couple.

Let the truth be acknowledged: every marriage is to some extent a gamble against risks. The balance between maturity and love on the one hand, and tension and stress on the other, is often precarious. Construction engineers know that, if they impose upon a steel beam greater weight than it was fabricated to carry, they take a chance that the whole building will collapse. The same thing is true in marriage, though unfortunately the weight which can be carried by any specific couple cannot be calculated with anything like the precision available to the builder. The additional burdens inherent in an interreligious or interracial marriage—over and above those to be carried by every couple—increase the risk enormously. One of the most agonizing frustrations faced by every marriage counselor is the difficulty of impressing this upon the couple contemplating mixed marriage. All such couples without exception, admitting the danger in principle, are firmly convinced of their own ability to surmount all obstacles. The fact that many of them return later to acknowledge the grim truth is of little consolation or help to the conscientious counselors in their effort to aid the next couples.

The statistical evidence is convincing. It discloses the divorce rate in cases of mixed marriage to be between three and four times that in other marriages. In one of the earliest authentic scientific studies of marriage, Burgess and Cottrell concluded that the chance for marital success is eleven times greater where husband and wife agree on all religious matters than where they differ. A study made by the American Youth Commission revealed the number of young people in several categories who were found to come from broken homes:

Both parents Jewish .... 4.6 percent
Both parents Catholic .... 6.4 percent
Both parents Protestant .... 6.8 percent
Parents from mixed religions .... 15.2 percent
Parents with no religion .... 16.7 percent

It is the fourth of these figures which concerns us most directly here. It confirms the conclusions of all other available surveys.

There is no need to exaggerate. No one at all conversant with the matter would pretend that no mixed marriages ever succeed. Religious background is scarcely the only factor adding up to failure or success in marriage. But it is one of the more important considerations. At an earlier point I emphasized the importance of cultural compatibility. Religion is an important aspect of culture, far more important than is often realized by a young couple about to be married. A host of religious experiences and impressions has already been absorbed into the total personality of both bride and groom, many more than either of them may consciously remember. These cannot easily be erased or expunged.

Religion involves more than theological doctrine. This is especially true of Judaism, which has always been more a way of life than of belief. Judaism involves one's attitudes toward the meaning of life, frames of reference regarding sex, patterns of family behavior, idioms and idiosyncracies of expression, peculiarities of food, and holiday rituals. A Jew who is accustomed to observing Chanukah and Passover might find it painfully difficult to celebrate Christmas and Easter instead. A Christian who had been baptized and had regularly taken Communion could feel lost, even ineradicably guilty, in the absence of these practices. There are many subtle yet vital aspects of each person's life no less imperative for the fact that they may have been taken for granted—the absence or disruption of which can cause extreme unhappiness.

No couple can afford to ignore all this, not even if religion seems currently to bear no special importance to either partner. They perpetrate a gross injustice against themselves if they "freeze" their spiritual lives in what may well be only a temporary climate of indifference. We shall see in our next chapter that religion can and should be one of the most creative forces enriching the relationship between husband and wife. This often proves to be true even of couples who, at the time of their marriage, are still religiously neutral. At the very least, interreligious marriage precludes this entire area of sharing. It may also transpose what should be a positive, love-inducing phase of life into a cause of friction and hate.

Christian authorities have no need to be concerned with Jewish survival or with the persistence of their own religious traditions. Since the direction of assimilation will most often be toward rather than away from them, in strictly mundane terms they stand to gain, not to lose from mixed marriages. The fact that they are nevertheless so frequently and emphatically opposed is based on the danger such marriages pose to the couples involved. No doubt this is what motivated the General Conference of the Methodist Church to declare in 1956 that "recent research has emphasized the importance of common cultural and religious backgrounds as the foundation of successful marriage. . . . Ministers are urged to discuss with both youths and parents the likelihood of failure in mixed marriages."[5] In 1959 the Lutheran Church Missouri Synod adopted a statement affirming that "religious agreement between a husband and wife is undoubtedly one of the major factors in securing that peace and harmony that makes possible the normal functions and development of Christian family life."[6]

Secular experts on marriage are generally in agreement. Thus Dr. Clarence Leuba, professor emeritus of psychology at Antioch College, concludes:

> In every marriage there are bound to be some outstanding differences in interests, attitudes, and beliefs; but a marriage cannot stand too many of them. . . . Cultural, religious, or racial differences are of this sort; they are likely to have far-reaching effects on marital adjustments. . . . Where the marriage partners come from different religious, economic, political, or social backgrounds, there are endless possible sources of irritation.[7]

TUG OF WAR

All these considerations are true in the first instance in the immediate relationship between husband and wife. What gives them very special urgency, however, is the problem of children born to a mixed couple. If one wanted to be callous or crude, one could simply say that two people who disregard so many compelling factors in marriage deserve whatever of grief they thereby bring upon themselves. But their children are entirely innocent—they made no choice, they had no alternatives, they did not even ask to be born. Yet how often they are the most piteous victims of the religious divergence between their parents!

Orthodox and Conservative Jews subscribe to the traditional view that the child of a mixed marriage automatically follows the religion of the mother. With or without the conversion of a Christian husband to Judaism, then, so long as his wife remains Jewish, their children are considered Jews. Reform

Judaism relies more on parental intention than on the mother's faith. In the eyes of Reform, no matter which parent is Jewish, regardless of whether the Christian partner was converted, the fact that parents choose to enroll their children in a synagogue school and see them through to *Bar Mitzvah* and Confirmation qualifies these youngsters as Jews. But these fine distinctions among the several branches of Judaism have little to do with the gnawing insecurity from which the offspring of a mixed marriage are likely to suffer.

Children's most desperate need is to know where they belong. If born to religiously mixed parents, they are not likely to achieve this security. They will probably be made to suffer certain disadvantages by virtue of the fact that one parent is or was Jewish—wondering from time to time why they cannot choose to be identified instead with the other who is not Jewish —oblivious to the positive pride which comes from knowledge of Judaism and which can provide an effective antidote to painful prejudice.

Again, this is more than just theory. I remember a woman who came to me years ago, insisting that I convert her to Judaism prior to officiating at her marriage to a Jewish man. Her unexpected vehemence elicited my curiosity. When questioned, she said: "Rabbi, I am myself the product of a mixed Protestant-Catholic marriage. I know in my own blood and bones the terrible uncertainty which afflicts such a child. Under no circumstances would I ever cause such pain to any child of mine. This is why I insist that my marriage be based on a religiously unified home!"

Where unity is not achieved, children often become hapless victims of an emotional tug of war; if not between their parents, then perhaps between competing grandparents. It is extremely difficult for two families of divergent religious loyalties not to press their respective points of view, however subtly, upon their grandchildren. And the consequence—more often than some of us would like to contemplate—is a confused, neurotic child.

Sometimes even intelligent parents deceive themselves on this score. They act as if all the problems posed by interfaith marriage have been solved, but their children reveal the truth

—in erratic behavior when they are young, or in confidential conversation with trusted advisors when they reach high school or college age. It is not uncommon for a rabbi, psychiatrist, or college professor to hear from the offspring of such marriages that even at a tender age they detected the religious animosity between their parents and felt a devastating war being waged through and over themselves.

Not only do parents often use their children as pawns in working out their unresolved religious conflicts, children also play their parents one against the other. Several of my colleagues have been confronted in recent years with adolescent, usually post-*Bar* and *Bat Mitzvah* children who refused to continue their religious education. Their justification was that, since only one parent was Jewish, they reserved the right to follow the one who was gentile. The problem is serious, potentially disruptive enough even when it is thus expressed on a conscious level. When repressed to the unconscious, it becomes much more explosive, both to the marriage and to the mental health of the youngsters.

Neat intellectual solutions agreed upon in theory before the wedding seldom stand up to the stubborn demands of life. The agreement of the parents cited at the outset of this chapter —to stagger their children's religious education between synagogue and church—would be funny if it were not so tragic. The cost to the children, in confusion and hopeless despair, is inordinately high. The crux of the difficulty is that not even the wisest and most perceptive of young people can anticipate in advance just how the experiences of parenthood will affect them. To agree intellectually in advance that one's child will be reared in no religious tradition, or in that of one's mate, may seem at the time like such a simple, sensible solution. But when the child is actually here, snuggled in one's arms, suddenly the whole experience becomes overwhelmingly emotional, not just intellectual. Circumcision, *Bar/Bat Mitzvah,* and Confirmation for the Jew—Baptism and Communion for the Christian—no matter how little these seemed to mean to each at an earlier stage of life, may now loom as matters of utmost urgency.

A Lutheran in my community once came to see me. Or at least I had known him for several years as a Lutheran. Only after several highly charged false starts sitting at the opposite side of my desk did he reveal to me that he had been born a Jew. Religion had meant so little to him that he felt no sense of sacrifice at all in glibly agreeing with his Lutheran wife that their children would follow her faith. In the case of their elder child, a daughter, this hadn't seemed to pose any unusual problems. But he had come to see me in desperation now because his son was just six months short of his thirteenth birthday. "Rabbi," he blurted out sporadically between tears, "I have suddenly realized that this boy of mine will be the first male in our family for centuries not to celebrate a *Bar Mitzvah.* I haven't been able to sleep one night since this thought came to me. What can I do?"

No one in such a situation at the age of twenty-five can be entirely immune from this kind of shattering experience a decade and a half later.

"WHAT CAN I DO?"

Have I betrayed my self-imposed charge not to play God in other people's lives? Have I come down so hard in intervening pages on the couples contemplating mixed marriage as actually to attempt dissuading them? I hope not, for this has not been my intention. I wanted rather, with all my mind and heart, to apprise them of the rough road most probably ahead in the hope that I might help them prepare for their journey. If I knew the trip two people had planned for themselves was charted over a route scarred with ridges and pits, would I not be responsible for warning them in advance? I feel the same sort of responsibility toward the reader who may be on the threshold of a mixed marriage.

It was too late for an effective answer to my Lutheran friend's anguished "What can I do?" Had he asked me the same question sixteen years earlier, I might have been able to help.

How? First, by doing precisely what I have attempted in the preceding paragraphs: spelling out the kind of problems he would have to face. To proceed as if they didn't exist, or blithely to assume that "we're different, we'll be the exception, our love will be strong enough to surmount any obstacle . . ." is to invite disaster.

My second way of helping would have been to suggest the desirability of his non-Jewish sweetheart's studying Judaism, even considering conversion to Judaism, before their marriage took place. This is not an easy kind of advice to give. Not for one who is firmly convinced, as I am, that religious conversion should never be undertaken purely for expediency. My faith means far too much to me to permit that it be treated cheaply or lightly. The only person who has a moral right to convert, the only person whom I as a rabbi would ever be willing to help convert, is one who, after carefully studying Judaism, has arrived at the genuine conviction that it holds out a set of values and practices which can enhance his or her life.

Obviously I have this possibility in mind in suggesting that the prospective gentile mate of a Jew undertake the study of Judaism. But no commitment should be either expected or accepted until that course of study nears its completion. Even if it does not lead to conversion, it holds the patent advantage of helping the non-Jew understand the background of the Jew and some of the problems with which their marriage will have to contend.

My rabbinic experience has revealed an annoying and aggravating pattern regarding conversion. More often than I would ever have suspected, the Christian partner to a proposed mixed marriage is discouraged from conversion only by the reluctance of the Jew involved. At times I have even suspected that the Christian was almost waiting to be asked, would indeed have welcomed the thought, but sensed the resistance of the prospective mate. Such reticence, to be sure, is usually couched in the language of lofty universalism. "What right do I have to ask my future mate to become Jewish when I would never consider becoming a Christian?" The heart of the matter, however, is usually that Judaism means little or nothing to the Jewish groom or bride. If it did, if the possibility of conversion were introduced, not as a dictatorial decree, but for the sake of a happier marriage and healthier children, there would be more Jews by choice as well as more successful marriages.

Every rabbi is confronted by couples who have agreed that their children will eventually be reared as Jews, but who stop short of actual conversion prior to being married. Such couples need to think through in greater depth the implications of their decision. Most cases of mixed marriage involve a Jewish groom and a gentile bride. For the Orthodox Jew, this immediately poses a problem; according to rabbinic law a child automatically follows the faith of its mother. But even those who no longer accept such laws literally must recognize that the religious flavor of the home is determined in most cases more by the mother than the father. One must wonder, then, just how feasible it is for a non-Jewish mother to succeed in rearing Jewish children. Even where the prospective husband is the gentile, the domestic tensions and competitions already discussed remain as potential aggravations unless conversion precedes marriage.

Why do I suggest only that the non-Jew consider conversion to Judaism? Why not conversion in the opposite direction? My first and primary reason emerges from our previous discussion on Jewish survival. One of my most sacred responsibilities as a rabbi is to do my utmost to increase the prospects for meaningful Jewish survival. It is only through a unified *Jewish* home that this becomes possible.

But there is another reason, perhaps even a more practical one, for thinking only in terms of a change to Judaism. Most couples of mixed religious background soon discover that in any event all or nearly all their social life turns out to be with Jewish friends. Their children, moreover, are generally considered by their peers to be Jews. This means that such couples and their families are Jews *de facto,* that they experience the superficial and often negative aspects of Jewish life, whether or not they choose to participate in the positive and creative advantages of being Jewish.

RABBIS' DILEMMA

My telephone rang insistently. A good friend was calling to tell me of her daughter's engagement and wedding plans. Of course, I congratulated her. She asked me to consult my calendar for a date and time, assuming that as her rabbi and family friend I would officiate. Only after we had completed all the arrangements did she mention—almost as an afterthought—that her future son-in-law was not Jewish.

Should I officiate at the wedding? My love for the bride and her family encouraged me to say *yes*. My responsibilities as a rabbi forced me to refuse.

No Orthodox or Conservative rabbi will officiate at a mixed marriage wedding ceremony. Neither will the great majority of Reform rabbis; a minority will, though the Central Conference of American Rabbis has officially urged its members not to. I stand with the majority in believing that—as a rabbi—I have a right to officiate only where two Jews are involved and the prospect for Jewish survival is good. I cannot and must not forget the statistics about Jewish identity given earlier in this chapter. My obligation as a rabbi is to maximize, not minimize, the probability that there will be a viable Jewish community in the United States five hundred years from now.

I am aware also of the fact that all too often couples asking rabbis to officiate for a mixed marriage are actually "using" them—either to give the appearance that theirs is a Jewishly valid marriage . . . or to appease their guilt . . . or to mollify unhappy parents or grandparents. My Judaism is too precious to allow my complicity in such a ploy. Like the overwhelming majority of American rabbis, therefore, I am always willing to meet with such couples, if they wish, to discuss with them the very real problems they will face, to help them in any way I can, consistent with my principles and conscience. And I accept them as a couple—as friends and members of my congregation if they so desire, regardless of how or by whom they are married. As a rabbi, I owe them no less than that. They, in turn, owe me respect for my integrity and understanding of my position.

It is significant, incidentally, that a very high proportion of those who call me to inquire about my officiating aren't in the least interested in coming to see me no matter how politely or generously I offer to help. Their concern is less with Jewish survival or adding a genuinely religious note to their ceremony or even with their own ultimate happiness than with finding a rabbi who will oblige. To consent to exploitation as an expedient, to be "used" in order to make such a marriage more palatable to parents or grandparents, is less a favor to the insistent couple than to force a hard, penetrating confrontation with reality. The couples unable or unwilling to reach a definitive resolution of their many problems prior to marriage will not find it easier to do so afterward, when more than a few additional complications will have entered the picture.

A religious marriage ceremony can be Jewish or Christian or Moslem. To force an uneasy synthesis, to pretend that it can be all three or even two, is to make a mockery of all religious tradition. Better an honest civil ceremony than one which pretends to the impossible. I have respect for many of my colleagues who officiate at mixed marriage ceremonies, however serious the mistake I am convinced they are making. I have no respect for those who officiate together with a minister or priest, making of the Judaism I love only an ingredient in a recipe or stew which is calculated to produce indigestion.

Do rabbis who refuse to officiate at a mixed marriage thereby reject the couples, driving them forever away from Judaism? Not unless such couples are searching for an easy rationalization to justify their own rejection of Judaism. Not if the rabbi is considerate and they are mature. Whenever possible, the rabbi's reasons should be expressed, not in a perfunctory telephone conversation or letter, but in a relaxed personal interview. He or she should make it clear that the refusal to violate one's professional conscience does not constitute personal rejection, that Judaism and the synagogue are willing to accept the couple as human beings and to acknowledge the validity of their marriage even if it has been solemnized at a civil ceremony.

Naturally, a rabbi is convinced that something important is lost when such a ceremony replaces the religious ritual. But couples who pose complicated problems must not expect the rabbi to be a miracle worker who can find perfect solutions for them. They may have to settle realistically for the best of several imperfect alternatives. It is they, after all, not the rabbi, who created the problem. The rabbi's responsibility is limited to compassionate understanding, to truthful explanation, and to an open door policy which will encourage the couples to return, if they wish, for continued discussion even after they are wedded.

THE SPECIFICS OF CONVERSION

In all major branches of American Judaism the primary prerequisite for conversion is a thorough process of study. The curriculum and method of instruction will vary from branch to branch, even from rabbi to rabbi. In Orthodoxy the content of the candidate's instruction is likely to center mostly on the ritual laws involved in maintaining a Jewish home. In Reform these procedures will be less central than the study of Jewish history and thought. A Conservative rabbi will probably strike some degree of middle ground between the other two.

Both Reform and Conservative Judaism have established unified classes for conversion in most metropolitan centers. In smaller communities the instruction is more likely to be given by an individual rabbi. A bibliography at the end of this volume contains material for any non-Jewish reader who is unable to consult a rabbi or class but desires to learn more about Judaism.

The ritual requirements for conversion vary among the branches of Judaism. Orthodox law demands that a male convert be circumcised and immersed in a מקוה (*mikveh*) or ritual bath; a female convert also requires immersion. These traditional procedures are waived by most Reform rabbis, retained by a few. Most Conservative rabbis will probably approximate the Orthodox pattern. In Reform Judaism the ceremony itself consists of a brief prayer service, often held in the synagogue or chapel before the opened ark. The converts promise to accept Judaism, to cast their lot under all circumstances with the Jewish people, and to rear their children as Jews. Though Reform Judaism does not insist on the circumcision of adult males, it generally does expect a pledge that any male children born to the couple will be circumcised.

A conversion to Judaism under Reform auspices is accepted by no Orthodox rabbi, by some but not all Conservative rabbis. This is likely to be an issue for converts in the United States under only two circumstances: if they or their children later wish to marry an Orthodox Jew; or if they should eventually settle in Israel. The situation in Israel is disturbing. In civil law there, one who is converted by a Reform or Conservative rabbi is included under the Law of Return, which provides immediate, automatic citizenship for any Jewish immigrant who desires it. Orthodox religious leadership in Israel has been unsuccessful in its attempt to change that law. Religiously, however, the official rabbinate in Israel does not consider such a person to be a Jew. A continuing and persistent effort has been mounted by non-Orthodox Jews throughout the world to bring Israel's religious practice into focus with civil law in this respect.

The conversion of a non-Jew to Judaism is frequently a traumatic experience for the Christian family. To a lesser degree, but sometimes in a troublesome way nonetheless, acceptance of a convert can be difficult for a Jewish family. Actually, it should not be. Our tradition is unambiguous on the matter. Though Judaism has not actively sought converts through the greater part of its history, it has always welcomed them warmly. Jewish law insists that a genuine convert is in nearly every respect a Jew. The only exception would be that a convert could not become a כהן (*kohen*), a priest. Maimonides was asked whether a convert to Judaism—in view of his biological background—should join the congregation in the prayer which commences, "Our God and God of our fathers. . . ." His answer was affirmative; he held that once a person has accepted our faith, that person is to be considered as if even the ancestors had been Jews. We are enjoined, moreover, by Jewish tradition never to remind converts of the fact that they were not born as Jews, lest they thereby be embarrassed.

It would be foolish to assume that, because of our tradition and law, every Jewish parent will immediately and fully accept a converted daughter- or son-in-law. Patience and love on the part of the involved couple can help; in some cases the assistance of a cooperative rabbi might also be sought. Both sets of parents should be treated respectfully and lovingly, unless they, by irrational and unreasonable behavior, make this impossible. Their needs are very real, often extremely urgent, and are not to be treated casually.

The Jew whose mate has converted for the sake of a happier marriage and a unified home assumes serious responsibilities as a consequence. The first of these is to study Judaism along with the candidate for conversion. Once or twice in the earliest years of my rabbinic career I experienced the unhappy suspicion that a man or woman whom I was converting may have known more about Judaism than the Jewish counterpart. To avoid this intolerable situation, I insisted that both parties study together.

The Jewish mate must accept also an obligation to practice a meaningful Jewish life, not to act indifferently toward that which the spouse has worked so hard to attain. I have been involved in two instances where a convert to Judaism desired many years later to revert to her original faith, simply because her "Jewish" husband seemed to have no use for Judaism, never observed the rituals of his faith at home, never attended services of worship. Surely we have no right to expect of converts a greater regard for Judaism than we who were born to it are ready to exhibit ourselves.

A final word on the subject of mixed marriage. Conversion is not a perfect preventive against all abrasions. The varying backgrounds of the individuals involved obviously cannot be obliterated. In a sense, all of us are at any given moment the sum total of heredity plus all the experiences we have ever known. Not even a sincere conversion based on study and commitment can erase the digits which add up to what each individual is at the moment of marriage. What it can do is to influence the future, if not the past; it can pave the way toward a unified quest for the ultimate meaning of life and a spiritually harmonious setting for the rearing of happy children.

CHAPTER FIFTEEN

Your Small Sanctuary

A rabbi who proclaims that religion is an important ingredient of successful marriage may be suspected of special pleading. There is much evidence from impartial sources, however, to substantiate this view. Reference was made just a few pages back to an American youth commission study. Even more alarming than the proportion of divorces it revealed among couples of mixed religious background was the evidence of failure by those who claimed no religious affiliation. Among students born to Jewish parents, 4.6 percent came from broken homes; the comparable percentage among those whose parents practiced no religion was 16.7!

Bishop James A. Pike of the Episcopal Church called our attention to surveys showing that the divorce rate among couples who are identified with neither synagogue nor church runs two and a quarter times that of couples who actively share a common religious tradition.[1] Evelyn and Sylvanus Duvall summarize a number of similar studies by saying:

> ... those who rate high in religiousness in all of the faith groups have a high happiness rating in marriage and a low divorce rate. Success in marriage is closely related to whether the married couple have religious or non-religious families.[2]

A survey made at the University of Southern California disclosed that among couples belonging to the same church 68 percent of the men were happily married; in a comparable group where neither husband nor wife was a church member only 31 percent of the men had achieved marital happiness.[3]

The Oklahoma City Family Clinic reached a similar conclusion. In attempting to reconcile 250 couples whose marriages were rocky, the clinic staff achieved much greater success with those who attended church services than with others. It was concluded that participation together in religious activities made reconciliation "almost a certainty."[4]

These impressive statistics should not be misinterpreted. They do not mean that active religious affiliation guarantees success in marriage. Certainly a religious identification which is only nominal—which amounts to no more than an annual payment of dues plus a semiannual antipasto of public worship —can exert little or no favorable effect on a marriage. What our studies do indicate is that, all else being equal, the active sharing of a religious life can be an important contribution to any couple's happiness. There seems to be almost an intuitive acceptance of this truth even among those who show no other evidence of religiosity. How else explain the fact that, despite the legal respectability of civil ceremonies, the overwhelming majority of Americans ask a rabbi, minister, or priest to officiate at their weddings? Or that so many who seldom frequent a synagogue or church are nonetheless anxious to have their marriage solemnized in a sanctuary?

The noteworthy correlation between religious affiliation and marital happiness should not surprise us. It can be explained in part by the fact that the personal characteristics which impel people toward the religious life in large part coincide with those which make for good marriages. Even more significant, however, is our earlier conclusion that the more two persons share of cultural background and interests in general, the happier their marriage is likely to be. If this is true with regard to aspects of culture such as literature, music, or art— how much truer with regard to religious faith! Two who share an active quest for the ultimate meaning of human life, who search together for their cosmic address, who strive to comprehend whether or not their love reflects an ineffable Source of Love in the universe—two such as these have touched together as deeply in their sharing as is humanly possible. Their marriage is likely to achieve a dimension which is attainable in no other way. Dr. James A. Peterson puts this point with exceptional clarity:

> Religious values, when sincerely believed and made a pivotal part of one's aspirations, must contribute to marital adjustment because these are the very values that are most necessary for it. . . . It matters in marriage whether a couple reach upward in their common interests toward that which is creative and lofty or whether they are content with that which is tawdry and inconsequential.[5]

ADDED EMPHASIS

It matters especially in Judaism. A religious civilization such as ours, which has always emphasized deed more than creed, must necessarily impinge on marriage at many points. Many centuries ago the Midrash recognized the importance of religion in marriage: "No man without a woman, nor a woman without a man, nor both of them without God."[6]

The rabbis indulged in an intriguing play on words to illustrate this truth. They observed that the Hebrew word for man is איש (*ish*), while that for woman is אשה (*ishah*). The first of these words contains the letter י, which is missing from the second; the second contains the letter ה, which is not found in the first. These two letters together spell one of the Hebrew abbreviations for God. When they are removed from the Hebrew for *man* and *woman,* there remains in each case the word אש (*esh*), meaning *fire*. From this our rabbis deduced that, when God is removed from the relationship between man and woman, nothing but consuming fire remains. Only if God is present in all they experience together, is it possible for their marriage to be fully human.[7]

Thus—and in many other ways—did the ancient teachers of Judaism emphasize the importance of religion to marriage. There are numerous contexts within which a sensitive person can feel a close personal relationship to God. We sense God in the beauty of the universe, in a mystical awareness of kinship between ourselves and the rest of nature, in the emergent thrust of life toward higher evolutionary goals, in our own moral aspirations and values, in the exquisite excitement of discovering a new truth, in our recognition of cosmic purpose to which, if we will, we can contribute.

But in the love of husband and wife—more than in any other experience accessible to human reach—we come close to the divine spirit which permeates the universe. And in the love act which unites both body and soul, through which they can initiate a new life—more than in anything else they do—married couples become God's creative partners. To experience and appreciate this is to know marriage in its noblest dimension.

On almost every page of this volume we have encountered some insight of Judaism on love and marriage. Memorizing them will not automatically assure your happiness. It is important to know the marriage and family ideals of Judaism, but also to realize that there is often a gap between intellectual understanding and emotional acceptance. The distance between head and heart is not always twelve inches; sometimes it proves to be many miles. Not everyone is capable of achieving the kind of marriage envisaged by our tradition.

All of us are moved by unconscious as well as conscious factors. This is likely to be especially true in our sex lives. Most of us are ordinarily able to live comfortably without exploring our unconscious. We manage to keep our intentions and performances sufficiently aligned to maintain good health and self-respect. Where this is not the case, where even the most diligent effort seems unavailing in an individual's desire to implement the marital ideals of his or her faith, it may be that psychotherapy is indicated.

But this will be the exception rather than the rule. Just as most of us can go through life successfully without surgery, so most have no need of psychotherapy, which perhaps might be defined as a form of emotional surgery. The important thing to remember is that our conduct is motivated, not only by the unconscious pushing us from below, but also by our conscious values and ideals pulling us upward from above. It is here that the values emerging from Judaism can be of such vital help.

"MY BELOVED IS MINE"

Because our rabbis appreciated the immense importance of religion in marriage, they devised a marriage ceremony of singular significance and beauty. They called it קִדּוּשִׁין *(kiddu-shin)*, coming from the same root as קִדּוּשׁ *(kiddush)* and קַדִּישׁ *(kaddish)* and expressing the idea of sanctity. Originally designating the betrothal ceremony, קִדּוּשִׁין became the term most commonly used for the combined rituals as we know them today. The details of a Jewish wedding ceremony vary from group to group; the essentials are the same. There are seven Hebrew blessings which acknowledge God as the universal Source of Love and identify the couple being married with the whole of Jewish tradition. Bride and groom drink from either one or two glasses of wine, symbolizing the fact that henceforth they will taste together both the happiness and sorrow of life. As the groom places a ring on the bride's finger, he recites the following formula: הרי את מקדשת לי בטבעת זו כדת משה וישראל *(Hare at mekudeshet li betaba-at zo kedat mosheh veyisrael)*—"By this ring, you are consecrated unto me (as my wife), in accordance with the faith of Moses and of Israel." In traditional ceremonies the ring must be a plain gold band, without engraving or stones. Reform rabbis permit use of the ring the bride plans to wear permanently, even if it is adorned. The ring symbolizes a sum of money which earlier Jewish grooms handed to their brides during the ceremony.

Increasingly in modern times the bride also places a ring on her groom's finger. Apparently this practice was known even in ancient days, for the Talmud suggests a formula for her to recite.[8] That formula seems never to have been adopted, however, as common usage. Some rabbis today simply ask the bride to repeat the groom's declaration with a change of gender, making it: הרי אתה מקדש לי בטבעת זו כדת משה וישראל *(Hare atah mekudash li betaba-at zo kedat mosheh veyisrael)*—"By this ring, you are consecrated unto me (as my husband), in accordance with the faith of Moses and of Israel." Other rabbis direct the bride to address her groom in words taken from Song of Songs: דודי לי ואני לו (Dodi li va'ani lo)—"My beloved is mine and I am his."

Jewish tradition suggests that at the very end of the ceremony the groom break a glass by stomping on it with his foot. Most Reform rabbis deem this to be an optional part of the ceremony, following the wishes of the couple. This custom probably goes back to pre-Jewish primitive times, when among various nations and tribes it was customary to break a piece of ceramic or glass on happy occasions. People who were rejoicing over a birth or a wedding considered themselves to be especially vulnerable to attack by evil spirits. By breaking some object of value, they thought perhaps they could either frighten these spirits away or convince them that they were really suffering enough already and should be left alone.

Many religious rituals of modern faiths can thus be traced back to their origins in prehistoric superstition. This does not necessarily invalidate them. The important thing is not the inception of a given custom but the reason attributed to it later by a developing tradition. In this case our rabbis explained that a Jew should pause even in the happiest moment of life to remember the destruction of the Temple in Jerusalem. Hence, the breaking of the glass.

Another explanation offered in the Talmud makes a point very much needed in our own time.

> Mar bar Rabina made a marriage feast for his son. He observed that the rabbis present were very gay. So he seized an expensive goblet worth 400 zuzim and broke it before them. Thus he made them somber. When Rab Ashi made a marriage feast for his son, he also noticed that the rabbis were rejoicing excessively. So he took a costly cup of white glass and broke it before them. This filled them with sorrow.[9]

I shall resume this thought in a moment. Suffice it to say for the present that if the rabbi is willing to leave the decision on the breaking of a glass up to the bride and groom, they should consider the reasons summarized above and decide in accordance with their own desires.

We return to the ceremony. Among Orthodox and Conservative Jews the bride and groom stand beneath a marriage canopy known in Hebrew as a חופה *(chupah)*. Sometimes in Reform or Conservative ceremonies a simulated חופה is used, made of flowers. As part of their ceremonies Orthodox and Conservative rabbis read what is known as a כתובה *(ketubah)*, a contract in which the groom accepts certain legal obligations and financial responsibilities toward his bride. Reform rabbis use either a simple marriage certificate or a revised form of the כתובה , one in which husband and wife assume mutual responsibilities to each other.

Why have a wedding ceremony at all? Why not just require both parties to appear before the proper authority and sign a document indicating their intention to live together? From time to time every rabbi hears such proposals made seriously. Often it takes the form of a direct challenge: "What does a piece of paper add to the way we feel toward each other?"

Well, I suppose the most immediate answer is that not all pieces of paper are identical. The wrapper of a candy bar is a piece of paper. So are a piece of Kleenex . . . an Israel bond . . . this page . . . the Constitution of the United States . . . a graduation diploma . . . a Bible verse . . . a treasured family photograph . . . a love letter. The piece of paper on which your כתובה or marriage certificate is printed is important only as it finalizes the dramatic ceremony symbolizing the most significant partnership in which you will ever participate. If your marriage comes even close to the high ideals of Judaism, if it even approximates the rich relationship it can and should be, then it is worth celebrating and remembering. If, on the other hand, it is just a casual agreement, an interim experiment, a temporary trial, then it isn't worth either a special ceremony or a "piece of paper."

In every civilization, human beings have felt the need to dramatize the most meaningful moments and transitions of their lives—most notably birth, puberty, marriage, death. The

Soviet Union has been far from successful in its attempt to eliminate religious ritual from the lives of its people. The government, as a matter of fact, has tried at times to create so-called secular rituals to satisfy an apparently insatiable human need for dramatic ceremonies to mark life's most exciting and crucial experiences. Marriage is certainly such an experience. Our Jewish wedding rituals lift the new relationship between wife and husband to its loftiest level, uniting the couple spiritually to each other, to their people, to the cosmic Source of Love. More about ritual in a moment.

A LIMIT TO AFFLUENCE

We may safely assume that what bothered Mar bar Rabina and Rab Ashi was not excessive joy as such but rather a lack of proper dignity and restraint. In many periods of our history this has been the concern of Jewish religious authorities. The eminent historian, Dr. Salo Baron, attests to this in the following paragraphs:

> Beginning with the fifteenth century, more and more communal organs, regional as well as local, felt the need of issuing a *pragmatica,* or some other ordinance, describing in great detail the articles of clothing which might be worn by various individuals on certain occasions, the number of guests and musicians who might be invited to certain functions, and the amount and type of food which might be served at such celebrations. Various reasons were advanced in justification of such sumptuary ordinances: the envy of ever suspicious gentile neighbors usually aroused by a display of costly garments or jewelry and by revelry in feasting; the attempt to keep up with the neighbors which led to the impoverishment of numerous families and converted many a celebration into a sorrowful occasion; the frequent indebtedness of extravagant celebrants to Gentiles and the ensuing enmity in the case of bankruptcy; the obliteration of what were considered legitimate dis-

tinctions between rich and poor or, on the contrary, the underscoring of such distinctions. . . .

. . . The Castilian Synod of 1432 . . . ordered the communities to call within thirty days a meeting for the purpose of regulating expenditure for food "at the time of betrothals and weddings and the birth of a child and other seasons of rejoicing." The need for such regulation was felt most strongly in Italy, where the gay and colorful life of the general population invited imitation. . . . The Conference of Forli in 1418, acting for many North Italian communities and prompted by the consideration that the Jews spent on banquets "more than they could afford and more than the wealthy Christians among whom we live," reduced the number of guests who might be invited to a wedding to a maximum of twenty men, ten married women, and five girls in addition to relatives up to the third degree (second cousins). Transgressors were to be punished by a fine of one ducat for each guest in excess of the permitted number. . . . The communities of the County Wied-Runkel thought that they were adopting "a truly profitable and acceptable ordinance" when they forbade the invitation of any guests except relatives to the third degree for weddings, to the second degree for other festivities. . . .[10]

There are intriguing contemporary overtones at various points in the foregoing; certain phrases sound almost as if they had been written today. Yet if our problems are quite similar, the circumstances surrounding them are vastly different. We no longer have Jewish communities with the power to issue compulsory decrees and to police them. Whatever restraint is exercised today, therefore, must be voluntary, resulting from the discipline and good taste of the individual rather than the power of the community. While there are one or two American cities in which rabbinical associations have imposed rules governing the locale of weddings and the outer limits of sumptuary embellishment, for the most part the influence of the rabbis is based only on education and persuasion.

Jewish religious authorities are agreed that the wedding ceremony should be one of simple dignity, that the spiritual significance of the occasion must not be obliterated or over-balanced by ostentation. The social celebration should augment the religious ceremony, not outshine it. So far as possible, we should strive to emulate the spirit of Jewish law which insisted that, if a prospective bride lacked the means for a respectable wedding gown, it became the responsibility of the community to provide one. Where bride and groom face financial problems in their early years of marriage, how much more appropriate and sensible it is for their parents to offer continuing assistance over a period of time in lieu of an extravagant splash following the wedding ceremony. Even where no financial worries are anticipated, an expression of family joy through contributions to important philanthropies in honor of the wedding is far more admirable than garish display. This paragraph should not be misinterpreted to be harshly critical of all wedding receptions; it is a plea only for proper proportion. The probability of achieving such balance is greater when the ceremony takes place in the bride's synagogue or home than when it occurs in a hotel or club.

NOT AN ISLAND

The wedding ceremony is not an isolated event. Its religious flavor is likely to reflect that which has been characteristic of both bride and groom in the past and to foreshadow the quality of their religious life in the future. Jewish tradition provided a period of spiritual preparation preceding the marriage ritual. The bride was expected to visit the מקוה (mikveh) or ritual-bath, where her physical immersion in water symbolized an ethical and spiritual cleansing in anticipation of her nuptials. Both partners were obliged to fast on the wedding day itself and to seek atonement for their sins. Despite the fact that literal observance of these customs has been discarded by all but the most Orthodox among American Jews, we would do well to prepare for the marriage ceremony in the spirit dictated by the Shulchan Aruch:

It is essential that the groom and bride upon entering the nuptial ceremony purify themselves before God, by repenting of their sins, by reviewing all their deeds from the day of their birth up to that day, by confessing their sins and beseeching Him, blessed be His name, to grant them pardon, forgiveness, and atonement.

They should firmly resolve thenceforth to devote themselves to the worship of God, truly and sincerely, and to be holy and pure, and thereafter they should enter under the nuptial canopy and pray unto the Holy One, blessed be His name, that He may make His divine presence rest among them, as the wise, of blessed memory, said: "The Divine Presence rests between a husband and his wife."[11]

How thoroughly appropriate and constructive it would be if the hilarity—sometimes even vulgarity—which often attends the separate celebrations held for the bride and groom on the night preceding their wedding were to be replaced by a joint חשבון הנפש (*cheshbon hanefesh*), a spiritual audit of the past and solemn dedication of themselves to the future. Here again Jewish tradition is instructive. For centuries it has been common practice for the prospective groom to be called to the Torah on the Sabbath before his wedding. In many modern synagogues a prayer for the welfare of bride and groom is incorporated in the Sabbath service and they are invited respectively to recite the Torah blessings and kindle the Shabbat candles. At its best, this augurs well for their future participation in the life of the congregation.

After the ceremony too prayer can play an important role. A prayer voiced together by husband and wife in times of crisis or stress will be much more meaningful if they are already accustomed to regular prayers of appreciation and thanks. And the silent communion of each with God can add immeasurably to the spiritual dimension of the relationship.[12]

Public affiliation of a young married couple with the synagogue is no less important than the private practice of prayer. Most congregations today sponsor special clubs or groups for such couples and offer lower rates of membership dues for those who cannot yet afford the normal higher levels. There is a good chance that the pattern of synagogue affiliation or indifference which you establish at the very outset of your married life will prevail permanently. Hence the extreme importance of a good beginning. In a large city which offers a variety of congregations, many newly-weds will want to attend religious services in several places and meet a number of rabbis before deciding upon the group with which they wish to become affiliated.

Suppose bride and groom originate from different types of congregations—one from a Reform background, the other from either a Conservative or Orthodox group? What is required under such circumstances is an acceptance of each other's habits and needs, coupled with a willingness to maintain open minds and hearts as they seek together for a solution which comes closest to satisfying the religious needs of both. The very least such a couple should do is to attend services in both types of synagogue, always with the objective of welcoming a new learning experience and attempting to appreciate novel religious values. While there is no formula which will cover all such cases, the husband and wife who possess in all other respects the prerequisites for a good marriage will be able, by mutual understanding and love, to solve this problem.

The subject of synagogue membership should not be closed without brief comment on the value of such association prior to the wedding ceremony. The husband and wife who can approach their officiating rabbi as a personal friend, who can seek premarital counsel from one who knows them and has perhaps taught and confirmed them, who can be married by a spiritual leader whose ceremony is personal has every advantage over those for whom the rabbi, as a stranger, can be only a professional officiant.

RITUAL OR ROTE?

My comments a few pages back about the Jewish wedding ceremony lead us now to consider in general the role of religious ritual in the home of the newly married couple. For many, the word *ritual* itself has unfortunately acquired a pejorative connotation, implying either the performance of meaningless rote or acting out neurotic compulsions or attempting by magic to influence the fates. It would be foolish to deny that ritual has indeed sometimes degenerated to all of these immature manifestations. But the fact that any form of human behavior is subject to abuse should not blind us to its possible value. Patriotism and parental love have also been disastrously distorted. Yet who would seriously propose that they therefore be totally condemned? Our task, then, must be not to repudiate ritual but rather to inquire into its creative role.

At its best, ritual is a poetic symbol, through which we undertake to express in movement a value, an attitude, a feeling, an ideal which words alone are unable fully to articulate. Shaking hands is a ritual. Though we have long outgrown what appears to have been the original reason for this custom—demonstrating that one is not carrying a concealed weapon in his hand—it still symbolizes our openness to friendship, our readiness to accept the person by whom we would ourselves like to be accepted. By a firm and affectionate handshake one friend can communicate to another far more than can be expressed with even the most eloquent of words.

Saluting the flag is a ritual. Whether it is an empty gesture or a meaningful symbol depends on the experience and intent of the individual. During my chaplaincy, in the Second World War, on Iwo Jima, at the very moment when the famous flag-raising occurred on Mt. Suribachi I was officiating at burials in our Division Cemetery near the foot of the mountain. For the rest of my life I shall never again salute an American flag anywhere without feeling again something of the spine-tingling emotion I experienced when I just happened to look toward Suribachi's top that morning and saluted as I witnessed the flag being hoisted on a piece of temporary piping. The man standing at my side during a parade may be indulging in the very same physical movements perfunctorily, with no awareness of what undergirds his raised hand. For him the salute is mere rote; for me it is a poetic symbol of surpassing value.

The true value of ritual was impressed upon me in 1964

as I watched on television the funeral of Winston Churchill. From a strictly utilitarian point of view, a simple, private ceremony would have sufficed. Instead, there were massed troops, processionals of distinguished international leaders, bagpipes and bands, trumpeters and choirs, and the slow, mournful cadence of the funeral march.

The ceremony was indescribably impressive. In poetic, dramatic manner it symbolized the precious ideals of history and the British people. The movements and motions expressed more than any words alone could have articulated. The day following Churchill's funeral, James Reston, one of America's most eminent journalists, speculating on whether we may not have become so practical a people as to be almost sterile, wrote that the rich ritual of the preceding day "reminded Washington of the imponderables of life. It suggested that sentiment and history, that ideas and philosophy, are also powerful. . . . The ceremony, for a few hours, brought . . . the past and the present together and made men here wonder whether, in this computerized modern world, they were not casting aside something from the older world that was essential to the future."[13]

In both its secular and its religious forms, ritual serves indeed as a bridge from past to present. It also helps to guarantee the future. The specific ritual employed for the Churchill funeral was not just an arbitrary or artificial choice; it emerged through the years as a custom of the civilization it enhances. So it is with our Jewish religious rituals. They are indigenous to Jewish history. The breaking of a glass to conclude the wedding ceremony, for example, as a reminder of the destruction of the Temple in Jerusalem would be meaningless to any people except our own, for no other people ever had a Temple in Jerusalem which was demolished as was ours. The סדר (seder) on Passover makes sense only for the one people in the world which has a tradition of having escaped Egyptian slavery. Through the intelligent performance of such rituals, Jewish couples associate themselves with their people's past, as well as with every Jew who has ever lived on this earth, who lives on it now, or will in the future.

The best of our Jewish rituals identify us also with the universe and its inherent Creative Power. The husband and wife who precede each meal in their home with the מוציא *(motzi)* blessing are symbolizing their gratitude for a universe which provides both their physical and spiritual needs and are reinforcing their sense of personal responsibility for the proper use of nature's gifts. Thus does religious ritual enhance their lives theologically no less than sociologically and psychologically.

A word should be added regarding the pedagogic value of ritual. The intelligent domestic practice of religious ceremonies can effectively remind both parents and children of important episodes and ideals out of their people's past. It can also spur them to live by the noblest of our ethical values. Couples who jointly observe שבת *(Shabbat)* at their dinner table are reminded weekly of their marital responsibilities and opportunities. This can provide no small impetus to their quest for a happy marriage.[14]

YOUR CHOICE

We Jews are especially fortunate with respect to ritual. No religious tradition supplies its people with a richer treasury of ceremony and symbol. The most important moments and emotions of life—birth, growth, adolescence, love, marriage, death—are encompassed and expressed by rituals which emerge from the Jewish past and establish a foundation for its future.

Through the regular practice of ritual as an expression of both ethnic solidarity and deep-seated religious faith, the Jewish home acquired a unique aura of sanctity. So much so that it merited the designation of מקדש מעט *(mikdash me-at)*—a small sanctuary. Indeed, through the ages the home attained importance at least equal to the synagogue as the principal locale for worship.

Over and above their enormous value for all Jews, our religious rituals—precisely because, as poetic symbols, they appeal mostly to the emotions—can do much to enrich the relationship between husband and wife. The Jewish bride and groom associate themselves with their people and its ideals when—standing before the rabbi at their wedding—they repeat words and enact a drama in which Jewish couples have participated for centuries. In a sense they thereby invite all Jews, past and present, to share in their life, to give it a richness and strength they would be unable to evoke by themselves. The same deep dimension can prevail throughout their life together to the degree that the rituals of Judaism become part of their home.

True, the married couples who practice Jewish ritual are contributing to the survival of Judaism and the Jewish people. But they simultaneously add experiences of indescribable beauty and meaning also to their marriage.

Which traditional rituals should a young Jewish couple observe? For the Orthodox Jew, the answer will include everything that has been sanctified by usage. The Conservative and Reform Jew will wish to be selective, retaining some traditions while rejecting others. The choice in terms of specifics must be made autonomously by each couple. Before a particular custom is cast aside, however, every honest effort should be made to understand its original significance and how it can be reinterpreted for modern meaning. I, for one, would not want to catalogue for others the specific religious customs and ceremonies which are worthy of being observed. It would be preferred that young couples go through their own process of evaluation and selection. The one point I would urge, however, is that there be enough overall flavor of Judaism and Jewishness in their home so that they, their friends, and one day their children will have no difficulty in identifying them as a Jewish family. This is more important by far than their acceptance or rejection of any specific ritual.

Should the newly-wed Jewish couple maintain a kosher home? This is as good an example as any of the type of ritual choice which I believe must be made by each husband and wife on their own. For those who are Orthodox, the decision has already been made by tradition. Conservative and Reform couples will decide on the basis of contemporary criteria. Some will feel that כַּשְׁרוּת (kashrut) is a discipline which can sanctify their homes; others will look upon it as a burden. Some will be convinced that the dietary laws provide us with a superb mechanism for distinguishing the Jewish home, thus enlarging the probability of Jewish survival; others will view these same laws as nothing more than an archaic remnant of the past. Some will want to insure that any Jew of any persuasion—including, perhaps, their own parents or grandparents—will be able to eat in their homes; others will rely on the willingness of even the most Orthodox guest to eat dairy foods from paper plates. It is on the basis of alternatives such as these that couples can decide for themselves. The answer will be relatively easy where both bride and groom come from either a kosher or non-kosher background. Where their familial homes differ in this respect, the dilemma regarding כשרות can be an effective testing ground of their ability to achieve major compromises. Such a decision should in every instance, however, be confronted and resolved prior to their wedding. A bride emanating from a non-kosher home can always receive instruction on how to observe כשרות from a Conservative or Orthodox rabbi, from her future mother-in-law, or an observant friend.

Let me add a word concerning one syndrome of ritual, that which is associated with Shabbat. A proper observance of שבת can immeasurably enhance a marriage. This can and should become the family day *par excellence*. The religious rituals of the Friday night dinner table bring all the members of the family together more closely than any other occasion. Saturday itself can be utilized for a variety of enterprises calculated to increase family unity and affection. These would, of course, include synagogue worship but by no means be limited to that. The husband and wife who try to spend שבת together —reading, walking, listening to good music, attending the opera, visiting museums—will find the positive effects of this one day flowing over into the remaining days of the week. What a pity it is that so many husbands and wives pick precisely שבת to be apart—going their respective but isolated ways on the golf course or at luncheons. Nothing is potentially more enriching for marriage and the family than a modern observance of Shabbat in the spirit of Jewish tradition.

The הבדלה (*havdalah*) ceremony which concludes שבת is

no less inspiring than the קדוש (*kiddush*) which commences it. Unfortunately הבדלה is one of the more neglected rituals in contemporary American Jewish life. For the sake of a beautiful Jewish home as well as marital happiness, it is worth reviving.

Frequently newly married couples agree intellectually that many advantages can accrue from the performance of Jewish ritual, yet, because they have not been accustomed to such usages in the homes of their parents, they feel self-conscious and awkward. Many congregations sponsor adult classes precisely to help them overcome such embarrassment. In the last analysis, the best way to overcome self-consciousness is to grow accustomed to ritual through practicing it regularly. The bride and groom who chant קדוש together six consecutive Friday nights will no longer feel awkward or clumsy.

PARENTS AND CHILDREN

Sometimes a prospective bride and groom accept the importance of religious ritual but say they intend to wait until their first child is old enough to understand before practicing these ceremonies. This is a serious mistake. For one thing, the domestic patterns established at the outset are likely to prevail permanently. A decision to practice the rituals of Judaism only in some indefinite future will most probably remain forever in the realm of unrealized intention.

Even more important, however, is the quality of the rituals practiced and how they will come through to the offspring of such a couple. Ceremonies and holidays observed only "for the sake of the children" become something of an artificial act. Even the youngest boys and girls possess an uncanny, intuitive ability to distinguish the genuine from the spurious in the behavior of their parents. They are likely to resent an *act* instituted primarily to impress them, but they will cherish an invitation to share in something which has long since become a precious part of their parents' lives. The best time to commence the practice of religious ritual is at the very beginning.

Needless to say, religion is a crucial area for agreement

between husband and wife. One parent to whom religious belief and practice are meaningful and one who is indifferent or antagonistic to them will probably produce a child who is spiritually confused. This is far more crucial than mere intellectual disagreement between mother and father. Because religion is so largely a matter of emotion, because it involves not just facts but loyalties, values, and ultimate goals, the child who constitutes a battleground for spiritual conflict between parents is profoundly to be pitied. This is more than speculation or theory. I have always felt special concern for youngsters in my confirmation classes who invariably attended religious services with one parent, never with the other. Or even worse: with neither parent. The consequences of such conflict are often reflected in the child.

But suppose husband and wife honestly disagree on religion? Is it fair to demand that one capitulate to the other? If the parent whose attitude to religion is genuinely negative is expected to participate nonetheless, doesn't this smack of hypocrisy? Isn't it the kind of play-acting for the benefit of children which has just been decried?

These are valid questions—not to be dismissed easily or lightly. They underscore our earlier recommendation that an examination in depth of religious attitudes and convictions be an integral part of the courtship experienced by all couples. If their convictions about the ultimate meaning of life and the value of religious practice are so divergent as to rule out any agreement short of enforced hypocrisy, there is reason to wonder whether they ought to consider marriage in the first place.

Where the religious gulf between two Jewish parents appears to be beyond easy reconciliation, at the very least an honest effort should be made toward cooperation. A nonreligious father can without personal hypocrisy say, both by action and in word: "I don't agree with mother in this matter, but I must allow room for the possibility that I am wrong. In any event, since religion means so much to mother, I love her and you enough to cooperate. We'll celebrate the holidays together and I'll attend services with you—as often as I can, with an open mind. We'll search together as a family; only at the end of such searching can we know whether or not something like substantial agreement will be possible." If it becomes a bone of contention, an issue for relentless controversy, religion can jeopardize a marriage. If it serves as at least a common search, undertaken together in a spirit of love, it can provide immense reinforcement and strength.

A few practical problems about parents and children remain. They should at least be briefly mentioned even in a book which does not purport to cover such matters systematically. There is, for example, the question of the ברית מילה (*berit milah*), the circumcision ceremony for male children. Orthodox parents will insist that this be done by a מוהל (*mohel*), a specially trained religious functionary who can conduct both the surgical and religious phases of the ceremony with competence. Even in Orthodox tradition the surgery may be performed by a Jewish physician if no מוהל is available; the religious ceremony would then be conducted simultaneously by a rabbi. There can thus be no real objection on religious grounds to the increasing practice among Conservative and Reform Jews of asking a Jewish surgeon to remove the foreskin.

What is deplorable, however, is the tendency among some young Jewish parents to treat circumcision as a purely hygienic procedure, ignoring the religious emphasis entirely. For Jews circumcision should be something more than that. According to our tradition it was enjoined upon all Jewish parents as a sign of the covenant between each individual male Jew and his God. It initiates the child into a whole cycle of identifications with his people and its faith. The מילה begins a spiritual process which continues through the observance of his first day of Jewish education, his *Bar Mitzvah,* his confirmation, his marriage, his becoming a parent himself. During the circumcision ceremony a most meaningful prayer is recited:

זה הקטן גדול יהיה. כשם שנכנס לברית כן יכנס לתורה לחופה
ולמעשים טובים.

(*Zeh hakatan gadol yiheyeh; keshem shenichnas laberit, ken yikanes letorah, lechupah, ulma'asim tovim.*)—"May this little one grow in vigor. As he has entered into the covenant of Abraham, so may he in due course enter into the study of Torah, into a fulfilling marriage, into the performance of good deeds."

This is too precious a heritage to be taken lightly. The Jewish parent who ignores it, who loses a priceless opportunity to emphasize the beauty of holiness on the birth of a child, thereby impoverishes self, marriage, and family. Most American congregations today make provision for impressive public naming prayers for both boy and girl infants.

A brief word about the naming of children: It is both appropriate and desirable for a Jewish child to be given a Hebrew name. This is another means of identifying the child Jewishly, of giving it from the very beginning a living relationship to tradition. But the naming of a child becomes a travesty when there is no intelligible relationship between Hebrew and English names. If משה (*Mosheh*), which should be Moses, is translated Montgomery, if שרה (*Sarah*) becomes Cynthia—it would be better for the Hebrew name to be skipped. Either a closely related name should be given, or the entire pretense had better be dropped. The translation of names from Hebrew into English and vice-versa is not always simple. Where the name is one commonly used during the biblical or talmudic periods, a direct equivalent can be found. Otherwise, however, sometimes the best we can accomplish is a reasonable approximation.[15]

The naming of a newborn child is often an extremely sensitive area in the relationship between the infant's parents and grandparents. The latter have every right to express their preference, none to dictate or insist. They had their chance to choose names for their own offspring. It is the baby's own parents who—after listening with respect and love to any suggestions the grandparents desire to make—have the right and duty to decide.

Central to the hopes and dreams of almost all couples is the eventual establishment of a family. Know, then, from the outset that children reflect the quality of their parents' marriage. All other factors being equal, parents who enjoy a wholesome, sensitive, loving relationship with each other will rear wholesome, sensitive, happy children. There is no other master key to successful parenthood. This is why at least these few paragraphs on parents and children are appropriate for consideration by the couple just contemplating marriage.

Alexander Magoun was perceptive and wise when he wrote:

> The child who cannot find God in his parents will not have an easy time finding God anywhere. The parent who cannot see God in the face of his child has never known God.[16]

CHAPTER SIXTEEN

Facing Forward

How happy will your marriage be?

N*o surer answer can be given this question now than when it was* asked at the outset. But at least we should be more aware of the important conditions on which the answer will depend. Neither the supreme happiness which comes to some married couples nor the abject misery which attends others is as inexplicable as we sometimes make them out to be. Over four decades of counseling many hundreds of couples have led me to associate certain factors with success, others with failure. Individuals differ. So do circumstances. The complex of attitude and behavior which works well with one couple may be quite inappropriate for another. Yet there are rules, and those who strive to learn and follow them will, on the average, enjoy a far greater degree of success than those who don't care or don't try.

I never face the husband and wife during their wedding ceremony without wondering what their future will be. Because I refuse to officiate at all without one or more premarital conferences, usually I have at least some idea of the factors operating for and against them. But the eventual balance of these factors is beyond the power of anyone exactly to anticipate. There are, of course, elements of luck in every marriage, as there are in every life. Some couples may be fortunate in never facing at any one time a combination of tensions and stresses too onerous for their love to sustain. Others, with pretty much the same carrying power and endurance, may have such heavy burdens heaped upon them that even their strongest beams of support snap and crumble.

Yet it would be a massive mistake to conclude that the balance in marriage hinges exclusively on luck. The incidence of failure is very much greater among those who trust only to luck than among those who calculate as carefully and accurately as they can and who then act in accordance with their calculations. A happy marriage doesn't just *happen*. It is always the result of intelligent planning and wise action, planning and action which must come both before and after the wedding ceremony.

How happy will your marriage be?

That depends on how well the two of you understand the meaning of love and how capable you are of giving and receiving love; on how mature each of you is as an individual and whether the relationship between you is a mature one; on the breadth and depth of your compatibility; on the effort you expend year by year to enhance and enrich your marriage; on whether your sex life is arrested on the level of animality or is truly and beautifully human; on how wisely you have used your courtship as preparation for marriage; on your familial affection for your parents and your children; on the religious dimensions of your life.

We can ask the question now. Only the future will reveal an answer, and you two will be partners in determining what that answer is to be.

WEIGHING IN

Periodic inventory is good for a marriage. What better, more productive use for each wedding anniversary than to evaluate the past and plan for the future? Not in a ponderous, oppressive manner—nor in a mood of criticism and complaint—rather in a spirit of gratitude for the good things which have already issued from the relationship, of appreciation for the values and strengths already made manifest, of hope that yesterday's failure can be transformed into tomorrow's success.

The table below is one which I have worked out for discussion groups of young married couples who are attempting to measure the success of their marriages. It should be filled out first by each mate alone; only after both have finished should their answers be compared. There will be no profit from this procedure unless both spouses respond with total truth. A further word of caution: better that the whole idea be forgotten than that these questions be utilized to secure ammunition for contention. If there appears to be danger in that direction, the likelihood is that these particular couples are already in need of aid more substantial than cooperative self-analysis.

How Successful Is Our Marriage?
(Check one response for each item—1 through 17.)

1. I love my mate today:
   ☐ more than on our wedding day.
   ☐ as much as on our wedding day.
   ☐ less than on our wedding day.

2. If I knew a couple in the identical circumstances we were in during our courtship, I would advise them to:
   ☐ marry sooner than we did.
   ☐ marry the same time we did.
   ☐ wait a little longer than we.

3. Alexander Magoun has divided marriages into three categories. Check the one you think most accurately describes your marriage:
   ☐ Some marriages are sheer hell.
   ☐ Most marriages are pretty mediocre.
   ☐ A few marriages are positively delicious.

4. My marriage has:
   ☐ more than met my expectations for happiness.
   ☐ just about met my expectations.
   ☐ not met my expectations.

5. I believe myself to be:
   ☐ emotionally very mature.
   ☐ reasonably mature.
   ☐ quite immature.

6. I believe my mate is:
   ☐ emotionally very mature.
   ☐ reasonably mature.
   ☐ quite immature.
7. Most of our major decisions are made by:
   ☐ me.
   ☐ my mate.
   ☐ both of us.
8. We resolve most of our disagreements:
   ☐ easily.
   ☐ fairly well.
   ☐ with difficulty.
9. In comparison to what I thought when we were married, today I think my mate and I have:
   ☐ more in common.
   ☐ less in common.
   ☐ as much in common.
10. Our financial problems have been:
    ☐ serious.
    ☐ not serious.
    ☐ nonexistent.
11. Our sex life has been:
    ☐ excellent.
    ☐ good.
    ☐ fair.
    ☐ not good.
12. To my mate sex has been:
    ☐ too important.
    ☐ of proper importance.
    ☐ not important enough.
13. Our progress toward marital adjustment has been:
    ☐ excellent.
    ☐ good.
    ☐ fair.
    ☐ poor.

14. With reference to rearing our children, we agree:
    ☐ always.
    ☐ most of the time.
    ☐ occasionally.
    ☐ seldom.
15. We spend our leisure hours together:
    ☐ always.
    ☐ most of the time
    ☐ occasionally.
    ☐ seldom.
16. The role of religion in our marriage has been:
    ☐ important.
    ☐ casual.
    ☐ insignificant.
17. On religious matters my spouse and I are:
    ☐ in strong agreement.
    ☐ in mild agreement.
    ☐ in mild disagreement.
    ☐ in strong disagreement.

    (For items 18 through 22 mark True or False.)

18. I now see virtues in my spouse of which I was not
    aware when we were married.   _____
19. I now see faults in my spouse of which I was not
    aware when we were married.   _____
20. My parents have interfered in our marriage.   _____
21. My spouse's parents have interfered in our
    marriage.   _____
22. I have had moments of doubt as to the wisdom
    of our marriage.   _____

    (Fill in answers to items 23 through 28.)

23. Our most serious problem in marriage thus far:

24. The things I know now which I wish I had known before we
    were married:

25. I wish my mate would improve in the following respects:

26. I wish I could improve in the following respects:

27. Marriage has helped me grow in the following ways:

28. Marriage has helped my spouse grow in the following ways:

A loving and responsible comparison of the answers recorded separately by husband and wife should enhance most marriages. It would be wise also to compare the answers given one year to those of the preceding year. If this is done, however, the previous replies should not be consulted until after the new ones have been written.

FINALLY

I have tried in these pages to describe the ideal marriage, aware of the fact that very few couples will fully achieve it. There are no perfect marriages because there are no perfect human beings. Woodrow Wilson is said to have reflected that the value of having a goal is in knowing by how far one has failed to attain it. The couple striving to approximate an ideal beyond accomplishment will reap richer rewards by far than if they were satisfied just to improvise year by year. It is as destructive to be entirely without a plan or goal as to castigate oneself for falling short of perfection.

Each experience adds into the sum total of marriage. Every word spoken by husband and wife to each other accumulates, for good or bad, to affect the balance. Whenever an expensive mahogany table is polished, its luster becomes more luminous. When a nail is driven into its surface, then extracted, not even the most skilled finisher can disguise the fact that damage has been done. So it is with marriage. Every rude, thoughtless, insensitive word spoken by either husband or wife leaves its permanent impression. Apologies can repair the harm but seldom obliterate its entire effect. Every act of sweetness and consideration is as rich wax, rubbed softly on the finest of woods. No one can live one kind of life and expect to reap a different kind of marriage.

Is there a secret to marital happiness?

Surely no simple or easy one. Perhaps the closest anyone has come to an all-embracing formula for success is reflected in the story of Abraham's faithful servant, whom he sent back to his native land to find a wife for Isaac. The servant's responsibility was heavy. Abraham had specified only one criterion: the girl must come from his own stock. He had said nothing about any other standard of choice. En route to discharge his franchise, the servant voiced this significant prayer:

> O Lord, God of my master Abraham, grant me good fortune this day, and deal graciously with my master Abraham. As I stand here by the spring and the daughters of the townsmen come out to draw water, let the maiden to whom I say, "Please, lower your jar that I may drink," and who replies, "Drink, and I will also water your camels"—let her be the one whom You have decreed for Your servant Isaac. . . . (Gen. 24:12 ff.)

Was this just an arbitrary sign which Abraham's servant requested? A careful reading of his words will disclose that it was not. What he really sought was a girl who would immediately offer to do more than was requested or expected of her. He would ask for water only on his own behalf; she would volunteer at once to provide drink both for him and his camels.

The husband and wife who do only the normally expected things for each other can probably get along all right. They may even enjoy a modest kind of success in their marriage. But the highest levels of happiness are reserved for those who give each other more than the norm.

There are no guarantees. Neither for you nor for any couple. There is only the bright promise of immeasurable happiness . . . and knowledge enough within your grasp for that promise to be fulfilled.

Bibliography

1. ON JUDAISM:

The Torah (A New Translation), Jewish Publication Society, 1963

The Torah, A Modern Commentary, Union of American Hebrew Congregations, 1981

The Prophets (A New Translation), Jewish Publication Society, 1978

The Writings (A New Translation), Jewish Publication Society, 1982

Bernard J. Bamberger, *The Story of Judaism*, Union of American Hebrew Congregations, 1957

Abraham Cohen, *Everyman's Talmud*, E. P. Dutton, 1949

J. Cohen, *The Case for Religious Naturalism*, Jewish Reconstructionist Press, 1958

Ira Eisenstein, *What We Mean by Religion*, Jewish Reconstructionist Press, 1959

———, *Varieties of Jewish Belief*, Jewish Reconstructionist Press, 1966

Albert H. Friedlander, *Out of the Whirlwind*, Union of American Hebrew Congregations, 1968

Roland B. Gittelsohn, *Man's Best Hope*, Random House, 1961

———, *Wings of the Morning*, Union of American Hebrew Congregations, 1969

———, *The Modern Meaning of Judaism*, Collins & World Publishing Co., 1978

Robert Gordis, *A Faith for Moderns,* Bloch Publishing Co., 1960
———, *Judaism for the Modern Age,* Farrar, Straus and Cudahy, 1955
Mordecai M. Kaplan, *The Meaning of God in Modern Jewish Religion,* Behrman House, 1932
Lydia Kukoff, *Choosing Judaism,* Union of American Hebrew Congregations, 1981
Harold S. Kushner, *When Children Ask about God,* Jewish Reconstructionist Press, 1971
———, *When Bad Things Happen to Good People,* Schocken Books, 1981
W. Gunther Plaut, *The Rise of Reform Judaism,* World Union for Progressive Judaism, 1963
———, *The Growth of Reform Judaism,* World Union for Progressive Judaism, 1965
Abram L. Sachar, *A History of the Jews,* A. A. Knopf, 1951
Maurice Samuel, *Certain People of the Book,* Union of American Hebrew Congregations, 1977
Hayyim Schauss, *The Jewish Festivals,* Union of American Hebrew Congregations, 1938
———, *Lifetime of a Jew,* Union of American Hebrew Congregations, 1950
Leo W. Schwartz, ed., *Great Ages and Ideas of the Jewish People,* Random House, 1956
Abba Hillel Silver, *Where Judaism Differed,* Macmillan and Co., 1956
Milton Steinberg, *A Partisan Guide to the Jewish Problem,* Bobbs-Merrill, 1945
———, *Basic Judaism,* Harcourt, Brace, 1947
Elie Wiesel, *One Generation After,* Random House, 1970
———, *A Jew Today,* Random House, 1978

2. ON MARRIAGE:

(Items marked * are especially recommended for the prospective bride and groom.)
D. S. Bailey, *Sexual Relations in Christian Thought,* Harper & Bros., 1959

*Eugene Borowitz, *Choosing a Sex Ethic*, Schocken Books, 1969

James H. S. Bossard and Eleanor S. Boll, *One Marriage, Two Faiths*, Ronald Press Co., 1957

David M. Feldman, *Birth Control in Jewish Law*, New York University Press, 1968

Frederic F. Flach, *A New Marriage, A New Life*, McGraw-Hill Book Co., 1978

*Erich Fromm, *The Art of Loving*, Harper & Bros., 1959

Roland B. Gittelsohn, *Love, Sex, and Marriage: A Jewish View*, Union of American Hebrew Congregations, 1980

Morton and Bernice Hunt, *The Divorce Experience*, McGraw-Hill Book Co., 1977

Herant A. Katchadourian and Donald T. Lunde, *Fundamentals of Human Sexuality*, Holt, Rinehart & Winston, 1972

*F. Alexander Magoun, *Love and Marriage*, Harper & Bros., 1956

James Leslie McCary, *Human Sexuality, Second Brief Edition*, Wadsworth Publishing Co., 1979

Notes

Note: Unless otherwise indicated, all talmudic references are to the Babylonian (Bavli) Talmud. The letter Y preceding a tractate indicates use of the Jerusalem (Yerushalmi) Talmud.

CHAPTER 1
Hope . . . and Despair

1. F. Alexander Magoun, *Love and Marriage,* p. 346, Harper & Bros., 1956.

CHAPTER 2
"I Love You"

1. F. A. Magoun, *Love and Marriage,* pp. 4f., 7.
2. Erich Fromm, *The Revolution of Hope,* p. 40, Harper & Row, 1968.
3. E. Fromm, *The Art of Loving,* p. 1, Harper & Bros., 1956.
4. *Ibid.,* p. 40.
5. *Ibid.,* pp. 22ff.
6. For the full account of this tender, poignant tale, see Philip and Hanna Goodman, *The Jewish Marriage Anthology,* pp. 38f., Jewish Publication Society, 1965.
7. Lucien Price, ed., *Dialogues of Alfred North Whitehead,* p. 11, Little, Brown & Co., 1954.
8. Eugene Borowitz, *Choosing a Sex Ethic,* pp. 73f., Schocken Books, 1970.
9. *Midrash Aseret Hadibrot.*
10. *The New York Times,* 15 February 1979. © 1979 by the New York Times Company. Reprinted by permission.

CHAPTER 3
More Than a Matter of Age

1. *Zohar Chadash* I:4b.
2. James H. S. Bossard and Eleanor S. Boll, *Why Marriages Go Wrong*, p. 110, Ronald Press Co., 1958.
3. *Ibid.*, p. 118.
4. *The New York Times*, 31 October 1965.
5. Sylvanus Duvall, *Before You Marry*, pp. 10f., Association Press, 1949.

CHAPTER 4
Water and Oil

1. P. and H. Goodman, *The Jewish Marriage Anthology*, p. 46.
2. *Yevamot* 63a.
3. Lillian S. Freehof, *Third Bible Legend Book*, pp. 80f., Union of American Hebrew Congregations, 1956.
4. *Pesikta Buber* 11b–12a.
5. *Sotah* 2a.
6. *Zohar* I:91b.
7. *Pesachim* 49a.
8. Samuel Caplan and Harold U. Ribalow, eds., *The Great Jewish Books*, p. 229, Horizon Press, 1952.
9. *Kiddushin* 70.
10. *Pesachim* 50.
11. *The New York Times*, 11 May 1966.
12. *Sanhedrin* 76.
13. *Yevamot* 101b.
14. *Bava Batra* 110a.
15. F. A. Magoun, *Love and Marriage*, p. 229.
16. John E. Crawford and L. E. Woodward, *Better Ways of Growing Up*, p. 222, Muhlenberg Press, 1948.

CHAPTER 5
Promise Is a Seed

1. F. A. Magoun, *Love and Marriage*, p. 32.
2. *Cleveland Plain Dealer*, 22 November 1976. Reprinted by permission.
3. *The New York Times*, 24 September 1973.
4. Louis I. Newman, *The Talmudic Anthology*, p. 269, Behrman House, 1945.
5. From pp. 45–46 in *To Have or to Be?* by Erich Fromm, Volume Fifty in *World Perspectives*, planned and edited by Ruth Nanda

Anshen. Copyright © 1976 by Erich Fromm. Reprinted by permission of Harper & Row, Publishers, Inc.

6. F. A. Magoun, *Love and Marriage*, p. 318.
7. *Bereshit Rabbah* 54.
8. *Being Male and Female: Summary of a Campus Institute*, Kansas State University, Manhattan, Kansas.
9. Rosemary R. Ruether, *Religion and Sexism*, pp. 24f., Simon & Schuster, 1974.
10. R. Restak, *The Brain*, Doubleday and Co. For disagreement with Restak's views, see article by Martha Mednick and Nancy Felipe Russo in *Boston Globe*, 9 September 1979.
11. *The New York Times*, 25 March 1980.
12. James A. Peterson, *Toward a Successful Marriage*, p. 98, Charles Scribner's Sons, 1960.

CHAPTER 6
Money Is the Root . . .

1. J. A. Peterson, *Toward a Successful Marriage*, p. 112.
2. *Kohelet Rabbah* 7.
3. L. Newman, *Hasidic Anthology*, p. 304, Charles Scribner's Sons, 1935.
4. George F. Gilder, *Sexual Suicide*, p. 69, Bantam Books, 1975.

CHAPTER 7
Sex and Love

1. E. Fromm, *The Art of Loving*, pp. 88f.
2. Julian Huxley, *New Bottles for New Wine*, pp. 218f., Harper & Bros., 1957.
3. Harlan Ellison, *Love Ain't Nothing But Sex Misspelled*, Trident Press, 1968.
4. *Saturday Review*, 26 September 1953.
5. E. Fromm, *The Art of Loving*, p. 92.
6. Evelyn M. Duvall, *Why Wait till Marriage?*, p. 75, Association Press, 1965.
7. E. Borowitz, *Choosing a Sex Ethic*.
8. R. L. Tyler, in Dolora and Dolora, *Intimate Life Styles*, p. 397, Goodyear Publishing Co., 1972.
9. E. Borowitz, *Choosing a Sex Ethic*, p. 107.
10. *Ibid.*, p. 18.
11. From *The Pleasure Bond: A New Look at Sexuality and Commitment*, by William H. Masters and Virginia E. Johnson, pp. 47, 173f. © 1970, 1971, 1972, 1973, 1974 by William H. Masters and

Virginia E. Johnson. Reprinted by permission of Little, Brown & Co.

12. From *Human Sexuality, Second Brief Edition,* p. 135, by James Leslie McCary. Copyright © 1979 by J. L. McCary and S. P. McCary. Reprinted by permission of Wadsworth Publishing Company, Belmont, CA 94002.

CHAPTER 8
"As You Sow . . ."

1. See "The Art of First Intercourse," in Eleanor Hamilton, *Sex before Marriage,* Hawthorn, 1969.
2. *The New York Times,* 21 July 1978.
3. W. H. Masters and V. E. Johnson, *The Pleasure Bond,* p. 57.
4. *Kiddushin* 2b.
5. *Sotah* 2b.
6. *Ibid.,* 25a.
7. *Ibid.,* 47b.
8. *Red Book Magazine,* April 1962.
9. Frank S. Caprio, *Marital Infidelity,* pp. 7, 11, Citadel Press, 1953.
10. *Boston Globe,* 23 June 1975. Reprinted courtesy of the Boston Globe.
11. *The New York Times,* 5 October 1977.

CHAPTER 9
"Be Fruitful and Multiply . . ."

1. United Infertility Organization, P.O. Box 23, Scarsdale, NY 10583.

Resolve, P.O. Box 474, Belmont, MA 02178.

Barren Foundation, 6 East Monroe St., Chicago, IL 60603.

A good book on this subject is *Infertility: A Guide for the Childless Couple,* by Barbara E. Menning, Prentice-Hall, 1977.

2. See Solomon B. Freehof, *A Treasury of Responsa,* pp. 211 ff., Jewish Publication Society, 1963.

3. Adoptive Parents Committee, 210 Fifth Ave., New York, NY 10010.

Concerned Persons for Adoption, 16 Fawn Drive, Montville, NJ 07045.

See also *The Adoption Adviser,* by Joan McNamara, Hawthorn Books, 1975.
4. S. Freehof, *Reform Responsa,* pp. 217ff., Hebrew Union College Press, 1960. See also *A Treasury of Responsa,* pp. 307ff.
5. Jewish Telegraphic Agency, 30 August 1977.
6. F. Rosner, "Artificial Insemination in Jewish Law," *Judaism,* Fall 1970, pp. 452ff.

CHAPTER 10
Miles Apart

1. I Corinthians 7:9.
2. D. S. Bailey, *Sexual Relations in Christian Thought,* p. 14, Harper & Bros., 1959.
3. *Ibid.,* pp. 23, 99.
4. *Ibid.,* p. 63.
5. Quoted by Robert E. Hall, M.D., in *The Nation,* 5 October 1964.
6. For a more lenient modern Catholic view, see Anthony Kosnik, *Human Sexuality: New Directions in American Catholic Thought,* Paulist Press, 1977.
7. R. Jolivet, *Introduction to Kierkegaard,* pp. 157f., translated by W. H. Barber. © E. P. Dutton, Inc., 1952.
8. *Yoma* 13a.
9. *Sanhedrin* 39a.
10. S. Glasner, in *Encyclopedia of Sexual Behavior,* p. 576, Hawthorn Books, 1961.
11. *Even Haezer* 76:1.
12. *Kiddushin* 13a, *Yevamot* 52a.
13. *Pesikta Rabbati* 17b.
14. *Responsa,* Prague #199.
15. *Yoreh Deah,* Ch. 381, Sec. 6.
16. From *Iggeret Hakodesh,* generally attributed to Nachmanides, though there is some doubt whether he was in fact the author.
17. Abraham B. Shoulson, ed., *Marriage and Family Life,* p. 56, Twayne Publishers, 1959.
18. *Eruvin* 100b.
19. *Niddah* 31b.
20. Gershom G. Scholem, *Major Trends in Jewish Mysticism,* pp. 105f., Schocken Books, 1954.
21. For the development of Catholic thought on contraception, see A. W. Sulloway, *Birth Control and Catholic Doctrine,* Beacon Press, 1959.

22. *Raia Mehemna* III: 34a.
23. *Zohar* I: 187a.
24. *Yevamot* 12b, 100b, *Ketuvot* 39a, *Niddah* 45a, *Nedarim* 35b; *Tosefta Niddah* II.
25. *Yearbook,* Central Conference of American Rabbis, 1927, p. 377.
26. For a fuller exposition of the attitude of Judaism toward abortion, see David M. Feldman, *Birth Control in Jewish Law,* New York University Press, 1968.

CHAPTER 11
Men, Women, and God

1. *Zohar Chadash* IV:50b.
2. *Sanhedrin* 22a.
3. *Ruth Rabbah* I.
4. *Pirke de-Rabbi Eliezer* 12:1.
5. *Ketuvot* 61a.
6. *Shabbat* 152.
7. *Chullin* 84b.
8. *Bava Metzia* 59a.
9. *Ibid.,* 59a.
10. *Yevamot* 62.
11. *Bava Metzia* 59a.
12. *Ketuvot* 62a.
13. *Kallah* II.
14. *Zohar* 233a.
15. *Zohar* IV: 259b.
16. *Or Yesharim* p. 109.
17. *Yevamot* 65a.
18. See article "Polygamy," *Jewish Encyclopedia, X:* 120, Funk and Wagnalls Co., 1905.
19. *Yevamot* 37.
20. *Sanhedrin* 22a.
21. *Song of Songs Rabbah* I.
22. E. M. & S. M. Duvall, *Sex Ways in Fact and Faith,* p. 98, Association Press, 1961.
23. *Deuteronomy* 24:1.
24. *Yad Ishut* 14:8.
25. Sidney E. Goldstein, *The Meaning of Marriage and Foundations of the Family: A Jewish View,* pp. 178 ff., Bloch Publishing Co., 1942.
26. *Leviticus Rabbah* 9.

CHAPTER 12
New Times . . . New Problems

1. I Corinthians 14:34f.
2. R.R. Ruether, *Religion and Sexism*, pp. 229f.
3. *Nedarim* 20b.
4. *Kiddushin* 41a.
5. *Megillah* 14a.
6. *Sotah* 11b.
7. *Taanit* 23a, b.
8. *Betzah* 23b.
9. *Genesis Rabbah* 17:7.
10. *Rosh Hashanah* 22a, *Sotah* 47b.
11. *Nu* 27:8; *Bava Batra* 110a, b.
12. Herbert Loewe, in Claude G. Montefiore and Herbert Loewe, *A Rabbinic Anthology*, p. 656, Macmillan & Co. Ltd., London, 1938.
13. *Siddur Rashi* #267.
14. G. Gilder, *Sexual Suicide*, pp. 26f. (See also p. 14.)
15. A fuller discussion of this problem may be found on pp. 104–107 of Yosef Criden and Saadia Gelb, *The Kibbutz Experience*, Herzl Press, 1974.
16. Herant A. Katchadourian and Donald T. Lunde, *Fundamentals of Human Sexuality*, p. 484, Holt, Rinehart & Winston, Inc., 1972.
17. C. Hefferan, *U. S. News & World Report*, 27 November 1978, pp. 82f.
18. *Harper's Bazaar*, July 1978, pp. 100ff. Copyright © 1978 by the Hearst Corporation, courtesy of *Harper's Bazaar*.
19. J. A. Peterson, *Toward a Successful Marriage*, p. 130.
20. *Boston Globe*, 9 October 1978.
21. *The New York Times Magazine*, 18 November 1979.
22. *Moed Katan* 23a. I am indebted on this point to Rabbi Solomon B. Freehof, who wrote an extensive and illuminating responsum in April 1979 to my personal inquiry.
23. Stepfamily Foundation, 333 West End Ave., New York, NY 10023.

   Remarried Consultation Service, Jewish Board of Family & Children's Services, 120 West 57 St., New York, NY 10019.

   Stepfamily Foundation, Palo Alto, CA 94303.
24. Jeanette Lofas and Ruth Roosevelt, *Living in Step*, McGraw-Hill Paperbacks. Also John S. and Emily B. Visher, *Stepfamilies*, Brunner-Mazel, Larchmont, NY.

25. For the positive aspects of becoming step-parents, see: Frederic F. Flach, *A New Marriage, A New Life*, p. 160, McGraw-Hill Book Co., 1978; Morton and Bernice Hunt, *The Divorce Experience*, p. 259, McGraw-Hill Book Co., 1977.
26. W. H. Masters and V. E. Johnson, *The Pleasure Bond*, p. 94.
27. Isidore Rubin, *Sexual Life after Sixty*, p. 152, Basic Books, 1965. (See also pp. 148–153.)

CHAPTER 13
"You Shall Teach Them . . ."

1. David Sidorsky, ed., *Future of the Jewish Community in America*, pp. 78ff., Jewish Publication Society, 1973.
2. L. Newman, *Hasidic Anthology*, p. 45.
3. *Shabbat* 10b.
4. *Exodus Rabbah* I:1.
5. Introduction, *Tikkun Zohar* 6a.
6. *Zohar* II:93a.
7. *Kiddushin* 30a.
8. *Ibid.*
9. *Zohar Chadash* to *Sidrah Lech Lecha*.
10. *Kiddushin* 30a.
11. *Shabbat* 119b.
12. L. Newman, *Hasidic Anthology*, p. 45.
13. *Zohar* I:50a.
14. L. Newman, *Hasidic Anthology*, p. 118.
15. *Ibid.*
16. *Ibid.*
17. *Yevamot* 6a.
18. *Kiddushin* 31b–32a.
19. *Kiddushin* 32a.
20. *Peah* 15c.
21. *Zohar* III: 93a.
22. C. G. Montefiore and H. Loewe, *A Rabbinic Anthology*, p. 503; L. Newman, *Hasidic Anthology*, p. 304; Abraham Cohen, *Everyman's Talmud*, p. 183, E. P. Dutton & Co., 1949.
23. *Kiddushin* 31b.
24. *Y. Kiddushin* 61b.
25. *Niflaot Hayehudi*, p. 45.
26. *Kiddushin* 31a.
27. *The New York Times*, 23 April 1978.
28. Mary Jo Bane, *Here to Stay*, Basic Books, 1976.
29. *Boston Globe*, 6 December 1974.

30. M. J. Bane, *Here to Stay.*
31. *The New York Times,* 26 August 1976.
32. *Pirke de-Rabbi Eliezer* 32.
33. P. and H. Goodman, *The Jewish Marriage Anthology,* p. 46.
34. *Yalkut Shimoni* 95.
35. A. B. Shoulson, ed., *Marriage and Family Life,* p. 67.
36. J. H. S. Bossard and E. S. Boll, *Why Marriages Go Wrong,* pp. 188f.
37. For a full, objective discussion of premarital intercourse, see Chs. 11, 12, and 13 of Roland B. Gittelsohn, *Love, Sex, and Marriage—A Jewish View,* Union of American Hebrew Congregations, 1980.

CHAPTER 14
Mixed Marriage

1. J. H. S. Bossard and E. S. Boll, *Why Marriages Go Wrong,* p. 150.
2. J. H. S. Bossard and E. S. Boll, *One Marriage, Two Faiths,* pp. 100f., Ronald Press Co., 1957.
3. Morris Fine and Milton Himmelfarb, eds., *American Jewish Yearbook, 1963,* pp. 18f., Jewish Publication Society.
4. *Ibid.,* pp. 30f.
5. E. M. and S. M. Duvall, *Sex Ways in Fact and Faith,* p. 61.
6. *Ibid.,* p. 62.
7. Clarence Leuba, *Ethics in Sex Conduct,* pp. 127f., Association Press, 1948.

CHAPTER 15
Your Small Sanctuary

1. James A. Pike, *The Next Day,* p. 95, Doubleday & Co., 1957.
2. E. M. and S. M. Duvall, *Sex Ways in Fact and Faith,* pp. 88f.
3. J. A. Peterson, *Toward a Successful Marriage,* p. 104.
4. *Ibid.*
5. *Ibid.,* pp. 107f.
6. *Genesis Rabbah* 8:9.
7. *Pirke de-Rabbi Eliezer* 12.
8. *Kiddushin* 6b.
9. *Berachot* 30b, 31a.
10. Salo W. Baron, *The Jewish Community,* Vol. II, pp. 301–306, 315, Jewish Publication Society, 1942.
11. Solomon Ganzfried, *Code of Jewish Law,* Vol. IV, pp. 6–13, Hebrew Publishing Co., 1927.
12. For a discussion of what prayer can mean in the life of the modern Jew, see R. B. Gittelsohn, *Man's Best Hope,* Chs. 13, 14, Random

House, 1961; or R. B. Gittelsohn, *Wings of the Morning*, Ch. 15, Union of American Hebrew Congregations, 1969.

13. *The New York Times*, 31 January 1965.

14. For detailed help on specific Jewish rituals, see Simeon J. Maslin, ed., *Gates of Mitzvah*, Central Conference of American Rabbis, 1979; W. Gunther Plaut, ed., *A Shabbat Manual*, Central Conference of American Rabbis, 1972.

15. For suggested translations of names as well as their origins and meanings, see Alfred J. Kolatch, *The Names Dictionary*, Jonathan David Co., 1967.

16. F. A. Magoun, *Love and Marriage*, p. 420.